T0320151

The Governance of Privatization Funds

The Governance of Privatization Funds

Experiences of the Czech Republic,
Poland and Slovenia

Edited by

Marko Simoneti

*Assistant Professor of Finance, University of Ljubljana and
Executive Director, Central and Eastern European Privatization
Network – C.E.E.P.N., Slovenia*

Saul Estrin

Professor of Economics, London Business School, UK

Andreja Böhm

*Deputy Director, Central and Eastern European Privatization
Network – C.E.E.P.N., Slovenia*

Edward Elgar
Cheltenham, UK · Northampton, MA, USA

Published by
Edward Elgar Publishing Limited
Glensanda House
Montpellier Parade
Cheltenham
Glos GL50 1UA
UK

Edward Elgar Publishing, Inc.
6 Market Street
Northampton
Massachusetts 01060
USA

A catalogue record for this book
is available from the British Library

Library of Congress Cataloguing in Publication Data

The governance of privatization funds: experience of the Czech
    Republic, Poland, and Slovenia / edited by Saul Estrin, Marko
    Simoneti, Andreja Böhm.
        Includes index.
            1. Privatization—Czech Republic. 2. Privatization —Poland.
    3. Privatization—Slovenia. 4. Corporate governance—Czech
    Republic. 5. Corporate governance—Poland. 6. Corporate
    governance—Slovenia. I. Estrin, Saul. II. Simoneti, Marko.
    III. Böhm, Andreja.
    HD4160.3.G68 1999
    338.943—dc21   98–42880
                                                                     CIP

ISBN 1 84064 013 8

Printed and bound in Great Britain by Bookcraft (Bath) Ltd.

Contents

Figures

Tables

Contributors

Andreja Böhm, Deputy Director, Central and Eastern European Privatization Network, Slovenia

Saul Estrin, Assistant Professor, London Business School, United Kingdom

Jan Hanousek, Research Director, The Center for Economic Research and Graduate Education, Czech Republic

Božo Jašovič, Research Director, Central and Eastern European Privatization Network, Slovenia

Evžen Kočenda, Associate Professor, The Center for Economic Research and Graduate Education, Czech Republic

Jozef Kotrba, Assistant Professor, The Center for Economic Research and Graduate Education, Czech Republic

Janusz Lewandowski, Chairman of the Board of Trustees, The Gdansk Institute for Market Economies, Poland

Domenico Mario Nuti, Visiting Professor, London Business School, United Kingdom and Professor, University of Rome, Italy

Marko Rems, Senior Advisor, Agency for Privatization, Slovenia

Marko Simoneti, Associate Professor of Finance, University of Ljubljana and Executive Director, Central and Eastern European Privatization Network, Slovenia

Roman Szyszko, Researcher, The Gdansk Institute for Market Economies, Poland

Milica Uvalic, Associate Professor of Economics, University of Perugia, Italy

Acknowledgments

The Central and Eastern European Privatization Network (C.E.E.P.N.) undertakes comparative and applied research on the issues of economic transition in cooperation with the leading research centers in the countries in transition and EU.

The papers included in this book were prepared in the framework of the C.E.E.P.N. international research project on the governance of privatization investment funds in the Czech Republic, Poland and Slovenia. The project was coordinated by Marko Simoneti and it was carried out with a grant from the European Commission – Phare ACE Programme.

The editors would like to acknowledge the work of Murray Bales in language editing, Milojka Bizajl in manuscript preparation and Christine Boniface in overseeing the production of the book.

Introduction

Marko Simoneti and Andreja Böhm

Privatization funds, as *sui generis* institutions of mass privatization programs, have been intended to provide for a corporate governance solution to the problem of widely dispersed ownership in the newly privatized companies in transitional economies in Central and Eastern Europe. They have emerged as major outside institutional shareholders of newly privatized companies and as 'true' owners they are expected to play an active role in their corporate governance. But governance of privatization funds themselves exemplifies the typical problems of corporate governance of widely held public companies. The fundamental question of their governance has therefore to be addressed: 'Who will guard the guardians?'

The papers included in this volume focus on the governance issues of privatization funds and to a lesser extent on their role in corporate governance of enterprises. They are the results of the CEEPN research project on Governance of Privatization Funds – Experiences of the Czech Republic, Poland and Slovenia which was conducted in 1996/97 with the financial support of the ACE Programme of the European Commission. The main argument of research was that improved governance of funds would have in turn a significant, multiplier effect on improved corporate governance of the newly privatized companies. Motivated owners are by far the basic condition required for the massive task of company restructuring after mass privatization. Moreover, in many countries in transition, including the Czech Republic and Slovenia, privatization funds have become important shareholders in practically all newly privatized companies and are large shareholders especially in those companies that require major restructuring. Their failure or success will therefore have macro-economic effects. The research project covered a topical theme of post-privatization in the countries in transition, which bore practical policy relevance region wide. At the same time, it embarked on the subject of privatization funds, which lacked understanding by both academic and consulting circles.

A large variety of approaches to designing and regulating the privatization funds has been attempted in the countries in transition. The three advanced transitional economies – the Czech Republic, Poland and Slovenia – selected

1

for research made up a representative sample for the region in terms of diversity of approaches and solutions to the typical problems of governance of privatization funds. The Czech and Polish models have been extensively followed, with variations, in other countries. The Slovenian model has been launched as a regulated variant of the Czech model. The choice of those countries has proven particularly relevant to emphasize the observed common trends of convergence of diverse original forms of privatization funds with standard forms of financial intermediaries in their operation and transformation.

Recent theoretical research focusing on the corporate governance of enterprises after mass privatization, has proposed possible scenarios for transformation of privatization funds based either on the Anglo-Saxon model relying on active trading of shares on the market as a means of external control by shareholders, or on the German model emphasizing voting as a more direct mechanism of internal control by shareholders. Taking into account wide evidence from the three countries the main thrust of the papers in this book is that privatization funds appear to lack effective external control and internal control by shareholders.

The main reason for the lack of effective governance of privatization funds is their institutional structure, which is in many respects not appropriate for the tasks that they are to accomplish in portfolio companies. In the Czech Republic and Slovenia, the funds would have to be active in supervising and restructuring many non-listed companies if they are to increase the value of assets for their shareholders. The adopted institutional framework of the closed-end diversified institutional investors in listed securities is inadequate for that task. It essentially restricts or gives only very limited incentives to fund managers for the active restructuring of portfolio companies.

The implications of the conflict between the active role of the funds in companies and the standard Western type regulation for passive institutional investors are not well understood by the consultants who offer policy advice to the governments of transitional countries for transformation or abolition of privatization funds after mass privatization. In response to the observed wide differences between the net asset values and market values of the funds' shares in the Czech Republic, they have proposed an automatic opening of the closed-end funds as a way of protecting small shareholders against ineffective managers. There must be complete misunderstanding of the reality if an open-end mutual fund structure is recommended for the required restructuring activities of privatization funds. It is highly unlikely that accountability of funds' managers and the controlling ability of shareholders (i.e., governance of funds) could be significantly improved, unless the fund managers would be allowed and given the right incentives to undertake adequate portfolio activities leading to increased values of portfolio companies (i.e., have incentives for an active role in corporate governance of portfolio companies). As a first step, effective exercise of ownership rights of funds in the portfolio companies with the possibilities for active trading of listed shares or block voting with non-listed shares would have to be ensured (like in Poland). In consequence, it would be possible to strengthen the accountability of fund managers with adequate control and incentive mechanisms. In other words, stronger accountability of company managers to the funds is the precondition for enhanced accountability of fund managers to their shareholders.

The second reason for the current lack of internal and external controls by fund shareholders can to a great extent be attributed to the generally poor conditions precluding effective corporate governance in transitional economies: (i) shareholders who have emerged in mass privatization programs are not yet accustomed to exercise the ownership rights either by exit or by voice, (ii) well functioning securities markets as a precondition for effective control of shareholders by exit have not yet been developed and (iii) the required concentration of ownership after free distribution of shares to citizens as a precondition for effective internal control of shareholders by voice has not yet been completed. Those limitations will be gradually diminished as the economic transition progresses but currently there are still too many regulations in place in order to 'protect' new shareholders in underdeveloped markets. Those restrictions affect both trading with fund shares and concentration of fund ownership and in turn impede development of both capital markets and effective corporate governance mechanisms.

In the initial underdeveloped markets the external control mechanism is constrained, therefore 'strengthening' of mechanisms of internal control is required. But with active secondary trading of shares the external control will become effective on its own. The privatization funds are hybrid and temporary institutions, which will eventually exit from the transition process as either standard diversified institutional investors, venture capital funds or holding companies. Depending on the exit route either the internal control will be strengthened by concentration of ownership or the external control will be further strengthened by active secondary trading of dispersed small investors.

In the CEEPN research project a two pronged approach was adopted to study the large variety of forms of privatization funds in the Czech Republic, Poland and Slovenia and the pertaining issues of their governance, and to draw policy conclusions and lessons for improved governance and adequate transformation of privatization funds: country research and comparative surveys.

Initially, research studies were mounted at the country level. Guidelines were prepared to serve as a framework for the preparation of country reports. They included common formats of questionnaires for interviewing the managers and supervisory boards of privatization funds. The approachability of privatization funds and their acceptance to participate in research was different in each country due to specific contexts of the privatization funds industry in each country. The Czech privatization funds were, for example, far less responsive than the Slovenian ones as the competition in the fund industry and external oversights were entirely different in those countries. Different external oversights implied different accessibility of relevant information such as the overall statistical data on privatization funds or the mailing addresses of members of supervisory boards. The mere numbers of privatization funds – close to 350 in the Czech Republic, below 100 in Slovenia and 15 in Poland were not only the indicators of the sizes of mass privatization programs but compelled methodological adaptations. Finally, to a certain degree country studies reflect distinct profiles of researchers and their professional preferences.

The common format of the country papers in Chapters 1–3 covers three parts. The **first** one is a quantitative and qualitative overview of the role of mass privatization programs in the overall country privatization programs and a detailed account of the supply and demand sides of those programs. The issues tackled are the criteria and process of selection of enterprises and financial institutions, the total size of supply and the shareholding earmarked for voucher privatization at the enterprise level, the total population of voucher holders and specific characteristics of vouchers including their distribution and modes of usage. The **second** part deals with the role of privatization funds in privatization and post-privatization. It covers the intended objectives and adopted legal and regulatory frameworks, the size by collected vouchers, identity of management companies, primary investment policies and portfolio characteristics and portfolio adjustments in secondary trading in relation to their intended and actual role in governance of privatized companies. The **third** part focuses on the governance of privatization funds as internal and external control of fund shareholders. It discusses the conflicts of interests between the shareholders and managers of funds, incentive structures for fund managers, the respective roles of competition among fund managers, corporate control markets, supervisory boards, regulation and external supervision, and the transformation of funds.

The Czech study (Chapter 1) discusses an example of the voucher privatization which is encompassing a significant part of the economy and privatization investment funds that have been established 'bottom-up'. Allowed with 'free entry' and loosely regulated on the standard model of institutional investors with a diversified portfolio, the funds engage primarily in trading of portfolio shares but as major shareholders they also make appointments to the supervisory boards of companies. Lacking effective external supervision, many funds have been placed in forced administration because of the tunneling of assets on nontransparent Czech capital markets. A number of others have been converted into ordinary joint stock companies. The authors are Jozef Kotrba, Evžen Kočenda and Jan Hanousek of the Center for Economic Research and Graduate Education at the Charles University. The paper draws extensively on the official statistical data of the Ministry of Finance, which was made available for the first time to the authors.

The Polish mass privatization program examined in Chapter 2 is limited to some 500 enterprises representing 10% of GDP. It has been uniquely designed to allow 'top-down' originated national investment funds to be essentially the restructuring funds. Experienced managers have been selected and given strong incentives for restructuring and privatization of companies whereby the funds will lapse by themselves. The funds are supervised by independent boards which will continue to represent the fund shareholders that are being consolidated on the transparent and highly regulated capital market. The authors are Janusz Lewandowski and Roman Szyszko of the Gdansk Institute for Market Economics. Lewandowski was Minister of Privatization for several years and played the key role in designing the mass privatization program and reaching the political consensus for it in the *Sejm*.

The Slovenian mass privatization (Chapter 3) is all-encompassing but the entry of the 'bottom-up' privatization funds has been closely regulated in the attempt to avoid typical situations of conflicts of interests. With no restriction on investments in individual companies, the choice of either a passive portfolio management or more active involvement in management of enterprises has been left to the funds themselves. The privatization gap is a specific feature of privatization funds in Slovenia, which has caused major (and rather unique) problems in their governance, among them long-delayed quotation of funds and total lack of competition among fund managers. The trend of converting funds into an ordinary joint stock company has been recently halted to allow for continued policy debates on how to fill the gap. The Slovenian study consists of contributions by Marko Simoneti, Božo Jašovič and Andreja Böhm of the Central and East European Privatization Network and Marko Rems of the Privatization Agency. The team undertook extensive empirical surveys of privatization funds and used them to draw the policy recommendations included in its extensive report to the government and Agency for Securities Markets.

The three country papers, notwithstanding their different scope and methodological approach, provided a solid basis for undertaking comparative analyses, which are included in the second part of this volume.

Chapter 4 prepared by Saul Estrin and Domenico Mario Nuti of the London Business School and Milica Uvalic of the University of Perugia is a comparative overview of the impact of privatization funds in corporate governance of enterprises in three countries. It compares the mass privatization programs, the origins and legal forms of privatization funds, portfolio characteristics of privatization funds and their role in corporate governance of companies and it attempts to estimate the implications of funds activities on performance of privatized companies.

Chapter 5 is a synthesis of the open issues of governance of privatization funds and provides an account of policy recommendations based on the evidence from the three countries. Most open issues and policy recommendations apply to specific country contexts; they are dealt with in depth in the country studies. This chapter attempts to generalize on them and to identify pertinent issues, which apply region-wide, and to draw policy conclusions relevant for a larger group of countries after mass privatization. The authors are Marko Simoneti who served as the coordinator and Andreja Böhm who was his assistant in this research project.

1. The Governance of Privatization Funds in the Czech Republic

Jozef Kotrba, Evžen Kočenda and Jan Hanousek

MASS PRIVATIZATION PROGRAM

Introduction

At the start of privatization, the economy of the Czech Republic (and of course Slovakia) was far more state owned than in any other Central and Eastern European (CEE) country. According to estimates of the former Federal Statistical Office and the Czech National Bank, in 1990 – i.e., in the first year after the end of the communist government – as little as 4% to 5% of the nation's GDP was generated in the private sector. Even the share of the non-state sector, which included cooperatives run in a fashion similar to state-owned enterprises (SOEs), was quite low (see Table 1.1).

Table 1.1   Private sector share in the Czech Republic

	1990	1991	1992	1993	1994	1995	1996
GDP generated in the private sector (%)	12	17	28	45	56	64	74

Source   Czech Statistical Office

Quite naturally, with the economy being so heavily state controlled, a great deal of attention was paid to privatization. First (ordered chronologically) came the restitution laws, prescribing the return of certain property to its previous owners. Second came 'small-scale privatization' used mostly for the privatization of smaller units through public auctions. Last, but most important due to its scale, was 'mass privatization' involving a whole range of privatization methods – from auctions and direct sales to the voucher method, based on a partly-free distribution of shares to the general public. Apart from that, some property was transferred to municipalities (municipalities were also beneficiaries of free transfers within mass privatization).

Another issue was the transformation of cooperatives, which was important particularly in agriculture, but also in retail trading and other branches.

From the quantitative point of view, the most important method was mass privatization: up until June 30, 1993, property worth CSK 597 billion[1] was approved for privatization, out of which property worth CSK 278 billion was distributed via vouchers. Second in importance were transfers to municipalities: around 6,000 municipalities received property worth CSK 350 billion in 1991, and they received some more property from mass privatization in the two subsequent years. Property involved in restitution amounted to between CSK 75 and 125 billion. Small privatization attracted sales amounting to CSK 31 billion. Foreign direct investment had contributed only CSK 58.2 billion between January 1, 1990 and September 30, 1993: its role is, in proportion to the amount of property privatized, relatively small. Because this study deals with those investment privatization funds emerging from 'large-scale privatization', we will omit further detailed discussion on restitution and/or 'small privatization'.

Key Institutions in the Privatization Process

Many institutions played an important role in the privatization process. At the time of the Czechoslovak federation, some of them already existed but only at the republic level. The Ministries of Privatization (one in each republic; on the federal level, their responsibilities with respect to federal property were held by the Ministry of Finance), the Fund of National Property (FNP; Czech, Slovak and, until December 31, 1993, also Federal FNP), and City and District Privatization Committees were all created solely for the sake of privatization. Many other institutions, such as Ministries of Finance (also one in each republic and a federal one), and the so-called 'founding ministries', took on privatization as an additional task.

The Ministry of Privatization (the official name is 'Ministry for the Administration of National Property and its Privatization') was founded in both the Czech and Slovak republics after the first free elections in 1990. Its agenda was broad: it was responsible for some restitution cases (receiving claims for financial compensation), and formally approved all businesses to be auctioned within small and mass privatization. Whereas its role in the former was restricted to a simple yes or no decision, its role in mass privatization developed into quite an active one: it often entered into negotiations with submitters of privatization proposals and made suggestions which sometimes resulted in significant changes to projects.

The Funds of National Property (of the Czech Republic, Slovak Republic and Federal) were established in 1991. All of them were designed with rather limited agendas: the Funds of the republics were recipients of sales proceeds from small and mass privatization, and they financed certain compensation claims as part of restitution. They were the vehicle for the formal exchange of property after a privatization project had been approved by all parties, but they were not supposed to alter or renegotiate the terms of the deal. The Funds are not under the authority of the government but are responsible to their respective parliaments.

Several ministries of the republics (before 1993 also at the federal level) played the role of founding ministries. In the planned economy period, each state-owned enterprise was subjected to one of the 'branch ministries', each being designed to control a particular branch of the economy: manufacturing, heavy engineering, construction, domestic trade and a few others. Since 1989, the number of such ministries has been progressively reduced. In the Czech Republic, two of them cover industry and trade, one covers agriculture, and the ministries of health and cultural affairs are responsible for selected enterprises. The founding ministries ensured that management of enterprises in their sphere, which were to be privatized, submitted a basic privatization proposal. They also submitted evaluations of all projects concerning 'their' enterprises.

The Federal Ministry of Finance had two roles: it had responsibilities to the privatization ministry with respect to those enterprises directly controlled by the federal government. It was also in charge of organizing the demand side of voucher privatization (i.e., for distributing vouchers to citizens and documenting their distribution) as well as of running the matching mechanism to equalize demand with the (fixed) supply. For this purpose, a special branch of the ministry, the 'Center for Voucher Privatization' was founded. The first wave of voucher privatization was organized only at the federal level (no Centers for Voucher Privatization were formed in the republics). The second wave was under the control of the Ministry of Finance and the Center for Voucher Privatization of the Czech Republic.

Mass Privatization

The first proposal for a mass privatization program occurred within the Czechoslovak context as early as December 1989 (Svejnar, 1989). It was basically a proposal to transform state-owned companies into joint-stock companies and, in the second step, to distribute their shares for free amongst the citizens. The following strategies for distributing company shares were discussed in Czechoslovakia:

- give the shares (a) to the citizens through shares in several mutual funds holding shares of firms. The shares of the mutual funds would be distributed freely to inhabitants, (b) to pension and health insurance companies, (c) to local governments or to other entities (Svejnar, 1989). Very similar proposals were (and still are) discussed in Poland (Lipton and Sachs, 1990 or Frydman and Rapaczynski, 1991);
- distribute shares through holding companies, so that each firm would be controlled by one company (Blanchard *et al.*, 1991); and
- issue free or almost free vouchers, entitling holders to demand shares of any privatized firm. This method leaves all decisions up to citizens (those who choose to participate).

Finally, the approved program for mass privatization in the Czech and Slovak Republics was quite flexible in terms of privatization methods: it allowed for direct sales, auctions, transformation into a joint-stock company and the sale or voucher distribution of shares, or a combination of different methods. Within the voucher scheme, there was also some freedom of choice: citizens could either bid with their vouchers for stocks of some particular companies, or allocate them to mutual funds. Unlike in plans discussed in Poland, those funds were established based solely on the decision of private or semiprivate entities to run such a fund; most of the funds were controlled by financial institutions. On the other hand, flexibility in the use of vouchers did not go as far as vouchers used in Russia. Vouchers could not be used for any other purchases (i.e., in small-scale privatization). Further discussion on voucher privatization can be found in Coffee (1996).

Legal framework of mass privatization

The legal basis for mass privatization consisted of several laws and administrative regulations. The Law on the Conditions of Transferring State Property to Other Persons (#92/1991), passed on February 26, 1991 (effective since April 1991) gave basic guidelines for the privatization of state-owned enterprises, banks, insurance companies and other institutions, including shares and other property assets owned by the state or the above institutions of other enterprises (e.g., a Czechoslovak property share on joint ventures, owned either directly by the state or by a state-owned enterprise). The law also established a Federal Fund of National Property. Unlike in restitution laws, the new owners could be either domestic or foreign entities. The property to be privatized included all assets, liabilities and claims of an enterprise; all contracts, wages and other agreements of the enterprise remained valid after being privatized. The only exceptions were property falling within natural restitution or privatized in small privatization and areas where the law requires state ownership.

Mass privatization was carried out through the five privatization methods possible:

- transformation into a joint-stock company and further transfers of the shares (i.e., by voucher privatization);
- direct sale to a predetermined buyer;
- public auction or public tender;
- transfer to municipal property; and
- transfer to social security, health insurance and other publicly beneficial institutions.

The privatization of each enterprise was based on an officially accepted privatization project. According to the law, each enterprise chosen by the government for privatization in one of two privatization waves (all state-owned enterprises were listed either in one of the waves or as enterprises temporarily exempt from privatization[2]) was obliged to submit its basic privatization project.

Responsibility for doing so lay on the founding institution, mostly a ministry. Those projects were primarily designed by the management of an enterprise. Moreover, anybody could present a competing project which, if it satisfied certain requirements, would be considered on an equal basis by all authorities involved in the privatization. After the projects were submitted, the founding ministry evaluated them (in some cases there were more than a dozen projects for a single firm) and passed its evaluation to the decisive body – the Federal Ministry of Finance (for former federal property) or to the republican Ministry for Privatization. In some cases, the right to decide was taken from those ministries by the government. This was mostly the case when a project was based on a direct sale without auction or public competition and/or when a foreign entity was the buyer.

Each project had to include a proposal to organize the privatized enterprise (for privatization, SOEs could be divided into new firms which could be sold or transferred separately), and one of the five approved privatization methods. Projects also had to contain information on the recent history of the privatized enterprise: for the period of 1989 to 1991 (for projects submitted in the first wave) it had to reveal data on employment, wages, capital, total sales and costs, profit and foreign trade.[3] To enable submitters of competing projects to provide this information (most of it was non-public in character), the management of privatized SOEs were obliged to provide information needed for the privatization project upon request.

The pricing of privatized enterprises differed according to the method of privatization and according to the status of the prospective buyer. In all cases, the book value had to be stated in a project: for this purpose, a copy of the enterprise's balance sheet had to be attached to determine net worth. Land and immovables had to be priced according to the existing pricing regulation[4] (which in most cases differed significantly from the book value) and an estimate of off-balance sheet assets had to be provided. For public auctions, tenders or direct sales to domestic buyers, this book value was taken as the basis for the starting or sale price; for transformations into joint-stock companies, it would determine its equity value. Foreign buyers had to propose a price based on an audit by an independent accountant, which was then subjected to further negotiations. The lawmakers intended this provision to present an advantage to local buyers; in fact, book values were often based on assets of dubious worth, so that direct sales to both domestic and foreign buyers used values estimated by auditing firms.

After a project was approved by the proper decision-maker, the property of an SOE was transferred to the Federal (or each republic's) Fund of National Property. This organizational peculiarity dissolved the firm without the founder liquidating it (founding ministry), and established a 'new' company by the Fund. The Fund's assets and their yields were separated from both federal and republic budgets. The Funds then sold or transferred the property according to the method(s) proposed in the approved project, possibly involving a provision that the Fund retain part of the property in its hands (in reality this only applied to some joint-stock companies). One of the methods of distributing shares was mass privatization with the use of the voucher scheme, which is later described in detail.

Table 1.2   Timetable for mass privatization

	Who was responsible	Date due
Approving and publishing lists of enterprises to be privatized in 1st and 2nd rounds and of those not to be privatized	Founding ministries, governments	June 1991
Submitting projects to founding ministries	Enterprises	31 Oct. 1991
Submitting projects to the Ministry of Privatization	Enterprise founders	30 Nov. 1991
Planned submitting of firm lists for voucher privatization with specified number of voucher shares	Ministries of Privat'n	15 Dec. 1991
Prolonged deadline for competing projects	Project submitters	20 Jan. 1992
Approving projects and subsequent privatizing of SOEs	Ministries of Privt'n, Governments	from 20 Jan. 1992[5]
Submitting of projects for second wave: exception for enterprises founded by Ministry of Health and for selected enterprises	Project submitters, founding ministries	16 Jul. 1992 31 Oct 1992 1 Jan. 1993
Submitting and publishing of preliminary list of enterprises to be privatized in second wave of voucher privatization	Ministry of Privat'n	1 Oct. 1993
Approving projects and subsequent privatizing of SOEs (2nd wave)	Ministry of Privat'n, Government	29 Oct. 1993

Mass privatization: scope and some results

Mass privatization involved most state-owned assets in industry, agriculture and trade. By way of illustration: the officially reported book value of capital in the Czech Republic in 1990 was CSK 2,604 billion, including houses, castles, railways and other non-privatized property. The book value of enterprises approved for privatization in the first wave was CSK 539 billion on June 30, 1993. The total value of the 2,800 enterprises planned to be privatized in the first wave amounted to approximately CSK 680 billion; some enterprises scheduled for the first wave were, however, moved to the second wave. The second wave had to cover around 2,000 enterprises worth approximately CSK 550 billion.

The first steps towards mass privatization had already been taken in 1991 (the relevant law being valid since April 1, 1991). It turned out that the process of compiling a project, the founding ministries processing it, the privatization authorities approving it and finally transferring the property to the new owner was rather lengthy. In fact, privatization started only in 1992 (see Table 1.2).

Apparently, after the rush in the second quarter of 1992 (within which one finds the beginning of the first wave of voucher privatization), the privatization process went much more slowly in the subsequent quarter and, in the fourth quarter of

1992, it basically stopped – property worth only 6.4 billion was approved for privatization, compared to the 32 billion in the third, or even the 366 billion in the 'voucher quarter'. This was due to several factors: after June 1992, a new administration came to power (unlike in Slovakia, there was only a minor shift in the political makeup of the government in the Czech Republic; however, in both republics there was a change in the head of the privatization ministry). Probably more significant was the fact that the least problematic projects were approved easily, and the 'troublemakers' kept the administration busy. Table 1.4 shows that there were a number of non-eligible projects from the first wave (submitted at the latest in the beginning of 1992) which were not decided before the end of 1993.

Table 1.3   Mass privatization: approved projects[1].

Privatization method			Number of privatization units Volume of property approved by Dec. 31	
	1992	1993	1994	1995
Public auction	336	639	2,000	2,128
	3,881	6,439	9,126	9,314
Public tender	300	599	1,117	1,394
	10,436	20,283	29,556	33,001
Direct sale	986	2,522	10,024	11,343[2]
	26,613	56,906	94,879	91,653[2]
Privatization of	1,218	1,716	1,870	1,883
joint-stock co.	420,171	696,998	744,525	768,101
Unpaid transfer	1,052	2,488	4,380	4,857[2]
	9,633	28,641	59,042	55,749[2]
Total	3,900	7,964	19,391	21,605
	470,734	809,267	937,128	957,818

Notes
(1)   Former federal property is not included.
(2)   In some cases, the approved privatization method failed (the buyer did not pay, the municipality refused to take over the hospital). In such cases, the privatization project was returned and reconsidered. Since direct sales, in particular, were 're-approved' as public tenders, the volume of property approved as of December 31, 1995 was lower than the previous year.

Source   Ministry for Privatization of the Czech Republic

In the beginning of 1993, mass privatization sped up again: projects for the second wave came in, and the bulk of large enterprises undergoing voucher privatization had to be finalized by October 1993. However, the speed achieved in the early period of privatization was not matched. After 1993, privatization projects of the major industrial firms had already been decided. Most privatization units approved were smaller agricultural and healthcare establishments so that, in spite of the seemingly sharp increase in the number of units, the value of property for privatization was stagnating. Tables 1.4 and 1.5 present a comprehensive breakdown of projects finalized by the Fund of National Property and final numbers of privatized enterprises according to such projects.

Table 1.4   Mass privatization: projects finalized by the FNP[1]

Privatization method	Number of privatization units Volume of property privatized by Dec. 31			
	1992	*1993*	*1994*	*1995*
Public auction	174 n.a.	278 2,885	558 4,210	777 6,787
Public tender	128 n.a.	285 10,081	400 17,813	570 18,432
Direct sale	587 n.a.	1,143 35,351	2,240 45,111	4,611 55,171
Restitution & direct sale	n.a. n.a.	73 5,259	262 5,889	244[1] 3,675
Privatization of joint-stock co.	1,210 n.a.	1,423 530,322	1,841 559,697	1737 754,652
Free transfer	559 n.a.	1,157 10,050	2,360 16,685	3,281 29,787
Total units privatized[2]	2,565 n.a.	4,359 593,847	7,664 646,505	11,220 868,504

Notes
(1)   Property returned and privatization cancelled in some cases. In total, 991 projects were returned from the Fund to the Ministry in 1995 alone. Some of the returned projects had already been implemented.
(2)   Excluding restitution administered by the FNP; these units are included in standard reports by the Fund, but not in 'approved units' by the Ministry.

Source   Fund of National Property of the Czech Republic

Table 1.5   Privatization projects and privatized enterprises in the Czech Republic

Status as of	Dec. 31, 1993		Dec. 31, 1994		Dec. 31, 1995	
Number of projects	Projects	Firms[1]	Projects	Firms	Projects	Firms
Submitted	23,607	4,335	26,614	4,638	27,901	5,087
Decided	14,374	2,694	21,144	3,842	24,259	4,424
Approved	4,646	2,470	6,737	3,278	7,367	3,552
Rejected	9,728	224	14,407	564	16,892	872
Undecided	9,223	1,641	5,470	796	3,642	663

Note
(1)   Number of firms for which projects were decided, undecided or all projects rejected.

Source   Report of Ministry of Privatization of the Czech Republic

One also cannot neglect the fact that although legislators and privatization authorities originally thought that in most cases only one project would be submitted for each firm, and the approval process would really be an approval process and not a decision-making one, this did not happen at all. Only about one quarter of the projects submitted were basic projects designed by the management of firms: for 4,493 firms 23,319 projects were submitted. Even though one firm could be privatized by more than one project (if it was being privatized in parts, there was no reason to sell all parts according to a single project) and, therefore, not all submitted projects really competed with each other, for most firms, privatization authorities had to select the winning project out of many. Table 1.6 summarizes those who submitted projects for enterprises included in the first wave of privatization.

Table 1.6   Submitters of projects in the Czech Republic

Project submitted by	1991 – Dec. 31, 1993			
	Total	*%*	*Approved*	*%*
Management of company	4,992	21.15	2,492	53.63
Management of establishment	711	3.01	203	4.37
Bidder for purchase of company	11,478	48.62	1,255	27.01
District Privatization Commission	1,123	4.76	176	3.79
Restitution claimants	630	2.67	134	2.88
Local government	715	3.03	55	1.18
Consulting firms	527	2.32	72	1.55
Employees	1,141	4.83	30	.65
Total	23,607	100	4,647	100

Source   Report of the Ministry of Privatization of the Czech Republic

THE ROLE OF INVESTMENT PRIVATIZATION FUNDS (IPFS) IN THE PRIVATIZATION AND POST-PRIVATIZATION PERIODS

Investment Privatization Funds

A brief paragraph of the Law on the Conditions of Transferring State Property to Other Persons (#92/1991) enabled investment privatization funds (IPFs) to participate in voucher privatization. Even though the By-law on the Issue and Use of Privatization Vouchers (#383/91) and particularly its amendment in early 1992 (#62/1992) set some regulations on the functioning of IPFs, the law on their regulation (248/1991 on Investment Corporations and Investment Funds) was passed only in April 28, 1992 – two months after the deadline for registration of IPFs. Until then, the establishing of IPFs was guided by the Law on Joint-Stock Companies (#104/1990) for companies established before December 31, 1991, and thereafter by the newly-introduced Commercial Code (Law # 513/1991).

The delay in passing the law on investment corporations had two major negative impacts on the first wave: one of them was a lack of regulation. Whereas that impact might have been welcomed by the founders of IPFs, the other one was not: the only possible form IPFs could take was as independent joint-stock companies, with all the complexities of corporate governance they can bring about. The Law on Investment Corporations and Funds allowed this legal form too but, in addition, it allowed open or closed mutual funds with far easier and cheaper management. Both closed and open mutual funds were widely used in the second wave.

To establish an IPF, its founder had to be a 'legal entity' (i.e., had to be incorporated) with equity of at least CSK 1,000,000 (i.e., US$ 33,000) per fund established. To apply to a ministry of privatization for approval, a founder had to submit a proposal for the establisher's plan and for the contract between himself and the IPF (which was a separate corporation) concerning the conditions of controlling the fund and a draft of the status of the IPF. The establisher's plan had to contain the following:

- conditions of managing the fund by the founder;
- number and qualifications of the proposed staff of the fund's administration;
- composition of the board of directors and supervising board of the fund, including some further information about its members;
- principles of the fund's policy towards branch specialization, attitudes towards risk sharing and so on;
- approval to furnish the fund with equity capital of CSK 100,000 before voucher privatization starts.

The contract between the founder and the fund had to include conditions for rewarding the founder for managing the fund. This reward could not exceed 2% of the nominal value of the shares gained in voucher privatization within the course of privatization or 3% of the property of the fund a year after privatization.

The founding institutions of the privatization funds, the founders, came from a broad spectrum of different legal bodies. A significant number of them were financial institutions of various types. Figures 1.1 and 1.2 provide basic information on this subject with respect to the number of points each fund attracted.

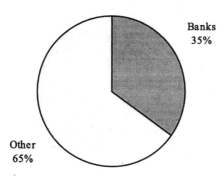

Figure 1.1   Fund founders: wave 1

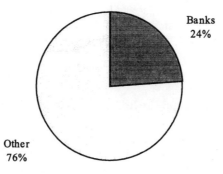

Figure 1.2   Fund founders: wave 2

In the first wave, privatization funds founded by banks captured 35% of the market with the points that were allocated to IPFs. In the second wave, this amount was somewhat lower, but the funds created by banks were still able to take 24% of the market. Under the term 'bank' are included not only typical banking houses and their sister companies but also insurance companies and their sisters as well. The rest of the market with voucher points to be allocated to IPFs was within the domain of funds that were created by other institutions. The majority of these institutions were manufacturing works. Their activities were supposed to be related to the business of a particular founder.

Each fund which intended to take part in voucher privatization had to be approved by the Ministry of Privatization; this was rather peculiar in the first wave since both voucher privatization and activities of IPFs were spread over all the Federation. The approved fund had to be established as a company (IPFs only), and after receiving an organization identification number, the fund could be registered, published in the official list of funds participating in the particular wave and become one of the options for the participants of voucher privatization in the 'zero round'. The first and second waves were quite different. We shall therefore discuss them separately.

The regulation of funds evolved slowly. The first step was an incompatibility clause, excluding top government officials from the boards of IPFs (via an amendment to the By-law on the Issue of Vouchers). The same norm restricted bidding by IPFs in the following way: an IPF could not invest more than 10% of its points in a single company, and could not obtain more than a 20% share of a company. IPFs established by a single founder were allowed to get 40%, but by a later law this was reduced to 20%, so that no single founder could receive more than one fifth of an enterprise privatized through vouchers. References to how other countries privatizing state-owned enterprises in terms of percentage stake acquisitions are discussed by Luftmann (1992) amongst others. However, since IPFs could merge (and they really did), the effect of this provision – if its purpose was to prevent a fund from controlling a firm – is questionable. Another provision of Law #248/1992 prevented the purchase of shares of financial institutions by IPFs founded by financial institutions (among other companies, shares of largest banks, insurance companies and savings and loans were offered in the first wave). Due to a lack of enforcement, this provision was also widely violated without noticeable consequences.

Voucher Privatization and the Role of Individual Investors and IPFs

The Law on Mass Privatization also allowed the distribution of shares of joint-stock companies via vouchers. Law #92/1991 stated who could take part in this process, but failed to give any detailed description of how the process should be organized. This was done by the by-law of the federal government #383/1991 on September 5, 1991 (effective September 30), which defined the technical procedure of voucher privatization and precisely described how an eligible person can obtain vouchers and set rudimentary guidelines for the functioning of Investment Privatization Funds (special mutual funds to which voucher holders could transfer their entitlement for free shares).

Unlike other privatization methods, voucher privatization depended heavily on the division of the process into privatization waves. In each wave, certain previously announced groups of enterprises (several hundreds to thousands) were offered for privatization. The voucher scheme was based on the matching of bids by voucher holders with a fixed number of supplied shares of enterprises, the goal being to sell off as much as possible.

The supply of enterprises to be privatized through vouchers was the outcome of the process of submitting and approving privatization projects as described in the previous section. The privatization authorities set a rough goal in terms of how much property should go into voucher privatization. In the process of submitting and reviewing the projects, privatization ministries had to submit information to the Federal Ministry of Finance. Since the process was federally organized, and citizens in both republics were allowed to bid for enterprises in their own republic as well as in the other, after registration it was necessary to adjust the amount of property supplied in each republic to the number of participating citizens.

The demand side of voucher privatization was formed by vouchers distributed to citizens. Starting in late 1991, post offices had to supply voucher books for the first round; the same procedure was used in late 1993 for the second round. Every Czechoslovak (Czech only for the second wave) citizen over 18 permanently residing in Czechoslovakia could register one such book for a fee of CSK 1,000 (approx. US$ 35). After doing so, the citizen was entitled to bid for shares of privatized enterprises within the given privatization wave: each voucher, formally worth 1,000 'investment points' was divided into ten 100 point parts. Before real bidding for shares began, participants could transfer the whole voucher, or a part of their point endowment, to the Investment Privatization Funds. Throughout the rest of the privatization wave, the funds would bid in the same way as other voucher holders (with some exceptions described later); shares of each fund were distributed proportionally among those who put their points into it.

Within each *privatization wave,* the following procedure applied: after eligible citizens registered their vouchers and privatization funds received their approvals from the ministries of privatization (for registration of citizens and funds, there were certain deadlines), lists of Investment Privatization Funds (IPFs) and of enterprises – joint-stock companies – were offered in a given round. For each enterprise, some essential information on its performance was revealed in the published list, including total sales, profits, employment, book value, outstanding bank loans, net worth for the previous three years (1989–1991 for first wave) as well as the percentage of shares offered for vouchers sold to foreigners or to domestic buyers or, in some cases, left in the hands of one of the Funds of National Property. Based on this information, voucher holders had to decide how many points to allocate on their own, and how many through IPFs. Assigning of points to IPFs was called the 'zero round', and was held before anybody was allowed to bid for shares. At the end of this 'zero round', all the points not given to IPFs had to be allocated individually by voucher holders.

Bidding for the shares of enterprises was organized within several *privatization rounds.* Each round had several phases:

- announcing the number and price of shares for each company (given in shares offered for 100 points) in a given round. In the first round, the price was uniform and published in the list of enterprises with all other information mentioned above. The published list of prices (from the 2nd round on) also summarized results of the previous round – the size and ratio of supply and demand in shares;

- ordering shares of particular companies by voucher holders: several hundred 'registration places' collected the orders and sent them to the central authority;
- processing of orders by the Center for Voucher Privatization in the following way:
  - (a) if demand was below or exactly equal to supply, all orders were met at the price valid for a given round;
  - (b) if demand exceeded the supply by less than 25%, the excess could be removed by a proportional cut in the demand of IFPs. However, this cut could not exceed 20% of the order of any mutual fund;
  - (c) if demand exceeded the supply and the provisions described above were not applicable, the orders were cancelled and points used in them were left to the voucher holders for the next round;
- the last phase was setting prices for the next round based on the performance of this 'market' for companies not yet fully sold; then a new round could start.

The way prices were cooked by the price commission of the Center is one of the little secrets of the process; estimations of price equations by Singer and Svejnar (1994) and Hanousek and Lastovicka (1993) show that the most important factors for setting the price of shares in a particular round were their price in the previous round, the ratio between demand and supply (both with positive coefficients) and the size of total supply (with a negative coefficient). According to both studies, each round had its own different set of coefficients; the exact formula for prices seems not to be retrievable by econometric estimations.

Conclusion of the process was left to the discretion of the Ministry of Finance: if it decided that it had converged enough, it could declare a particular round as being final; after this round ended, all points used for orders which were not satisfied were declared void, the results of all rounds were aggregated and each voucher holder got the shares for which he had successfully bid.

The Voucher Scheme at Work: First Wave

On the supply side, a total of 1,492 enterprises was offered in the whole Czechoslovak Federation (see Table 1.7). There were significant differences between privatization projects for voucher privatization in the Czech Republic and in Slovakia: whereas in the Czech Republic most projects combined the voucher method with other methods (only 39.7 % of them used vouchers as the only method), in Slovakia 90.1% of projects were based on only one method. (Federally-owned property was also mostly privatized with a combination of at least two methods.) Many projects combined the voucher method with sales to domestic or foreign investors or through the creation of a joint venture.

Table 1.7   Structure of privatization of joint-stock companies participating in the first wave of voucher privatization

| | Number of privatization units into which privatized state-owned enterprises were divided[1] | | | | |
	1	2–4	5–9	10 and more	Total
Czech JSC	600	248	99	41	988
Slovak JSC	320	108	70	5	503
Total CSFR	920	356	169	46	1,491
Second wave	324	160	74	118	676

Note
(1)   In some cases, more than one unit was privatized within voucher privatization. Each company was then counted separately. 1,491 joint-stock companies were established from 1,309 originally state-owned enterprises.

Source   Database published by the Center for Voucher Privatization

In some cases, the Fund of National Property kept part of the property. There were two main reasons for this. First, the Fund wanted to preserve a domestic majority or even influence the state in some important enterprises, i.e., major banking institutions (see Table 1.8). Second, pending negotiations with foreign or domestic investors, the Fund kept some of the property as part of a contract for a joint venture, passing shares of an FNP to a foreign partner when it actually provided the agreed number of investments. Such was the case with, for example, the monopoly producer of tobacco products Tabak, later sold to Philip Morris.

Table 1.8   Major financial institutions: state preserves influence

Institution	Book value	Vouchers	Other investors		FNP
Komerčni banka	4.56	53%	–		44%
VUB	2.04	52%	–		45%
Czech S&L	5.60	37%	Municipalities	20%	40%
Czech Insurance Co.	1.64	15%	CS Trade Bank	15%	23%
			Interbanka	7.7%	
			Komerčni banka	10%	
			Investični banka	10%	
			Savings Bank	10%	
			Employees	5%	
Investični	1.00	52%	–		45%

Source   Kuponova privatizace 6, 1992

On the demand side, development was rather dramatic in the first wave: between November 1992 and early January, only several hundred thousand persons registered their voucher books. Government estimates were that around 2.5 millions inhabitants would do so before the deadline for registration. This goal was roughly achieved by mid-January. Had the property been divided between the voucher holders registered at that time, each voucher book worth 1,035 crowns would have yielded property at a nominal value of 70,000 crowns. At that time, several private as well as state-owned bank-sponsored Investment Privatization Funds started aggressive campaigns to attract voucher holders to give their shares to them. One of the private companies controlling several funds, Harvard Capital & Consulting[6] focused on those who had not decided whether to take a part in voucher privatization by offering 10,035 crowns (ten times more than the cost of registration) to those who gave their vouchers to the fund. This strategy, copied by several funds (the Czech Savings and Loans bank offered immediate credit of 10,000 crowns to voucher holders who gave their points to its IPF), attracted far more citizens than anyone expected: 8,565,642 citizens, approximately 75% of those eligible, registered by the end of February 1992. This, of course, proportionally reduced the value of assets going to each participant to 35,000 crowns.

Four hundred and thirty-four IPFs founded by various entities entered into the zero round; those which turned out to be most successful were funds connected with large financial institutions, but all sorts of other funds tried their luck, too. The fact that many citizens decided to register for voucher privatization only because of the IPF campaign was reflected in results of the zero round. At least 72% of all voucher points were put into IPFs, leaving only 28% in the hands of individual voucher investors.

Table 1.9   The zero round: funds stand high

Millions of points	Czech Republic	Slovak Republic	Total
Held by citizens	5.980	2.580	8.560
Given to IPFs	4.320	1.820	6.130
– Czech IPFs	4.290	0.180	4.470
– Slovak IPFs	0.030	1.630	1.660

Apparently, the citizens of both republics tended to invest their points domestically, but Slovak citizens invested more in the Czech Republic than vice versa (see Table 1.9). This trend was even stronger in real bidding for shares in the first to fifth rounds. Another significant trend – possibly very important for the future role of funds in the Czech and Slovak economies – was the tendency to put points into large, well-known funds instead of funds specializing in some particular branch or region. Among the nine most successful, only one fund was not connected with a major financial institution: Harvard Capital & Consulting, and one of the others was founded by a foreign bank (Creditanstalt, an affiliate of a major Austrian bank). The thirteen largest IPF founders controlled over 56% of all points given to funds. The degree of concentration is illustrated in Table 1.10.

Table 1.10   Structure of IPFs according to size

Size of IPF in points received (million)	< 1.0	1–5	5–10	10–50	50–100	> 100
Number of IPFs	191	122	43	59	6	13

Table 1.11 shows the distribution of shares allocated to IPFs during the first privatization wave. The shares were distributed by a founder of the IPF.

Table 1.11   Distribution of shares allocated to IPFs, by founder (wave 1)

Founder	No. of points allocated	Market share	Cumulative market share	No. of IPFs
Česká státni spořitelna	950,918,800	15.494	15.494	1
První investiční, a.s.	713,837,100	11.631	27.126	11
Harvard capital and consulting	565,170,000	9.209	36.334	6
V+B INVEST, i.a.s.	500,668,100	8.158	44.492	1
IKS KB spol. s r.o.	465,708,300	7.588	52.081	1
Kapitál. invest. Společnost, a.s.	334,234,900	5.446	57.527	1
SLOVENSKÉ INVESTICIE, s.r.o.	188,041,300	3.064	60.591	1
CREDITANSTALT, a.s.	138,924,800	2.264	62.854	1
PRVÁ SLOVENSKÁ INVESTIČNÍ, a.s	136,348,000	2.222	65.076	11
Správce prvního privatiz. fondu	117,681,800	1.918	66.993	4
Živnostenská banka, a.s.	117606100	1.916	68.910	1
SLOVENSKÁ POISŤOVŇA, a.s.	108,710,600	1.771	70.681	5
Investiční společnost BOHEMIA	85,363,700	1.391	72.072	6
AGROBANKA PRAHA, a.s.	85,035,000	1.386	73.457	13
VSŽ, a.s. Košice	78,409,000	1.278	74.735	1
HC and CS, a.s.	73,454,900	1.197	75.932	2
LINH ART spol. s r.o.	72,141,000	1.175	77.107	1
DIVIDEND, a.s.	55,264,000	0.900	78.008	10
SLOVHOLDING, a.s. .	50,553,900	0.824	78.832	1
O.B.INVEST, spol. s r.o.	48,644,900	0.793	79.624	2
C.S. Fond, a.s.	46,154,000	0.752	80.376	3
Panok - Knight, a.s.	42,971,500	0.700	81.076	1
GUMÁRNE BARUM, a.s., Púchov	39,764,200	0.648	81.724	1

Table 1.11　(continued)

Founder	No. of points allocated	Market share	Cumulative market share	No. of IPFs
VSŽ, a.s., Košice + SŠTSP, š.p.	37,815,400	0.616	82.341	1
CZECH INVESTMENT COMPANY	35,944,400	0.586	82.926	1
SKLOEXPORT, a.s.	34,803,800	0.567	83.493	1
Evrobanka, a.s., Praha	32,321,300	0.527	84.020	2
SLOVENSKÁ ŠTÁTNA SPORITEĽŇA	31,525,300	0.514	84.534	1
Pivovar RADEGAST, a.s.	31,153,600	0.508	85.041	1
COOPEX INVEST, a.s.	29,103,100	0.474	85.515	1

Source　Authors' computations

The largest IPF, created by Česká státní spořitelna, captured almost one billion of the allocated points, which is more than 33 times the amount allocated to the least successful IPF. This is a strikingly high amount and, in reality, represents 15.5% of the market share. It is also evident that the second largest fund founder (První investiční) does not lag far behind with its 11.6% market share, which is divided among its 11 funds.

Thus, the two strongest IPF founders accounted for more than 27% of the market with allocated points in the first wave. The next three fund founders can be regarded as similar in size with about 8% of the market share each. However, Harvard Capital and Consulting spread its 9% share among its 6 different funds while První investiční created 11 funds. Altogether, the five largest IPF founders captured more than one half of the voucher scheme market. Such an uneven but understandable result is illustrated by Figure 1.3.

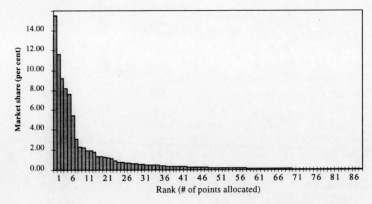

Figure 1.3　Wave 1: market shares of the managers of the biggest funds

The bidding procedure for both individual voucher holders and IPFs took five rounds, lasting from May 18 until December 22, 1992. All economic agents involved (with one small exception on the side of the price committee) behaved quite rationally: in the beginning, the prices of shares of all firms were set uniformly at 30 shares per 1,000 points (a whole voucher book). Bidders tried to get the most attractive shares at a low uniform price: this resulted in a very poor rate of allocation (only 29.9% of offered shares were sold with an extremely high participation of bidders). The second round was a round of waiting: prices of poor enterprises were still quite high (a maximum of 100 shares per 1,000 points), participation the lowest ever and the rate of allocation moderate. The third round was marked by the above mentioned irrationality of the Price Committee: prices for the cheapest firms were set as low as 970 shares per 1,000 points, with relatively high prices for the best firms. This resulted in the most active participation of bidders in the process (running into the cheapest firms) and, due to widespread excess demand, in the poorest result in terms of proportion of offered shares sold. Out of 132.1 million shares, only 32.4 million were sold, and total demand exceeded supply by 107.3 %. The fourth round, with lower extremes cut back, showed relatively good results with 93% of investment points used and 78.8% of shares sold, so that the next round was declared to be the last one. Participants were urged not to change their selections dramatically – in firms where excess demand had been observed in the previous round, prices were increased so that if all bidders were consistent in their demand, no excess demand would arise – and, surprisingly, this suggestion worked quite well. The last round had a record rate of allocation of points (93% of points used for bidding were successfully allocated) as well as shares: (40.9 million shares out of 62.5 million shares left were sold). During the whole bidding procedure, 99% of points available were used and 92.8% of shares offered were sold.

Empirical studies (Hanousek and Lastovicka, 1993; Singer and Svejnar 1994) also indicate that the investment behavior of funds and individuals was significantly different in each round. This was caused (apart from other factors like mis-specification of equations, which both groups of authors estimated) by the strategic considerations bidders had to take into account. The first and most straightforward factor determining demand in each round was the expected value of shares of each firm: those who value some particular title most, so that its relative expected value exceeds the relative price (compared to other firms offered) should bid for it. However, since the final round was not announced before its start (in the fourth round, nobody knew that the fifth one would be final), with each round, bidders had to consider the probability of placing their points. If they valued some firm a lot, they had to consider what the probability was of too many bids from others for the same firm, in order to prevent excess demand (and, therefore, zero allocation of points).

The Voucher Scheme at Work: Second Wave

Whereas in the first wave, shares representing CSK 212.5 billion of the book value of Czech enterprises were sold (the remaining 86.9 billion came from Slovakia), the second wave sold shares representing only 145 to 147 billion. Moreover, 21.1 billion came from unsold shares from the first wave. On the other hand, the participation of Czech citizens was high compared to the previous wave: in the first one, 5.83 million citizens registered their vouchers; in the second this number exceeded 6 million.

The second wave of large privatization offered quite modest outcomes in comparison with the first. Table 1.12 shows that the market share with respect to point allocation was somewhat more evenly distributed.

Then the 10 founding institutions with their 48 funds were needed to capture more than half of the market. However, roughly half of this portion could be credited to the first three funds, which were very similar in size (A-INVEST, Expandia, and Harvard). These three funds attracted around 300 billion points each. The combined number of points allocated to fund founders was, however, still less than that of the single leading founder from the first wave (Česká státní spořitelna), which formed one large IPF. Again, as in the first wave, Harvard Capital and Consulting spread its 7.5% share over a large number of funds – 23 this time.

Table 1.12   Distribution of shares allocated to IPFs, by founder (wave 2)

Founder	No. of points allocated	Market share	Cumulative market share	No. of IPFs
A-INVEST, investiční společnost, a.s.	309,243,300	7.896	7.896	2
Investiční společnost Expandia, a.s.	306,290,600	7.820	15.716	3
Harvard Capital and Consulting, a.s.	292,170,900	7.460	23.176	23
O.B.Invest, investiční společnost, s.r.o.	198,351,200	5.064	28.240	3
KIS, a.s., Kapitálová investiční společnost České pojišťovny	186,697,800	4.767	33.007	3
Investiční společnost podnikatelů, a.s.	159,263,500	4.066	37.073	2
Investiční společnost Linh Art, s.r.o.	156,432,100	3.994	41.067	3
Czech investment company investiční společnost, spol. s r.o.	151,666,300	3.872	44.939	1
Spořitelní investiční společnost, a.s.	124,161,800	3.170	48.110	1

Founder	No. of points allocated	Market share	Cumulative market share	No. of IPFs
Investiční kapitálová společnost KB, a.s.	124,063,500	3.168	51.277	1
PPF investiční společnost, a.s.	119,703,700	3.056	54.334	2
První investiční akciová společnost	97,629,000	2.493	56.826	5
C.S. FOND, a.s., investiční společnost	94,007,200	2.400	59.226	7
Moravská agrárně potravinářská investiční společnost, akciová společnost	89,932,800	2.296	61.523	1
Creditanstalt investiční společnost, a.s.	78,201,900	1.997	63.519	1
ŽDB, a.s., Bohumín	67,782,700	1.731	65.250	1
KREDITAL, a.s.	65,407,500	1.670	66.920	1
CS FIRST BOSTON investiční společnost, a.s.	65,213,900	1.665	68.585	1
Montované stavby Praha, a.s.	64,533,300	1.648	70.233	1
ŽB - Trust Investiční společnost, s.r.o.	59,538,200	1.520	71.753	1
SHD SPOLEČNÝ PODNIK MOST	56,214,600	1.435	73.188	1
Tradeinvest, investiční společnost, s.r.o.	49,514,000	1.264	74.452	1
Investiční společnost EVBAK, a.s.	46,952,500	1.199	75.651	5
Moravskočeská investiční společnost, a.s.	45,692,500	1.167	76.818	1
Plzeňská investiční společnost, s.r.o.	38,479,400	0.982	77.800	3
Kontinentální sdružení pro investice a obchod, investiční společnost, a.s.	35,255,500	0.900	78.700	2
Investiční společnost Bohemia, a.s.	32,140,500	0.821	79.521	2
Mercia, spol. s r.o.	29,658,300	0.757	80.278	1
COOP INVEST investiční společnost, a.s.	28,599,200	0.730	81.008	1
Česko-kalifornská investiční společnost, Praha, s.r.o.	25,692,500	0.656	81.664	3
České investice, s.r.o.	24,128,000	0.616	82.280	2
Region Invest investiční společnost, a.s.	23,922,300	0.611	82.891	1
Poštovní investiční společnost, a.s.	21,237,100	0.542	83.433	2
ZEMAP-INVEST, první kuponová investiční společnost, s.r.o.	20,282,300	0.518	83.951	3

Source   Authors' computation

Figure 1.4 presents the different market shares among the fund founders in the second wave.

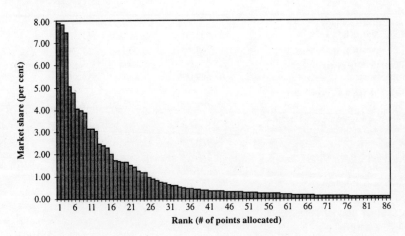

Figure 1.4   Wave 2: market shares of the managers of the biggest funds

The domination of the market by a small number of fund managing institutions in the first wave was then replaced by a somewhat strong leading tier, closely followed by a large group of fund managers of relatively similar size. In other words, the market became more dispersed. This was most probably a result of the learning process citizens underwent during the first wave (in particular, they became more adept at bidding) combined with the better marketing strategies of the fund founders, designed to attract much needed points.

Voucher privatization in the Czech Republic was remarkably successful in allocating shares of the targeted state enterprises quickly and efficiently. The bidding process was crude in many ways, especially in the administration of share prices and in the attempts by the privatization authority artificially to speed the process by over-adjusting prices. But in spite of the artificial price jolts, the market reacted logically, even predictably. In five or six short rounds over a few months almost all shares were allocated and almost all voucher points were spent. Individual investors, taking their cues from the mutual funds (to whom they attributed better information), tried to get the most value for their vouchers. However, these individuals paid less attention to the IPFs in the second wave than in the first, indicating growing investor self-confidence. The IPFs, guided by considerations other than short-term portfolio maximization, tried to acquire shares even at premium prices.

The open and public way that shares were transferred from the state to private hands ensured that no individual or group of investors could reap windfall gains at the expense of the general populace.

THE GOVERNANCE OF IPFs

Mass Privatization: Achievements and Problems

The extent of mass privatization undertaken in Czechoslovakia is globally unprecedented. As a result, it is impossible to evaluate the process and its outcome comparatively. Nevertheless, it is indisputable that the Czechs and Slovaks have proved that a program involving large-scale transfer of ownership of this kind is feasible and can be carried out in a relatively short period of time. The main problems associated with the Czechoslovak scheme appear to have been the following:

The legislative framework for mass privatization, especially for the voucher component, was too vague. Most of the laws spelled out general principles, relegating details to government decrees and *ad hoc* administrative decisions. This gave the governments a lot of discretionary power, which led to abuse. For example, the timing and method of concluding the first wave of voucher privatization was fully determined by a handful of officials. Investors were told that the voucher scheme could be concluded at any time with an *ex post* announcement from that group, with their leftover voucher points becoming worthless.

Voucher privatization also turned out to be difficult to organize. One of the important advantages anticipated by the Czechoslovak authorities when the method was accepted was that this method could turn the difficult decision process of 'who to sell to' into an easier approval process of 'whether to privatize this enterprise or not'. However, as soon as the method started to compete with and be combined with other standard methods, this expected advantage disappeared. The result was a laborious process that led to corruption.

On the other hand, one may argue that using the voucher method as a single privatization tool would have been too risky and that the benefits of diversification more than outweighed the complications brought about by the use of a combination of methods.

Forced Administration and Transformation of IPFs

How did the funds actually perform? Qualitatively, the worst situation was evident in the case of several funds being 'tunneled out'. This means that the real assets of the companies forming a fund's portfolio were to a greater or lesser extent sold and the resulting profits were extracted through various channels that would, in most cases, be illegal in any civilized country. This tunneling out of funds resulted in a forced administration regime. Tables 1.13 and 1.14 offer a breakdown of the funds that were put into forced administration.

Table 1.13   Wave 1: forced administration

Founder	No. of points allocated	Market share	Cumulative market share
Investiční společnost BOHEMIA	85,363,700	1.390918	1.390918
C.S. Fond, a.s.	46,154,000	0.752034	2.142952
CNIS, spol. s r.o.	20,358,400	0.331720	2.474672
Montované stavby Praha, a.s.	13,772,400	0.224408	2.699080
Mercia spol. s r.o.	507,500	0.008269	2.707349

The first wave resulted in five funds being put into forced administration. They represented less than 3% of the market and, thus, forced administration may have simply been due to mismanagement, competition, etc. However, in the second wave 10 'tunneled out' funds captured altogether more than a fifth of the market share, suggesting fraud of a much more pervasive nature than in the first wave.

Table 1.14   Wave 2: forced administration

Founder	No. of points allocated	Market share	Cumulative market share
A-INVEST, investiční společnost, a.s.	309,243,300	7.896	7.896
C.S. FOND, a.s., investiční společnost	94,007,200	2.400	10.296
Investiční fond AGB, a.s.	88,991,700	2.272	12.568
Creditanstalt investiční společnost, a.s.	78,201,900	1.997	14.565
CA-český infrastrukt. IF, a.s.	78,201,900	1.997	16.561
TREND-VIF a.s.	64,533,300	1.648	18.209
Moravskočeská investiční společnost, a.s.	45,692,500	1.167	19.376
Investiční společnost Bohemia, a.s.	32,140,500	0.821	20.196
IF Mercia, a.s.	29,658,300	0.757	20.953
NIS Litomerice	7,266,100	0.186	21.139

The privatization funds started to be transformed over time and based on legislation. Changes to the form of holding companies were by far the most important transformation of this type.

Figure 1.5 shows that 28% of IPFs from the first wave were transformed into holding companies and 3% of IPFs were put into forced administration, which obviously precluded any type of transformation until the authorities decided to remove the forced administration. The remaining IPFs were transformed into different structures or have not yet been transformed.

The second wave resulted in a different picture. Figure 1.6 is quite illustrative of the lower percentage of transformed funds. Roughly 21% of the IPFs were transformed into holding companies. An almost identical portion was, however, put under a regime of forced administration preventing their further transformation. This left the IPFs remaining from the second wave untransformed or transformed into other forms. In other words, the results of the second wave were less favorable than those of the first wave in that the number of IPFs transformed into holding companies decreased and the number of forced administration cases increased.

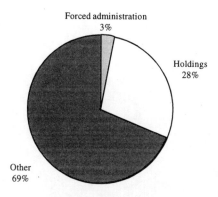

Figure 1.5   Wave 1: fund transformation

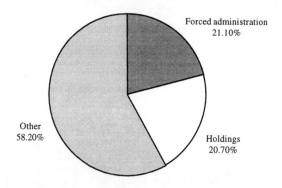

Figure 1.6   Wave 2: fund transformation

An interesting question is what was the actual market share of the privatization funds that underwent transformation? Figures 1.7 and 1.8 present some answers for the first and second waves, respectively. It is evident that the second wave resulted in more dispersed market control among the funds. In the first wave, seven funds captured 20% of the market, contrasting sharply with the fact that all transformed funds from the second wave were needed to capture one fifth of the available market. If we look more closely at the picture, we can see that one single leading fund took 9% of the market in the first wave, whereas its second wave counterpart was able to capture only half of that percentage share. There are several possible explanations for this trend: (1) individuals had learned how to bid from their experience in the first wave, (2) individuals had started to see the benefit of investing in companies that they were personally involved with, and (3) individuals had become distrustful of the privatization funds.

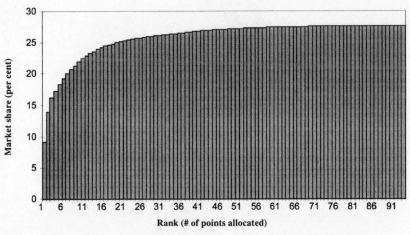

Figure 1.7   Wave 1: cumulative market share of the transformed funds

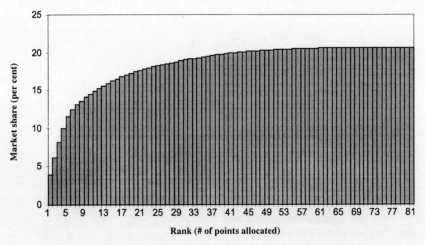

Figure 1.8   Wave 2: cumulative market share of the transformed funds

Managers vs. Managed IPFs

The founders or managers of privatization funds established different numbers of funds. Obviously most of them founded only one IPF. However, multiple funds created by the same manager were not at all infrequent. Naturally, there were some extreme cases. For example, in the first wave Agrobanka Praha created 13 IPFs and, in the second wave, Harvard Capital and Consulting founded an unbelievable number of funds – 23 in total (see Tables 1.15 and 1.16 for details).

Table 1.15   Portfolio structure by number of IPFs: wave 1

No. of fund founders	No. of IPFs	Average no. of firms in IPFs portfolio	Minimum no. of firms in IPFs portfolio	Maximum no. of firms in IPFs portfolio
301	1	39.46	1	514
20	2	144.95	1	1,420
6	3	51.17	19	92
2	4	513.5	15	1,012
1	5	202	202	202
2	6	222	47	397
1	10	80	80	80
2	11	210	154	266
1	13	249	249	249

Table 1.16   Portfolio structure by number of IPFs: wave 2

No. of fund founders	No. of IPFs	Average no. of firms in IPFs portfolio	Minimum no. of firms in IPFs portfolio	Maximum no. of firms in IPFs portfolio
191	1	70.15	1	854
29	2	44.72	2	202
11	3	98.72	18	680
4	5	66.75	17	107
1	7	54	54	54
1	17	65	65	65
1	23	13	13	13

As suggested before, the number of founders that created the numerous funds was rather low in both the first and second waves. In the first wave, 301 companies founded only one fund each. The portfolios of these funds consisted of 40 firms on average. In one extreme case, a portfolio consisted of only one firm, when an IPF was created for the sole purpose of buying a stake in a company to be founded and eventually privatized. At the other end of the spectrum, one portfolio consisted of over 514 firms. This excessive diversification was most likely the result of legislation, which limited a single fund within a company to a maximum 20% share of ownership. The huge number of points entrusted to the founder, Česká státní spořitelna, had to be spread among an inordinate number of companies, which in reality precluded any reasonable model of corporate governance. Naturally, all funds that encompassed such extensive portfolios happily reduced them later on because they encountered difficulties stemming from minority position problems and the inability to effect active corporate governance. Table 1.16, which presents the results of the second wave, offers a similar picture and suggests parallel conclusions.

Results of the Survey of Czech Investment Funds

As we needed to have a clear picture of the size, means and results of trading, together with the focus of the individual investment funds active in the Czech Republic, we sent questionnaires out to their managers. The questions therein were based on a survey used by our Slovenian partners, although some of them were modified to reflect the situation in the Czech Republic. The questions fall into five major groups:

- questions relating to the asset portfolio of the fund;
- questions relating to portfolio trading;
- questions relating to the fund's investment policy and to the supervision of investment companies;
- questions relating to the supervision of privatization funds; and
- questions relating to the investment company.

We are sorry to say that the response rate was very low. Out of more than 150 funds whose managers were asked to fill in our questionnaires, we received only 16 responses. Although this number may seem very low indeed, we still think valuable information about the investment funds sector of the Czech Republic can be retrieved from the data we have.

Individual investment funds can obviously be very different, particularly in terms of the amount of assets under control. It is, in our opinion, desirable to divide the investment funds into two distinct groups according to the amount of assets they manage. The first group, say, of small funds (12 in our sample), includes funds with a net asset value (NAV) below CZK 1 billion, and the big funds group (4 in our sample) consists of the funds with a NAV exceeding this value. The choice of this benchmark is a result of our subjective opinion based on the situation in the market. We are convinced that it is appropriate to analyze the characteristics of the small and the big funds separately, as there are some significant differences between these two groups.

Assets and Portfolio

Assets managed by the investment funds
The average net asset value managed by the small funds is CZK 135.710 million. The average book value for this group is CZK 146.903 million. The value of assets managed by small funds has, therefore, decreased on average since the end of voucher privatization. Only one fund out of twelve exhibits an increase in the value of assets (this increase amounts to 16.8%).

The average net asset value managed by the big funds is CZK 5,024.255 million. The average book value for this group is CZK 5,059.047 million. Hence, the value of assets under the management of big funds has on average stayed at the same level since the end of voucher privatization. Two of the big funds showed increases in the value of their assets, one of them being only minor, but the other revealed an increase of 32.4%.

Portfolio
Figure 1.9 shows that on average, the small funds invested 76.3% of their portfolio in shares (ranging from 65.2% to 88.5%).[7] The average investment in bonds was 7.9% (ranging from 0% to 18%). The average investment made by the small funds in receivables was 4.9% (ranging from 0% to 22%). The average investment in other assets was 10.9% (ranging from 0% to 30%).

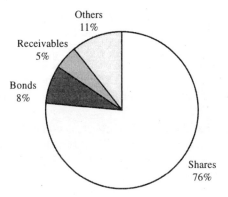

Figure 1.9   Assets in portfolio – small IPFs

The situation in the big funds group is relatively similar (see Figure 1.10). On average, the big funds invested 66.5% of their portfolio in shares (ranging from 48% to 85%). Bonds represent 13.75% (ranging from 0% to 45%) of their portfolio, receivables 6% (ranging from 0% to 18%), and other assets 13.75% (ranging from 7% to 30%). The only distinction worth noting is probably a higher proportional investment in bonds by the big IPFs. As bonds are a more complex instrument to understand (for example, they have higher sensitivity to macro-economic indicators such as interest rates), a comparison among the representative group of big investment funds may offer an explanation.

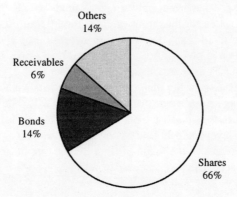

Figure 1.10   Assets in portfolio – big IPFs

Number of Companies Invested in by IPFs

The small privatization investment funds invested, on average, in 41.6 companies (ranging from 15 to 67) whereas the big investment funds invested, on average, in 82.25 companies (ranging from 50 to 113).

On average, small investment funds are co-owners of 35.3 companies they invested in. This number represents 85% of all the companies in the small investment funds portfolio. In the case of the big investment funds, the average number of companies where they share ownership with other investment funds is 82.25. This number represents 100% of the companies in their portfolio.

It is interesting that the average number of companies where the small investment funds are majority owners is zero. The big investment funds hold a majority in companies, on average, in 21.75 cases, or 26.44% of all the companies in their portfolio.

Structural Composition of Investment Fund Portfolios

The portfolio of small investment funds consists, in terms of NAV, of an average 65.3% (ranging from 40% to 93%) of mining, manufacturing industry and construction, 5.5% (ranging from 0% to 15%) of trade and the travel industry,

21.2% (7% to 44%) of financial services and 8% (0% to 31%) of others. The situation is illustrated by Figure 1.11.

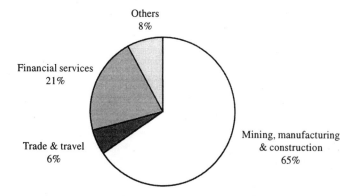

Figure 1.11   Assets by sector – small IPFs

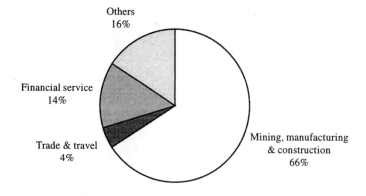

Figure 1.12   Assets by sector – big IPFs

The portfolio of big investment funds consists on average of 65.9% (ranging from 52.93% to 76.71%) of mining, manufacturing industry and construction, 4.3% (ranging from 2.30% to 7.51%) of trade and the travel industry, 14.1% (11.63% to 17.85%) of financial services and 15.7% (8.76% to 22.27%) of others (see Figure 1.12).

The only significant distinction between the portfolios of the small and big IPFs in terms of structural composition is the higher proportion of financial services securities in the big funds' portfolios. The only suggestion we can give the reader, by way of interpretation of this, is to point out that the four big investment funds originated in the financial sector.

Portfolio Trading

The small investment funds reduced their share in the companies in their portfolio on average 28.9 times (from 10 to 81 times). The average total value of these transactions was CZK 76.7 million, i.e., CZK 2.65 million per transaction. The small funds, on the other hand, increased their share in the companies on average 23.5 times (from 2 to 115 times). The average total value of these transactions was CZK 70.2 million, i.e., CZK 2.99 million per transaction.

The big investment funds decreased their share in the companies in their portfolio on average 71.25 times (from 22 to 163 times). The average total value of these transactions was CZK 3,037.5 million, i.e., CZK 42.63 million per transaction. The big funds, on the other hand, increased their share in the companies on average 21.5 times (18 to 25 times). The average total value of these transactions was CZK 2,070 million, i.e., CZK 96.28 million per transaction.

Investment Policy and the Supervision of Companies

All of the small funds view portfolio diversification as their major investment policy. Only two out of twelve small funds also include ownership concentration in their investment policy. Hence, not surprisingly, most funds (10 of 12) rely on a more passive market strategy based on selling shares according to market conditions. Only two funds implement an active policy based on their 'voice', i.e., enforcement of their interests. These are the same two funds, which include ownership concentration in their 'strategic package'.

The above data may offer an explanation for the very low average number of investment fund members on the supervisory boards of the portfolio companies, 0.9 (from 0 to 4). It is quite logical that the two funds relying on their 'voice' have nominated the highest number of representatives, 3 and 4, respectively. The average number of cases where the investment funds initiated or cooperated with other funds in replacing management is also very low, 0.5 (0 to 2).

The prevailing investment policy of the big funds lies, on the other hand, in concentrating their share in the companies. All four big funds chose this option. All the big funds also indicated that the potential sale of the share and the 'voice' strategy are of equal importance. The big investment funds were much more successful in placing their representatives on the supervisory boards or boards of directors of the companies in their portfolio than the small funds. On average, they nominated their representatives on the supervisory board or the board of directors in 42 cases (from 32 to 52). The average number of cases where the big investment funds initiated or cooperated with other funds in replacing management is 5.75 (from 4 to 8). We may therefore conclude that the big investment funds are much more active in the process of controlling the companies and imposing pressure on the companies' management.

As far as the goals of the investment funds are concerned, the opinions of the small funds' managers were surprisingly in accord. They were asked to choose from seven options and they did so in the following way:

- 'Value maximization through active portfolio trading and optimization' ranked first with an average rank of 1.08.
- 'Profit maximization through capital gains (interest rates and dividends)' took second place with an average rank of 2.0.
- 'Value maximization through active supervision of the companies (representation in the supervisory boards)' took third place with an average rank of 4.08.

Whereas the ranking of the above three options was quite clear, the ranking of the remaining four options – 'Value maximization through restructuring', 'Value maximization through investments (venture capital)', 'Support of progressive and successful management in selected companies', and 'Founding of a real estate investment fund' – was different from fund to fund.

The ranking of the options by the big investment funds was quite similar to the ranking by the small investment funds. 'Value maximization through active portfolio trading and optimization' and 'Profit maximization through capital gains (interest rates and dividends)' were placed first and second, respectively. The only difference between the opinions of the small and the big fund managers appeared at the third place where 'Value maximization through restructuring' replaced 'Value maximization through active supervision over the companies (representation in the supervisory boards'. This is a rather paradoxical result given the rate of representation in the supervisory boards discussed above.

None of the small fund managers surveyed viewed any of the above listed seven goals as contradicting the goals of the fund. In the case of the big funds, one of the four managers considered some of the seven options contradictory to his or her fund's goals.

None of the surveyed funds, neither big nor small, invests only locally. All the funds invest throughout the Czech Republic.

The managers of the investment funds were asked for their opinions on the ownership share of management, employees, and state in the companies they invested in. Tables 1.17 and 1.18 summarize their opinions.

Table 1.17   Co-owners welcome? – small investment funds' view

Opinion of the small investment fund managers on the ownership share of	Management	Employees	State
Positive	5	3	2
Negative	0	2	5
Indifferent	7	7	5
Not encountered	0	0	0

Table 1.18   Co-owners welcome? – big investment funds' view

Opinion of the big investment fund managers on the ownership share of	Management[1]	Employees	State[2]
Positive	4	0	0
Negative	4	4	4
Indifferent	0	0	1
Not encountered	0	0	0

Notes
(1)   All the big fund managers chose 'positive' as well as 'negative' claiming that their approach is case-by-case.
(2)   One manager chose 'negative' as well as 'indifferent'.

Supervision of Investment Privatization Funds

The funds were asked about the dividend policy they pursue. Eight of the twelve small fund managers opted for constant and regular dividend payments, three for constant and regular dividend payments plus extra dividends and only one for retained earnings. Half of the big funds (2 of the 4 respondents) pursue a policy of constant and regular dividend payments and the other two pursue a policy of constant and regular dividend payments plus extra dividends.

The other question concerned trading of the investment funds' shares. The shares of one small fund are already traded on the Prague Stock Exchange (PSE). The remaining eleven small funds managers think that the shares of their fund will never be traded on the PSE. Also none of them expressed an interest in publicly trading shares of the funds. All the big funds' shares are already on the Prague Stock Exchange.

Three managers of the small investment funds think that the amount of dividend payments affects the market price of investment fund shares. The remaining nine managers do not agree with this opinion. All of the small investment fund managers consider that the market price of the funds does not reflect their relative performance. In the opinion of the managers of the big investment funds, the amount of dividend payments does affect the market price of the fund. They also believe that the relative price of a fund's shares reflects the performance of the fund.

The average structure of the supervisory boards of the small funds is the following: one representative of the investment company, one representative of the shareholders of the fund, and one independent individual. It is interesting that the board of directors (BD) and the supervisory board (SB) of all the big funds consist only of independent individuals (both the BD and SB having three members).

The general shareholders' meeting of the small funds took place on average four times (from 3 to 7). In the case of the big investment funds, general shareholders' meetings took place on average 6 times (from 3 to 7). The average representation of shareholders of the small fund is 22% (from 14% to 59%). All the supervisory boards of the small funds have changed during their existence. The average presence of the shareholders of the big funds (in terms of number of votes) at the shareholders' meeting was 41.25% (from 35% to 50%). All of the supervisory boards of the big funds have also changed during the course of their time with the funds.

In the opinion of 10 small fund managers, the investment company represents the interests of the fund shareholders. Two other managers do not share this opinion. In the opinion of all four big fund managers, the investment company does not represent the shareholders of the funds.

To end the management contract in the case of the small funds, 31% of shareholder votes are needed.[8] In the case of the big funds, 76.25% (from 75% to 80%) of shareholder votes are needed to conclude the management contract with the investment company.

The Investment Company

The owners of the investment companies managing the small investment funds are mostly individuals and privatization companies. One hundred per cent of the investment companies who responded to our questionnaire are owned by financial institutions.

The compensation of the managers of the investment companies managing the small funds can be broken down in the following way: fixed (9), a percentage of the net profits of the fund (2), or a percentage of net profits of the investment company (1). The salaries and bonuses of the managers of the investment company are fixed plus a percentage of the portion by which the company exceeds expected results.

In the case of the small funds, the length of management contracts is either not determined (8), or averages at 3 years and 5 months in the remaining four cases. The average contract length for the big fund managers is 5 years and 3 months (from 3 years and 7 months to 5 years 10 months).

CONCLUSIONS

The extent of mass privatization undertaken in Czechoslovakia is globally unprecedented. As a result, it is impossible to evaluate the process and its outcome comparatively. Nevertheless, it is indisputable that the Czechs and Slovaks have proved that a program involving the large-scale transfer of ownership of this kind is feasible and can be carried out within a relatively short period of time.

There is no doubt that the process suffered from certain shortcomings. The legislative framework for mass privatization, especially for the voucher component, was too vague. Most of the laws spelled out general principles, relegating details to government decrees and *ad hoc* administrative decisions. This over-endowed the governments with discretionary power, which led to abuse. Voucher privatization also turned out to be difficult to organize. One of the important advantages the Czechoslovak authorities anticipated when the method was accepted, was that this method could turn the difficult decision process of 'who to sell to' into an easier approval process of 'whether to privatize this enterprise or not'. However, as soon as the method started to compete with and be combined with other standard methods, this expected advantage disappeared. The result was a complicated process that led to corruption. On the other hand, one may argue that using the voucher method as a single privatization tool would have been too risky and that the benefits of diversification more than outweighed the complications brought about by the use of a combination of methods.

There has indeed been a turbulent evolution in the investment privatization fund sector since July 1996 when rigorous regulation came into effect. A number of investment privatization funds were spontaneously converted into non-regulated holding companies, leading to sharp declines in their share prices and causing several disputes. Later on, this sort of conversion became possible only by buying out minority shareholders at the NAV. With the introduction of stricter supervision of capital markets in late 1996 and early 1997, forced administration was imposed on several funds and licenses were withdrawn from several others.

Issues of governance of IPFs are discussed in detail and supported by various data. The data come from two sources. The first source is the statistical data from the Ministry of Finance that have just been released for the first time and we have thus presented the first work on Czech investment privatization funds underscored by reliable statistical evidence. The second source consists of responses to questionnaires distributed to the managers of numerous IPFs. Unfortunately, the situation was not conducive to this type of research and management companies were reluctant to take part in our survey. The response rate was only about 10% and can be viewed as an almost complete failure. Nevertheless, there is still a certain amount of valuable information to be retrieved from the data.

Concerning the performance of the individual IPFs as asset managers, the big IPFs seem to have outperformed the small IPFs – the value of assets under small fund management has decreased on average while the value of assets under the big fund management has on average stayed at the same level since the end of voucher privatization. This fact may be attributed to better information being available to the big fund managers, as well as to their superior qualifications since they often have significant experience from the financial sector.

There is quite a difference between big and small Czech IPFs. While the small funds do combine their assets with other investment funds in order to control a majority share in any company, the big investment funds, together with other IPFs, control over 26% of the companies in their portfolio. This is partly due to the amount of assets. The big IPFs manage sufficient assets so that their stakes in some companies remain significant in spite of their dilution due to portfolio diversification. However, it remains a mystery as to why the investment choices made by small IPFs and big IPFs were so different that the two groups did not 'meet' in any company where the IPFs hold a majority share.

Given the size of the stakes in the companies, the strategy of the individual funds differs between the two groups of IPFs. The small IPFs are generally only involved in trading their stakes in an effort to optimize their portfolio, without any significant interest in controlling the companies. The big investment funds, on the other hand, are much more proactive when it comes to controlling companies and imposing pressure on their management. The slow pace of restructuring in the Czech economy, however, suggests that the level of exercising ownership rights by owners in general, and the IPFs in particular, in Czech companies is quite poor. We hope that in the years to come there will be a significant shift in the big IPFs' strategy away from speculative trading towards active supervision and control over the companies in their portfolio.

The comprehensive results of the study corroborate the positive role of the investment privatization funds during privatization but simultaneously highlight the fact that the institutional and legislative set-up is still far from optimum.

NOTES

1. CSK stands for the Czechoslovak crown (koruna).
2. The 'Lists of Enterprises' were published in *Tydenik Hospodarskych novin* 31, 32, 37, 39 and 40/1991.
3. The Ministry of Privatization of the Czech Republic issued an obligatory plot of the privatization project (government by-law 324/1991), which specified the content and form of the projects in detail. A similar document was issued in Slovakia (*Tydenik Hospodarskych novin* 38/1991).
4. Public notice on the Prices of Immovables was issued by the Ministry of Finance of the Czech Republic on September 5, 1991 (published in *Hospodarske noviny*, September 13, 1991). This regulation increased official prices to a multiple of their former level.
5. For enterprises undergoing voucher privatization there was a strict deadline: the end of April, so that voucher privatization could start at the beginning of May.
6. The fund bears such an enigmatic name because its founder holds an MBA degree from Harvard University.
7. One investment fund did not supply these data.
8. Only two fund managers answered this question.

2. The Governance of Privatization Funds in Poland

Janusz Lewandowski and Roman Szyszko

MASS PRIVATIZATION PROGRAM

The Objectives of the MPP

Poland's version of the Mass Privatization Program (MPP) – called the National Investment Funds Program (NIF) – was elaborated in detail by mid-1991 on the basis of the idea of voucher distribution developed amongst advisors to 'Solidarity' in Gdansk (presented for the first time on November 17–18, 1988).

The Polish model represents a multi-functional design, going beyond mere distributive aims. It was designed to address the following objectives:

- widespread participation of citizens in the ownership changes enabling them to benefit from the process in a fair and equal manner;
- radically accelerating the privatization of the larger and medium-sized enterprises;
- providing a mechanism for actively restructuring companies through the investment funds and the agency of professional management skills; and
- extension of the capital market via the large range of new securities: certificates, NIFs' shares, and participating companies' shares.

The specific feature of the Polish MPP model involves 'top-down' investment funds, designed to solve the problem of dispersed shareholding and effective management structures. For this reason, the program was perceived as a heavily 'engineered' one, in contrast to the Czech scheme, enabling the rapid transfer of companies to the private sector, but without any specific inherent mechanism for their restructuring. The real difference, however, consisted in the political vacuum and intellectual disbelief surrounding the MPP concept in Poland in the early 1990s compared with the display of strong political will to implement mass privatization in the Czech Republic and Russia, as a vehicle for the rapid depoliticization of the economy.

44

Due to political blockades, the Law on the National Investment Funds was not enacted until 1993, effectively delaying the implementation of the program until 1994–95.

Position of MPP within the Overall Privatization Program

Polish MPP has never been seen as a global solution to the privatization challenge. From the very beginning, MPP was perceived as a major quantitative step within the multi-track approach to privatization.

The strong trade union tradition of 'Solidarity' and workers' councils control over state-owned enterprises (SOEs) during the 1980s appears to have been important in shaping the social, political and, consequently, legal context of Polish privatization. At the beginning of the 1990s, 47% of Poles were in favor of employee ownership – more than in the other former COMECON countries. The pressure on insider-oriented acquisitions influenced the Law on the Privatization of State-Owned Enterprises of July 13th, 1990 – as reflected in the privileged shareholding and employees' initiative in privatization.

Privatization actually started in 1990/91 on the basis of British-style initial public offerings and leveraged lease-buyout formulas. Insider-oriented deals still dominate in Polish privatization. By December 1996, only 180 SOEs had been effectively privatized through capital privatization, 2,700 through liquidation and direct privatization (1,200 of them through employee buyouts) and another 1,100 went bankrupt. Five hundred and twelve MPP companies were selected on a voluntary basis (a condition *sine qua non* of generating a parliamentary majority in favor of the NIF program in 1993). The Ministry of Privatization was required to consult with potential participants. Motions concerning the transformation of state-owned enterprises into companies in order to have their shares contributed to the funds were submitted. If neither the director nor the workers' council had forwarded an objection with reasons within 45 days of the notification of the enterprise, this was regarded as an expression of consent. Thereafter, a list of those not responding negatively could be submitted for approval by the Council of Ministers. The voluntary selection of SOEs imposed obvious limitations on the supply-side of the Polish program.

The Supply Side of MPP

In all, 512 larger and medium-sized SOEs, representing around 10% of industrial sector sales, were formally transferred to the National Investment Funds Program by an ordinance of the Council of Ministers. Their book value was around 7 billion zloty (US$ 2.8 billion). Participating companies are mostly in manufacturing and construction.

The initial shareholding structures of companies, following the contribution of their shares to National Investment Funds (NIFs), was as follows:

Shareholder	Per cent
Lead NIF	33
Other NIFs	27
Employees	15
State Treasury	25
Total	100

The lead shareholdings (33% in each of the 512 companies), together with minority shareholdings (27%) were contributed to NIFs by the Treasury in the form of non-monetary contributions.

Minority shareholdings were allocated in equal proportions to all NIFs. It is assumed that the NIFs are currently consolidating their minority stakes. In total, 60% of the shares in the 512 companies provide the supply-side of the Polish MPP, to be distributed amongst the public via NIF certificates.

Pursuant to the law, up to 15% of the shares in each company are to be assigned, free-of-charge, to employees and in certain cases up to a further 15% may be distributed amongst other entitled individuals (farmers and fishermen) who have contractual relations with the companies concerned. The remaining shares in each company – 25% – are held by the State Treasury as the basis for issuing compensation and reprivatization certificates.

The Demand Side of MPP

All 27.8 million adult Polish citizens were eligible to participate in the NIF Program. Commencing on November 22, 1995 for a period of one year (subject to certain allowances for processing entitlement claims), the Ministry of Privatization, acting on behalf of the State Treasury, made certificates available to all entitled persons. According to the Article 31 of the Law on National Investment Funds and their Privatization of April 30, 1993, all citizens of the Republic of Poland who were registered as permanent residents in Poland and who, at December 31, 1994, were at least 18 years old, were entitled to receive one universal share certificate. No further criteria for allocating certificates (i.e., by years of employment or age) were applied in the Program. Each person was allowed to acquire a single certificate on payment of a fee of 20 zlotys (about 7 dollars). The fee was intended to cover costs associated with the distribution of the certificates and did not in any way represent either a valuation of the assets included in the NIFs or an estimate of the likely price in secondary trading (note that in February 1997 certificates were traded at 160–165 zlotys on the Warsaw Stock Exchange).

The preparation of lists of entitled persons was delegated to the local authorities (*gmina*). The network of the distribution points, covering all *gminas* was provided by the PKO BP bank and appeared effective in handing out the certificates throughout the November 1995–November 1996 period.

In 1996, 25,675 million adult Poles, i.e., 95% of the eligible population, entered the NIF Program by collecting their certificates. The certificates were issued in a physical bearer form and were immediately tradable. Citizens were also permitted to open security accounts with brokers and trade certificates on the Warsaw Stock Exchange in dematerialized form.

Certificates do not carry voting rights. Any dividends attributable to share certificates will be paid through the dematerialized system into the account of a financial agent appointed by the Minister of Privatization. It is intended that the agent will accumulate any dividends and other revenue for the benefit of share certificate holders. Such revenue may be paid at any time at the discretion of the Minister of Privatization, but it is expected that it will be paid, at the latest, at the time the share certificates are converted into NIF shares.

As NIFs have filed their individual prospectuses and had them approved, NIF shares have been admitted to the Warsaw Stock Exchange. Thereafter, any holder of a securities account with a licensed bank or broker has been able to exchange his share certificate for one share in each relevant NIF, and the NIF shares have then been separately tradable in dematerialized form.

dematerialized NIF shares will carry all usual voting rights and shareholders will receive dividends through the existing securities investment account system maintained by licensed brokers, which requires servicing by listed companies themselves.

THE ROLE OF NATIONAL INVESTMENT FUNDS

Legal Form and Objectives

Fifteen National Investment Funds were established in December 1994. NIFs are 'top-down' closed-end funds, having the form of a joint-stock company. Except for cases specifically stated in the law, all Polish Commercial Code provisions on joint-stock companies apply to the NIFs. The rights of the State Treasury as a founder and shareholder of a fund are exercised by the Minister of State Treasury (replacing the Minister of Privatization in the course of the administrative reform of 1996). The Minister made non-monetary contributions to funds in the form of shares of 512 companies.

The formal statement of NIFs' objectives (Article 4 of the Law on NIFs and their Privatization) is as follows:

The purpose of the funds is to increase the value of their assets in particular by enhancing the value of shares in companies of which the funds are shareholders. In particular, the funds should endeavor to achieve this purpose through:

(1) exercising rights with respect to the shares of companies established as a result of the transformation of state-owned enterprises into companies wholly owned by the State Treasury and shares of other joint-stock and limited liability companies in particular for the purpose of improving the management of the companies in which the funds have a substantial shareholding, including the strengthening of their position in the market and obtaining new technology and loans for the companies;

(2) conducting economic activity through the purchase and sale of shares of companies and exercising of acquired rights; and

(3) granting and obtaining loans to accomplish the tasks set out in items 1 and 2 above, as well as other tasks defined in the statutes.

Going beyond the formal statements, one should see NIFs as being consciously designed hybrids of holding companies, mutual funds and venture capital entities.

The primary responsibility of the fund managers was to increase the value of the NIF assets as much as possible over the next ten-year period. This will require fund managers to pay considerable attention to those companies in which their NIF has lead shareholdings, giving guidance and using their expertise to ensure that the companies are managed in the best possible way. This will also include supervision of management's preparation and implementation of suitable business plans. In addition, fund managers will make decisions to buy or sell investments owned by the NIFs.

Fund managers are able to perform their role of supervising companies in which the NIFs are lead shareholders by exercising NIFs' rights to nominate almost a majority, including the chairman, of the members of the supervisory boards of the MPP companies. Although NIFs will not have a majority of the members of the supervisory boards of individual companies in which they have lead shareholdings, they may create alliances with other supervisory board members, thereby enabling a majority vote to be carried. In practice, the role of the fund manager with regard to a company in which the NIF has a lead shareholding is similar to that of active venture capital in Europe or the United States.

The major task of the fund manager is to participate in the meetings of each company's supervisory board, which is a forum for influencing and reviewing the strategy, plans and results of the company. It will not be a task of the fund manager to prepare business plans, management accounts etc., as they are the responsibility of the company's management board; but the fund manager supervises by commenting and giving direction about such efforts.

Conflicting views as to the fund's management strategy, resulting in tensions within NIFs, are discussed later in this chapter.

NIFs' Initial Performances

Implementation of the Polish MPP started in 1995, with fifteen NIFs being incorporated, their boards appointed, selected fund managers assigned to particular NIFs and management contracts signed. The enclosed specification of the NIFs reflects their starting position as in 1995 (see Table 2.1). Further institutional rearrangements and dynamics are studies for the benefit of the final country report.

The initial effort of the NIFs, after allocation of lead shareholdings was accomplished, was to establish a relevant database on the companies and to discover their true financial status. This appeared to be a critical aspect because of the quality of selected participating enterprises after 1993. Their small size and poor financial status – against the criteria originally envisaged for selection (better and larger SOEs) – proved more a burden than an asset for the NIFs. Together with the deterioration of many companies in the original group, waiting for the implementation of the Program since 1991–92 and the removal from the list of certain valuable enterprises, this contributed to immediate problems and *ad hoc* rescue schemes, instead of long-term strategies. In several cases, declaring bankruptcy was inevitable, attracting much public attention. On the other hand, more than 120 better companies were selected for listing, either on the Warsaw Stock Exchange or on the newly launched over-the-counter (OTC) market. Consolidating minority shareholdings and paving the way to new sources of financing supplemented the NIFs' activities in the early stage of their operations. NIFs managed to arrange foreign loans for 27 companies and domestic loans for more than 130 participating companies.

Table 2.1   National investment funds – names and sponsors of management companies at the beginning of the program[1]

Name (short form)	Management firm	Principal sponsors of the management firm
First National Investment Fund	BRE/GiroCredit Management sp z o.o.	Bank Rozowju Eksportu (Poland); GiroCredit (Austria)
Second National Investment Fund	Hevelius Management sp z o.o.	UNP International (Poland); Bank Gdanski (Poland); Murray Johnstone (UK)
Third National Investment Fund	Trinity Management sp z o.o.	Barclays de Zoete Wedd (UK); Bank Polska Kasa Opieki (Poland); Company Assistance (Poland)
Fourth National Investment Fund	Konsorcjum Raiffeisen Atkins Zarzadzanie Funduszami SA	Raiffeisen (Austria); WS Atkins (UK)
Fifth National Investment Fund Victoria	Polskie Towarzystwo Prywatyzacyjne Kleinwort Benson sp z o.o.	Kleinwort Benson (UK); Polski Bank Rozwoju (Poland)

Name (short form)	Management firm	Principal sponsors of the management firm
Sixth National Investment Fund Magna Polonia	Chase Gemina Polska sp. z o.o.	Chase Gemina (US/Italy); Wielkopolski Bank Kredytowy (Poland); Nicom Consulting (Poland)
Kazimierz Wielki Fund	Kazimierz Wielki Fund Management Co. AG	Lazard Freres (France); GICC Capital (US); Bank Gospodarstwa Krajowego (Poland)
Eighth National Investment Fund	KP Konsorcjum sp z o.o.[2]	Barents Group (US); Bank Handlowy w Warszawue (Poland); Paine Webber (US); York Trust (UK); Kennedy Associates (US)
Eugeniusz Kwiatkowski Fund	–	–
Tenth National Investment Fund	Fidea Management sp z o.o.	Banque Arjil (France); Agencja Rozwoju Przemys³u (Poland); Warszawska Grupa Konsultingowa (Poland)
Eleventh National Investment Fund	KN Wasserstein sp z o.o.	KNK Finance and Investment (Poland); Wasserstein Perella (US); New England Investment (Poland)
Twelfth National Investment Fund Piast	BNP-PBI Eurofund Management (Polska) sp z o.o.	Banque Nationale de Paris (France); Polski Bank Inwestycyjny (Poland)
Thirteenth National Investment Fund	Yamaichi Regent Special Projects Ltd.	Yamaichi International Europe (UK); Regent Pacific (UK/Hong Kong); ABC Consulting (Poland)
West Investment Fund	International Westfund Holdings Ltd.	Bank Zachodni (Poland); Central Europe Trust (UK); Charterhouse (UK); Credit Commercial de France (France)
Fifteenth National Investment Fund	Creditanstalt SCG Fund Management SA	Creditstalt (Austria); St. Gallen Consulting (Switzerland)

Notes
(1) The principal participants are those with 10% or more in the activity of the fund manager firm. The specification reflects the initial condition of the NIFs' incorporation.
(2) Management contract terminated.

THE GOVERNANCE OF NATIONAL INVESTMENT FUNDS

Sponsors of Management Companies – Control Structure

The sponsors of management companies in the National Investment
Funds are:

- foreign banks (commercial and investment);
- foreign fund (venture capital) managers;
- Polish commercial banks; and
- Polish and foreign consulting firms.

In nine out of fourteen cases, management companies have majority
control (50 or more per cent majority stake of a single shareholder in a
management company). In eight cases, the owner of a majority stake in a
management company is a foreign entity (usually controlled by commercial
or merchant banks). In two cases, a Polish entity controls the management
company (commercial bank and consulting firm). The remaining five
companies have balanced control structures. Typically, the structure consists
of three partners with roughly equal stakes in the management company
(see Figure 2.1 in relation to the last column of Table 2.1).

The objective of the control structure of representative management firms
of National Investment Funds is designed to ensure a proper blend of skills.
Foreign firms were supposed to offer experience and knowledge concerning
company restructuring and investment banking services. Polish partners were
assumed to contribute understanding of specific characteristics of the local
business environment.

A 'Chinese wall' between sponsors and management companies in the form
of legal and organizational separation was introduced to avoid conflicts of
interests. Nevertheless, it is implicit that sponsors of management firms
perceived National Investment Funds as an opportunity to cross-sell their
services. Polish commercial banks aspiring to the status of a universal financial
institution tried to get access to investment banking business as well as to
expand their loan portfolios.

All agreements between funds, or between one or more funds and third
parties, regarding acquisitions of shares are to be notified to the Anti-Monopoly
Office within 14 days of the date of the conclusion of an agreement. The
notification obligation does not apply to agreements whereby a fund acquires,
in total, less than 10% of the shares of a given company. The duty of notification
referred to above rests on the management board of the fund.

Unless the prior approval of the Anti-Monopoly Office is obtained, no
management firm can simultaneously provide management services to two or
more funds and no management firm can own shares in any fund to which it is
then providing management services.

No member of a supervisory board or management board of any fund shall simultaneously serve as a member of the supervisory board or management board of another fund. This prohibition applies accordingly to persons exercising the power of commercial representation (*prokura*) on behalf of a fund.

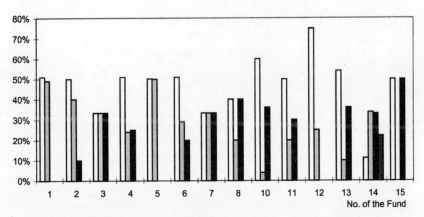

*Figure 2.1 Percentage of shareholdings in management companies –
at the beginning of the program*

In the event of non-compliance with the requirements and prohibitions, the Anti-Monopoly Office may issue a decision imposing upon the responsible member of the management board of the relevant fund or management firm a fine not exceeding half of that person's annual income for the previous fiscal year.

The prohibitions referred to above also apply to entities which occupy a 'dominant' or 'dependent' position with respect to the management firm.

Within three years of the date of registration of a fund, parliamentary deputies and senators are no longer permitted to be members of a supervisory board or management board of a fund or company in which the fund holds at least 20% of the shares.

The objectives of the program

Management boards and supervisory boards have diverse views on the objectives of the program (see Figure 2.2.). Management boards are focused on the net asset value (NAV) of their portfolios, whilst supervisory boards see restructuring of companies as the primary objective of NIFs. This discrepancy may be (and in many cases already is) a major source of tension in NIFs. This comes down to the question of to what extent NIFs are obliged to employ their resources in restructuring and improving the sometimes near bankrupt companies which they had to accept in the process of portfolio selection.

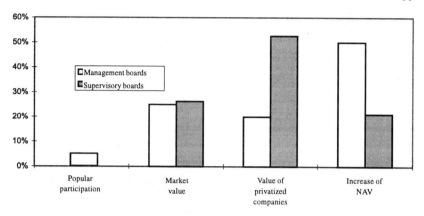

Figure 2.2   Objectives of the program

Conflicts of Interests in the National Investment Funds' Operations

The debate on the role of Fund Managers centers on two conflicting concepts. One is that funds and Fund Managers should adopt a long-term strategy and focus on restructuring their companies. The other is that the funds' priority should be to boost values of portfolios (particularly in view of their impending stock exchange listing), so they should concentrate their limited supervisory and advisory capabilities only on promising companies and selling off other firms as quickly as possible.

Differences of perception have caused serious tensions between some Fund Managers and supervisory boards, which often prefer restructuring. Less often, some supervisory boards object to severe restructuring measures that Fund Managers recommend. Supervisory boards often aspire to play a managing role in contradiction to their attributes and management contracts.

Problems of poor staffing of some management firms, and conflicting perceptions of Fund Managers' roles have been the source of disputes in three cases. Two ended with the cancellation of management contracts. In the third case, the Minister of Privatization dismissed most members of the supervisory board.

It appears that significant opportunities for cross-ownership between management companies' sponsors and investment funds are highly improbable. Banks which sponsor management companies are either already private or are too large to be the object of significant investment of the NIFs; illiquid assets and limits on NIFs' borrowings make such cross-ownership unfeasible. Moreover, acquisition of shares in a NIF to which a management firm provides management services is subject to the approval of the Anti-Monopoly Office. The limitation also applies to entities which occupy a 'dominant' or 'dependent' position' with respect to the management firm.

Arms-length transactions and insider information

According to surveyed members of supervisory boards, insider information and arms-length transactions are important issues in the governance of NIFs (see Figure 2.3). Members of supervisory boards acknowledge the existence of the problem but see it as not too pressing (there are no 'definitely not effective' responses). Management boards are almost evenly divided on the issue.

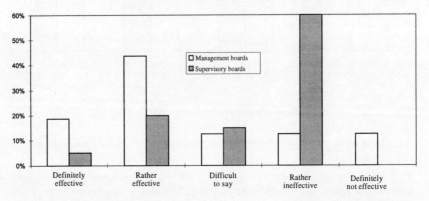

Figure 2.3   Assessment of safeguards against insider information and arms-length transactions in NIFs

Incentive Structures for Managers and Management Companies

A fund might have concluded a contract for the management of its assets with a management firm. The contract is executed on behalf of the fund by its supervisory board. Initially, fourteen out of fifteen National Investment Funds signed contracts with management firms.

Funds wholly owned by the State Treasury might have concluded management contracts exclusively with management firms selected by way of competitive tender by the Selection Commission.

Tenders were public as were selection criteria. The detailed procedures for conducting tenders were determined by the Council of Ministers.

The duties and powers of management firms are determined in the statutes of a fund and in the contract between the fund and the management firm.

Neither the statutes of a fund nor any contract between such fund and management firm shall exclude or limit the liability of the management firm for any damage or loss caused to the fund by intentional wrongdoing or gross negligence of the management firm.

Any modification of a material term of a contract between a fund and a management firm, in particular any modification of the terms and conditions of remuneration of the management firm, requires ratification by the general meeting of the fund.

A fund may terminate its contract with the management firm without giving cause with no more than 180 days' notice; in case of termination by the fund of a contract in circumstances for which the management firm is not responsible, the possible penalty for termination to which the management firm could be entitled shall not exceed one half of the annual fixed management fee.

Contracts between a fund that is wholly owned by the State Treasury and a management firm, provide for an annual fixed management fee, annual performance fee or a final performance fee.

The following principles of the remuneration of a management firm apply:

- the annual fixed management fee is established by way of tender;
- the annual performance fee, including any fee expressed in terms of a percentage of fund shares, is not to exceed 1% of the fund shares for each year of rendering services by the management firm, in an amount obtained from the sale of shares and the value of due dividends; and
- the final performance fee, including any fee expressed in terms of a percentage of fund shares, is in both cases not to exceed 0.5% of fund shares multiplied by the number of years of service of a management firm, in an amount obtained from the sale of shares and the value of due dividends; such fee is payable only after the termination of the contract with the management firm.

The fee referred to above shall not exceed an amount determined in proportion to the period for which the management firm provided services to the fund.

Once any shares of a fund are held by shareholders other than the State Treasury, the principles of remuneration of a management firm, which renders services to the fund, must satisfy the condition that the portion of fees paid to the management firm which is dependent on the financial performance of the fund, even when expressed in terms of a percentage of fund shares, may in no event exceed 2% of the shares of the fund with respect to each year of service of the management firm.

In principle, the fixed fee was considered to cover the operational costs of a management company. The fee is fixed in US dollars and will be increased in accordance with changes in the US Consumer Price Index. The amount of fixed management fee varies across the funds (see Figure 2.4). The average level of 2.3% of net assets constitutes more than a decent level of existence according to Polish standards. Yet it must be remembered that net asset value is calculated in accordance with movements in a company's book value. Thus, the net asset value can differ substantially from the market value of companies.

As variations in fixed management fees are not large and most elements of management contracts are standard, it is apparent that there was a good deal of

coordination on the side of the state treasury and its influence upon management
contract negotiation.

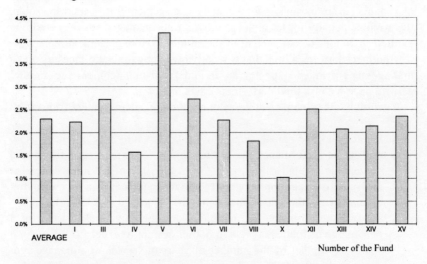

*Figure 2.4 The amount of fixed management fee as a percentage of net
asset value as in 1st quarter of 1997*

Tying the performance fee to the value of the fund was thought to offer incentives
for value increases. It is worthwhile noting that management firms are not entitled
to NIFs' shares in kind. The management firms obtain only the proceeds of the
sale of shares. To ensure long-term enhancement of a fund's value, limits on selling
shares to finance performance fees during the first six years of the contract were
introduced. Shares assigned to the fund to finance the management firm's
performance fee may be sold only after a period of time (from 1 to 3 years) from
when they were assigned.

In general, the incentive structure appears to be appropriately designed to align
the interests of management firms with those of shareholders. A substantial part of
remuneration in the form of cash proceeds from the sale of NIFs' shares appears to
offer a fair solution to the agent–principal conflict. Nevertheless, it must be noted
that the performance fee levels negotiated by supervisory boards are at the high
end of what is permitted by law. This could be seen as a clear indication of the
strong negotiating position of management firms. This is due, in turn, to the very
limited competition between management firms in obtaining contracts.

At the current stage of the program it is impossible to relate the level of
remuneration of a management firm to its restructuring activity. Data concerning
the whole group of portfolio companies suggests that until now NIFs have
concentrated more on supervising portfolio companies than on day-to-day
management (see Table 2.2).

Table 2.2   Breakdown of portfolio companies' responses to the question on the management style of NIFs

Definitely more supervision than day-to-day management	More supervision	Equal supervision and day-to-day management	More day-to-day management	Definitely more day-to-day management than supervision
19%	55%	20%	5%	1%

Fee structure

In general terms, there is a high level of satisfaction with the fee structure of management firms (Figure 2.5). Supervisory board members' comparatively less enthusiastic view of the fee structure may be due to their role as fund watchdogs exerting pressure on management boards to perform.

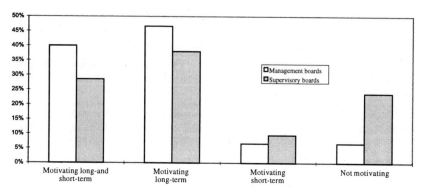

Figure 2.5   Assessment of the fee structure of management firms

The Role of Competition in the Governance of National Investment Funds

Competition in selecting portfolios

The portfolios of the National Investment Funds were created using a process of choice. The order of choice was random to ensure equal chances for all participants. The funds revealed their preferences by choosing the most valuable companies first.

Correlating the order of choices made by funds with companies' financial data available for that date gives a close estimate of fund managers' preferences (Figure 2.6). The procedure unveiled quite substantial differences between the funds.

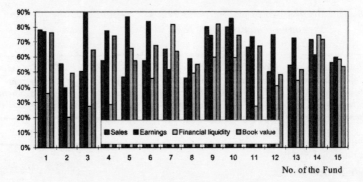

Figure 2.6   Correlation coefficients of choice order and companies'
           financial data – rank correlation of the order of choice and the
           order of the companies according to the value of sales, earnings,
           financial liquidity and book value, respectively

Correlating data on all funds allows the possibility of assessing the relative importance of financial results for the whole program (Figure 2.7). The most important financial indicator of fund managers' preferences is their historical earnings. The least important appears to be financial liquidity. While some funds concentrated on selected branches, most did not target any specific industry when building up their portfolios.

The composition of initial portfolios changed through swap transactions of minority stakes between NIFs. The rationale for these transactions was, according to fund managers, to limit information overload associated with the high number (over 400) of minority stakes in portfolio companies. Usually after swap transactions, minority stakes become consolidated at up to 10% – the minimum level of shareholder activity in Poland.

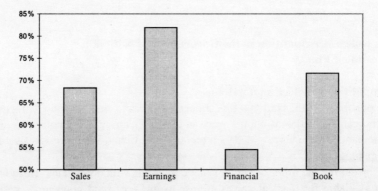

Figure 2.7   Coefficients of the relative importance of financial results for
           the whole program

Competition between management companies

Probably the most noticeable attribute of the Polish Mass Privatization Program is its extremely limited scope of competition between management firms. Competition was contained during the selection process (only firms offering the 'appropriate' blend of skills were considered as serious partners) as well as during management contract negotiation (supervisory funds had a limited choice of management firms to negotiate contracts; the number of firms was only marginally higher than the number of funds). This situation of high professional reputation expectation might have resulted in a sub-optimal fee structure. It is sometimes evident that the level of fixed fees obtained by management firms, in particular, is too high. Therefore, there is an incentive to concentrate on current spending versus long-term value boosting.

Apart from financial incentive problems, there is a strategic dilemma associated with the low level of competition between management firms. The supervisory board of an NIF, acting on behalf of the shareholders, faces a very difficult decision: either to put up with the sometimes less than satisfactory performance of the management firm or to cancel the contract and go without a management firm at all. Termination of the contract can be an attractive option from a cost-reduction point of view. It is undoubtedly cost effective to hire outside consultants on a case-by-case basis. On the other hand, operating without a management firm can decrease fund value in the longer term. It is mainly in the areas of large-scale finance arrangements that management firms with the strong participation of foreign sponsors may prove to be most valuable. Thus, a decision to improve current performance may impede the fund's ability to raise sufficient finance in the longer term. The decision is made even harder by the fact that supervisory board members are not yet appointees of private shareholders. As public trust persons with limited tenure, members of supervisory boards are in a very difficult position to make wealth-maximizing choices. Admittedly, the situation in which there is almost no alternative to the current fund management firm may alter with the development of Poland's financial system.

Monitoring of National Investment Funds through 'Exit' (External Controls)

Trading of NIF shares is conducted on the Warsaw Stock Exchange. As yet, the expectations of over-the-market trading of NIFs' company shares developing have not materialized.

Securities associated with NIFs are traded on three levels:

- unregulated market of share certificates;
- stock exchange trading of share certificates in dematerialized form; and
- stock exchange trading of NIFs' shares.

The one-way system of transforming share certificates in material (paper form), with no regulation and supervision of the market, into computer-based share securities is typical of the Polish market. Once any of the securities enter a higher level of trading, there is no possibility of entering the lower level again. This substantially limits the scope of arbitrage between markets.

As share certificates not converted into NIF shares will become worthless at the end of 1998, it is expected that most of the 26 million plus share certificates will be converted into ordinary shares of NIFs. Trading on the third level began on June 12, 1997 with little more than 10% of share certificates converted. The trading was preceded by the publication of the prospectuses of all NIFs. The analysts were surprised by the level of turnover of NIF shares in the first days of trading which accounted for around 25% of total turnover of the Warsaw Stock Exchange. Pricing was close to parity with share certificates (taking transaction costs into account). Both the liquidity and efficiency of pricing in the first days of NIF share trading had a very encouraging effect on the market perception of the reliability of securities associated with NIFs. Within the first quarter of the year after listing, the NIFs' shares were traded at a substantial discount on their net assets value. But their high level of liquidity makes them attractive alternatives to other securities on the Warsaw Stock Exchange.

The major challenge for NIF share trading is the question of to what extent the unregulated market of share certificates will be absorbed by the regulated public market. It has to be stressed that the Polish security market was, from the very beginning, created with the clear objective of providing investors with as much transparency and liquidity as possible. This resulted in a centralized, computer-based trading system with strict rules of market supervision applied by an American-style Security Exchange Commission. The distinctive features of the system are:

- monthly financial statements of listed companies;
- restrictions on trading outside the market;
- high listing requirements;
- revealing of substantial interests (above 5%); and
- market dominance of the Warsaw Stock Exchange.

In this context, the unregulated market for share certificates offers a window of opportunity for different sorts of otherwise illicit activities, including money laundering, accumulation of large interests and insider-trading. The degree to which this opportunity is exploited will not be fully visible until the listing of all NIF shares on the public market. As for now, opinion polls show that about half of share certificate recipients have already sold their NIF certificates.

Monitoring of National Investment Funds through 'Voice' (Internal Controls)

Legal form

As mentioned above, all the National Investment Funds participating in the Polish program were established by the State Treasury in the form of joint-stock companies.

Governance The ruling bodies of an NIF are: the management board, the supervisory board and the general meeting of shareholders.

- **Management Board.** The management board consists of one to seven members appointed by the supervisory board. The board members are responsible for the day-to-day management of the NIF. As long as the State Treasury remains the sole shareholder of the NIF, all members of the management board must be Polish citizens. (Under the Commercial Code, each member of the management board legally has the power to act on behalf of the NIF.)
- **Supervisory Board.** The supervisory board consists of five to nine members appointed by the general meeting to provide supervision over the activities of the NIF. In particular, the supervisory board is charged with reviewing the NIF's accounts and reporting to the general meeting. At least two-thirds of the members of the supervisory board of the NIF, including the Chairman, should be Polish citizens. The supervisory board acts by resolution of a simple majority of all supervisory board members, although it may delegate individual members with the exercise of special supervisory powers.
- **General Meeting.** The shareholders meet annually for the ordinary general meeting to elect the supervisory board, review the annual report, and determine whether to continue using the services of the management firm. Shareholders meet for extraordinary general meetings called by the supervisory board, the president of the management board or by shareholders holding more than 10% of the NIF's shares.

After the State Treasury ceases holding at least 75% of the shares of the NIF, the State Treasury will vote its NIF shares along with the other shareholders' votes, splitting its votes accordingly.

Rights and obligations of shareholders In the case of ordinary shares, profits are distributed proportionally to the paid-up contributions unless otherwise provided in the constitutional documents.

The constitutional documents may also provide for preference shares which give the right to any extra share of the profits within the limits of the calculation tables of the National Bank of Poland of the year preceding the accounting year, increased by two points. Preference shares may also carry greater voting rights.

Shares are freely transferable. Only the transfer of registered shares must be made subject to the company's consent and must be in writing. In the event of refusal of consent, the company must find a new purchaser, otherwise the transfer may go ahead.

Management   The management of a Polish joint-stock company is carried out by its management board nominated, in principle, by the company in general meeting (or, depending on the statutes, by the supervisory board). It is made up of one or several members. The members of the management board may be removed by the general meeting.

The management board is the legal representative of the company. If it has several members, the signatures of two members or a member and a nominee of the board are required for all documents binding on the company. The constitutional documents may make provision for limitations on their powers but these are ineffective in relation to a third party.

In practice, the board may nominate a chairman from among its members. The constitutional documents may authorize the chairman alone to bind the company or may give him this power within certain limits.

The supervisory boards   The constitutional documents may provide for a supervisory board or an audit commission, or both. The creation of a supervisory board is mandatory when the capital exceeds 500 million zlotys.

The supervisory board must be made up of at least five members elected by the general meeting, unless otherwise provided for in the constitutional documents (in the case of any joint-stock company, another mode of nomination may be provided for).

The supervisory board must supervise the company's activities. It must:

- examine the balance sheet and the profit and loss account;
- examine the reports of the administrative board and the decisions relating to distribution of dividends; and
- submit an annual report to the general meeting and its activities.

Its powers of control are very extensive. It may require reports from employees and examine the documents of the company and, in certain circumstances, appoint and remove members of the management board. Unless otherwise provided in the constitutional documents, decisions require an absolute majority.

The audit commission is subject to the same rules. Its role is to audit the accounts. This role may be extended if the company has no supervisory board.

General meeting of shareholders   An ordinary general meeting approves the accounts of the accounting year and must be convened by the management board within four months following the end of the accounting year. Any other matter may be put on the agenda of the meeting.

An extraordinary general meeting may be convened at any time to vote on any matter. The management board, or the supervisory board in the event of the management board's failure so to do, or any other person designated by the constitutional documents may convene meetings.

General meetings must be convened by two notices published in the Official Journal, the first appearing three weeks before the meeting, the second ten days before. These notices must set out the agenda.

No quorum is fixed by law. In principle, one share carries one vote. The constitutional documents may, however, restrict this right in the case of shareholders holding more than one share or may provide for shares with double voting rights. In the latter case, the number of votes per share is limited to five.

Unless otherwise provided in the constitutional documents, decisions require an absolute majority of votes. Decisions relating to amendments to constitutional documents, mergers, winding-up of the company or the sale of the business require a majority of three quarters. Decisions modifying the objects of the company require a majority of two thirds. In these cases, one share carries one vote.

Decisions amending the constitutional documents must be the subject of a notarial deed.

Winding-up and liquidation of the company   The Code sets out the grounds for dissolution of a company. These include the occurrence of conditions set out in the constitutional documents, insolvency and court-ordered liquidation. If winding up is preceded by a 'liquidation period' (i.e., a period for realizing the assets of the company), the liquidators are normally appointed from amongst the members of the administrative board.

Creditors must be reimbursed first. Any surplus is distributed amongst the partners proportionally to their contributions, within one year after the latest notice of the opening of the liquidation. The liquidators must notify the Ministry of Industry and Trade of the dissolution.

In a joint venture, the Polish partners have a pre-emption right over the assets, unless otherwise provided in the constitutional documents.

The business name of a National Investment Fund should contain the phrase, 'National Investment Fund – Joint Stock Company'. The business name of a fund should be sufficiently different from the business names of other funds.

Appointment of the initial supervisory boards and responsibility

The governing bodies of a fund are the general meeting, the supervisory board and the management board. Until the first general meeting is convened, in which shareholders other than the State Treasury may participate, the members of the supervisory board of a fund are appointed and recalled, and their remuneration determined by the appropriate minister (previously the Minister of Privatization, currently the Minister of State Treasury) with the consent of the President of the Council of Ministers.

The members of the supervisory board of Privatization Investment Funds are appointed by the appropriate minister from among persons selected through a competition conducted by a Selection Commission.

The Selection Commission is composed of:

- four persons elected by the lower chamber of parliament;
- one person elected by the higher chamber of parliament;
- one person designated in each case by the national inter-union organizations and national trade unions being representative of employees of the majority of state places of employment; and
- twelve persons appointed by the President of the Council of Ministers.

The President of the Council of Ministers appoints the Chairman of the Selection Commission and determines its rules of procedure.

The statutes of a fund determine the number of members of its supervisory board. The number is an odd number and no greater than nine until the first general meeting is convened in which shareholders other than the State Treasury may participate.

At least two thirds of the members of a supervisory board of a fund, including its chairman, should be Polish citizens.

The term of the first supervisory board expires on the day the first ordinary general meeting of the fund has been held in which shareholders other than the State Treasury may participate.

Until the first general meeting is convened in which shareholders other than the State Treasury may participate, powers of the general meeting which are not reserved by this law or the statutes of a fund to the exclusive competence of the general meeting, are exercised by the supervisory board.

Within the period referred to above, the statutes of a fund may not grant the supervisory board powers to decide on the following matters:

- change of statutes;
- issuance of new shares;
- merger of the fund with another company; and
- dissolution of the fund.

In addition to its powers arising under the Commercial Code, the supervisory board has the exclusive power to appoint the members of the management board, and to select the management firm.

The management board of a fund is appointed for a period of up to two years. As long as the State Treasury remains the sole shareholder of a fund, only a Polish citizen may be a member of the management board.

Within eight months of the end of each fiscal year of a fund, the management board shall be obliged to prepare and present to the supervisory board a balance sheet as at the last day of the fiscal year (the balance sheet date), an account of profits and losses for the previous year and a written report on the activities of the fund in the given year. In this respect, it is a more liberal regulation than the Commercial Code (three-month period).

The Minister of Finance may determine specific accounting requirements for national investment funds.

The management board of a fund shall convene a general meeting within ten months after the end of each fiscal year. In this respect, it is a more liberal regulation than the Commercial Code (five-month period).

Remuneration of NIF supervisory board members is based on the average wage in the Polish enterprise sector multiplied by 3.8 for chairmen of supervisory boards and 2.7 for all other members of supervisory boards. Financial rewards of supervisory members are not linked to the financial performance of funds. Supervisory boards were the primary vehicle of public control over the activity of NIFs. The boards took full responsibility for strategic management decisions; most notably cancellation of management contracts.

In the initial period of Polish mass privatization, management firms were envisaged as being a major element of the 'value added' in the program. The management firms were, at least in spirit if not by the letter of the law, responsible for running the business NIFs. The experience of governance in NIFs is that the business decision center has remained in executive boards. To ensure influence of management companies, personal links between the management company and the executive board of NIFs were established – top managers of management companies were nominated as presidents of executive boards. It is clearly a case of the dominance of the traditional two-tier (supervisory board and executive board) corporate structure over, contrary to the Polish experience, the concept of the management company. More generally, it is frequently apparent that differences in understandings of the 'mechanics of law' in continental and Anglo-American systems have been the major source of tensions between parties involved in the NIF program.

Control structure

Control structure of NIFs in Poland is far from fully developed. There is no efficient ownership control in all dimensions of governance (Figure 2.8). Empirical studies suggest that NIFs exercise strong control over their portfolio companies. Alliances with other NIFs enable a majority shareholder approach to controlling strategic issues in a portfolio company. This effect is attributable to the design of the program which ensured the substantial interests of NIFs in portfolio companies.

At the same time, listings of NIF shares on the stock exchange gave shareholders an efficient way to exercise their control through 'exit'. In this case, mass privatization took advantage of the well functioning and transparent capital market in Poland.

As to the internal control of portfolio companies and the external control of NIFs, we can assert that strong ownership control exists. We believe external controls of portfolio companies and internal controls of NIFs are areas of deficiency in governance. Regulations and policy-making decisions should focus on ameliorating these insufficiencies.

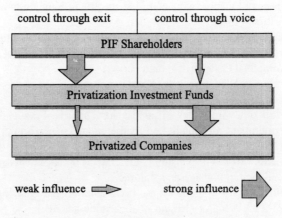

Figure 2.8   Control structure of NIFs in Poland (1997)

Role of private shareholders

Members of the governing bodies of NIFs expect that the active role of NIFs' shareholders will soon be apparent (Figure 2.9). Management of NIFs seem to pay attention to the financial performance of the funds. All funds went through a detailed process of provisioning for losses in the market value of their portfolio companies. The conservative approach to accounting practices may suggest that the funds are eager to show substantial value creation in future. This offers quite a powerful instance of management's will to perform well in the perception of the private shareholder.

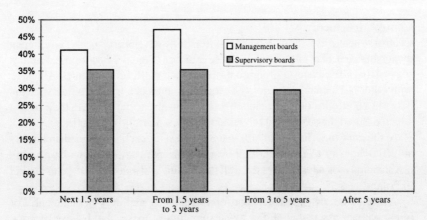

Figure 2.9   Time horizon of active role of private shareholders of NIFs

Regulation on takeovers

The perception of the level of restriction on the concentration of ownership and rules on mergers and takeovers as being appropriate is the dominant view among members of governing bodies of NIFs (Figure 2.10). Yet it is apparent that there is a certain level of uneasiness (especially on the side of supervisory members) as to the extent to which potential hostile takeovers should be avoided. The attraction of NIFs as takeover targets lies in their size which makes them valuable pools of collateral. The ability to raise finance securitized on NIFs' assets (large if not first class quality) constitutes an important advantage in a transition economy. In post-communist financial markets, it is still size that matters.

The activity of NIFs which are keen to issue commercial papers, convertible bonds and obtain bank loans (on attractive terms) confirms the importance of their role as a financial intermediary. In this context, it is crucial to ensure that they will be free to channel their funds into new ventures (see discrepancy in perceptions of NIFs' objectives).

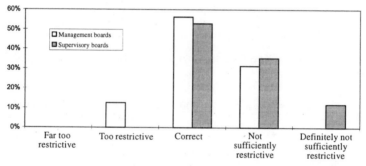

Figure 2.10   Opinion on restrictions on concentration of ownership and rules on mergers and takeovers of NIFs

Control over NIFs

In our opinion, the degree to which experience of the 'control game' over NIFs will contribute to developing an efficient market for corporate control is the most immediate challenge to the program. This issue has the highest priority (over external control on portfolio companies) in terms of creating mature corporate structure of investment funds in Poland. The view is apparently shared by the members of governing bodies who have no illusion as to the fact that regulation can be effective in protecting NIFs from takeover (Figure 2.11).

In the first days of September 1997, market participants received a signal that one of the funds (with a management firm owned by a large Polish commercial bank, a British investment bank and a Polish consulting firm) was going to take over another fund (with no management company). As the final result of the process is still unknown, it appears that in the Polish circumstances having a management company may prove to be an effective poison pill (a deterrent against hostile takeovers). This would be an interesting, though somewhat surprising, effect of the Polish approach to mass privatization, which certainly needs to be carefully researched.

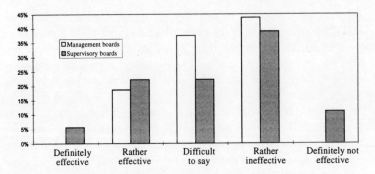

Figure 2.11   Assessment of the future effectiveness of restrictions on concentration of ownership and rules on mergers and takeovers of NIFs

The Role of Regulation and Supervision for the Improved Performance of NIFs

At the time of registration of a fund, the fund statutes should contain the following restrictions:

- a prohibition on acquiring securities issued by entities not based in Poland or by entities not primarily engaged in business in Poland;
- a prohibition on holding shares in general partnerships or other entities, or investments which would create unlimited liability for the fund;
- a prohibition on acquiring shares in any company if as a result of such acquisition the fund would have over 33% of the votes of the company, with the exception of a situation where:

    (a) shares exceeding the limit of 33% were obtained by the fund in the form of a rights issue;
    (b) shares exceeding the limit of 33% were obtained by the fund in the exercise of a preemption right due to all shareholders;
    (c) shares exceeding the limit of 33% were obtained by the fund in the performance of an obligation to make a cash offer to all remaining shareholders of the company to purchase all remaining shares;

- within three years of the registration of the fund, a prohibition on the fund on selling shares of a company in which the fund owns more than 20% of the share capital and is, at the same time, with the exception of state legal persons, its largest shareholder, if as a result of such sale the fund's holding in the share capital of such company would fall below 20%; this prohibition need not apply where such a sale takes place as a result of a public offer made by the fund or an offer for sale to a single investor or a group of investors, provided however that the buyer acquires all the shares of such company offered for sale in this way;

- a prohibition on the fund selling securities that the fund at the time of the making of the sale agreement does not own; unless at the time of making of such agreement the fund is entitled to acquire an appropriate number of securities of the same kind;
- a prohibition on the fund acquiring securities issued by another fund or entity which is engaged primarily in trade in securities, if as a result of such acquisition more than 5% of the net asset value of the fund would be invested in the acquired securities;
- a prohibition on the fund acquiring precious metals and entering into commodities contracts, options or futures contracts, except for:

  (a) transactions with the aim of reducing the risk within limits allowed by Polish law;
  (b) the acquisition of shares of companies that produce and process precious metals or commodities;

- a prohibition on the fund acquiring real estate (except for use as office space for the fund or any management firm with which the fund has contracted), or shares in companies engaged primarily in real estate investment, if as a result of such investment more than 5% of the net asset value of the fund would be invested in shares of such company;
- a prohibition on the fund borrowing money or issuing debt securities, if as a result the total value of the fund's debt obligations would exceed 50% of the net asset value of the fund;
- a prohibition on the fund acquiring securities, if as a result of such acquisition more than 25% of the net asset value of the fund would then be invested in securities of one issuer.

The fund statutes should also provide that any amendment to the statutes resulting in the elimination of any of the restrictions referred to above, which takes place within three years of the date of registration of the fund, shall require the unanimous vote of the general meeting of the fund. In such a case, the State Treasury will not be obliged by the provisions of the statutes to a particular manner of voting at the general meeting of the fund.

Level of regulation
There is a fairly unanimous perception of the NIF program being adequately regulated (Figure 2.12). It appears that managers and supervisors are generally

satisfied with checks and balances implemented in the regulatory framework of the program. As the result reflects only the current stage of the ten-year program, we propose a dynamic approach to assessing the regulatory framework of mass privatization programs. This would reflect changing the objectives and limitations faced by regulators.

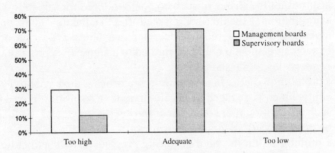

Figure 2.12   Assessment of the level of regulation of the NIF program

Three-phase regulatory cycle of mass privatization programs

- **Initiation phase** – with the focus on speed and fairness of the process; the Polish program (based on a regulated market approach) scored low in its speed of implementation (as outlined at the beginning of this chapter) yet popular participation seems to indicate favorable assessment of the fairness of the program.
- **Adjustment phase** – with the focus on boosting efficiency in privatized companies; research conducted by the Gdansk Institute for Market Economics indicates that NIFs managed to implement substantial improvements in organization, marketing and financial standing of privatized companies.
- **Maturity phase** – with the focus on the impact of the program on the investment fund market as a whole and its competitiveness; in the Polish case this issue is still open, especially in the context of the new regulation on closed-end funds which appear to be the natural final direction of the transformation of NIFs.

Final remarks

International comparisons clearly demonstrate that the Polish version of mass privatization is strongly influenced by state regulation and supervision. It can be argued that relatively high standards of regulation were an important contribution to the present success of the NIF program. Popular citizens' participation, accelerated privatization, extension of the well-regulated capital market and the perception of a reliable program can be, at least to some extent, attributable to this factor. Yet, paradoxically, the source of success in the first phase may prove to be a liability in later stages of the program.

It may be said that the technically successful program will be at odds with the essence of any privatization program – liberating the economy from the direct influence of politics. Until now, the program has attracted almost all conceivable types of political pressure. Passing necessary legal regulations was, for a prohibitively long period of time, blocked by parliament debate; the size of the program was a matter for a national referendum; centralized decision-making encouraged ponderous lobbying activity. It has, however, to be admitted that such lobbying activity was not limited to Polish participants in the program.

The current perception of the NIFs as being predisposed to political manipulation is to a large extent a derivative of the very logic of the program. The active role of government in creating and appointing controlling positions in NIFs naturally resulted in the creation of a political-lobbying-friendly environment. Strict government control to prevent unwelcome results of the program had its downside in the form of limits on entrepreneurial activities of the funds. It may be reliably claimed that the long-term success of the program will depend on the speed and efficiency with which NIFs lose their special status and become regular market controlled business entities; a situation which has yet to emerge in Poland.

3.   Governance of Privatization Funds in Slovenia

I.   The Role of Privatization Funds in Privatization and Post-Privatization

Marko Rems

MASS PRIVATIZATION PROGRAM

Overview of the Role of the Mass Privatization Program

Objectives of the mass privatization program

The Law on Ownership Transformation, which regulates the Mass Privatization Program (MPP), was passed in November 1992. The main objective of the Law was to transform all socially owned companies into joint-stock and limited liability companies with clearly defined ownership rights of the new owners.

Two different privatization concepts were applied within the Law on Ownership Transformation:

- a decentralized multi-track approach, with initiatives and decisions coming from the companies;
- privatization based on the free distribution of shares to the population through the privatization investment funds (PIFs).

The strong public opinion, that socially owned companies belong to the employees, the capable management of Slovene companies and the fact that there were not many potential domestic or foreign investors, suggested the use of the first concept. The idea of a preferential scheme for employees, which is realized by the discount in employee buyouts, can also be explained by the spirit of social ownership whereby employees were *de facto* owners of the companies.

The fair and broad participation approach of the population was achieved by distributing the vouchers to all the citizens of the Republic of Slovenia. The concentration of shares and redistribution were planned after the conclusion of the MPP.

A multi-track approach gave way to a variety of privatization techniques, the public offerings of shares being a fairly popular one. Since the companies that chose this method had to be listed on the stock exchange, the clear intention to develop the capital market could be found in the Law. The creation of PIFs additionally contributed to the expansion of the capital market.

The purpose behind the introduction of the PIFs and the distribution of 40% of the shares of each company to PIFs, Compensation Fund and Pension Fund,[1] was to find new owners outside the company, who would play an active role in the corporate governance of the companies, as well as to balance the prevailing role of the insiders.

Taking into consideration the Privatization Law and other supportive legislation, speed was not one of the primary goals. More attention was given to the organization and financial restructuring of the companies before undergoing privatization. The exclusion of agricultural land from the company's assets, the restitution in kind and compensation in shares, the harmonization of the financial statement with international accounting standards and the audit of the so-called 'wild' privatizations were the main transition issues, implemented hand in hand with the MPP.

As we can see, there were quite a few objectives to be achieved by implementing the MPP. Due to political disagreement related to these issues, which were declared as the objectives (the development of capital market, restructuring), the fulfillment of goals was relatively slow. Furthermore, some of the policy measures are not harmonious with these objectives and sometimes are even directed against them.

Overall privatization process and MPP

Before adopting the Privatization Law, the old Yugoslavian Company Law from 1988 was in force. It allowed private ownership of the companies and determined the transformation procedure. Many new private companies were formed by employees (managers in most cases) of socially-owned companies. The old socially-owned company employed them, while the most profitable operations were canalized through their private companies. Such behavior was significant in trade and services branches and activities, due to the low capital intensity and the lack of regulation. Quite a lot of assets were actually privatized this way. Up to the end of 1992, 44 companies were privatized through the federal law procedure. They were mostly medium size companies.

The companies that provide public services and utilities were regulated by the Law on Public Utilities, which was passed in 1993. It empowered the ministries to determine which company was subject to this Law and the ownership share to be privatized in accordance with the MPP. Fifty-five out of 151 public utility companies were subject to the MPP, while the rest of the shares were transferred to the state.

At the beginning of the MPP, the contribution of the private sector to the GDP was about 30%; 1,545 companies which were subject to the Privatization Law represented 40% of the GDP, while the rest could be connected to the public sector. The situation at the beginning of 1997, after a four-year period, shows that 958 companies completed their privatization program, 410 companies are in the process, while 116 companies still have not finished the preparation phase. By analyzing the 958 already privatized companies, we can see that they contribute about 30% to the GDP. So, the larger and most important companies have already been privatized. Following the current dynamic of the MPP, it is expected that the process is going to be completed by the end of 1997.

As mentioned in the previous section, the Slovenian model allowed companies (workers' councils) to make an autonomous decision on the choice of their privatization method, as well as when to start preparing and implementing their privatization program. The only limitation they had to take into consideration was the time-limited validity of vouchers, which has since been extended many times, due to the slow speed of the privatization program.

A combination of free distribution and commercial privatization methods were provided by the Law:

- A free transfer of 40% of ordinary shares to the funds: 10% of the shares to the Compensation Fund, 10% of the shares to the Pension Fund and 20% of the shares to the Development Fund. After the ownership transformation registration at the registry court, the Development Fund is obliged to sell these shares to the PIFs, which represent the Slovene version of the MPP. This method is obligatory and had to be used by all companies which were subject to the privatization program. These shares are tradable as soon as the company issues the shares.
- Internal distribution: 20% of ordinary shares can be offered in exchange for vouchers to employees, former employees and relatives of employees, the latter in case of low subscription. These shares are not tradable for a period of 2 years after privatization.
- Internal buyout: up to 40% of the ordinary shares can be sold to employees and former employees in exchange for vouchers[2] and cash. Shares are sold at a 50% discount and can be bought in 5 instalments. The shares, which are bought with vouchers, are not tradable for a period of 2 years after privatization, while the 'cash' shares are tradable immediately after they are issued.
- Sale of the shares: up to 60%[3] of the shares can be sold by means of public offering of shares, public tender or public auction. The voucher payments are allowed in public offering of shares, while only cash payments are possible in the other two techniques. The shares are tradable after they are issued, irrespective of the form of payment.

- Sale of all assets of a company and liquidation. The Development Fund assumes all liabilities of the liquidated company.
- Increasing the equity of the privatized company, by issuing new shares for more than 10% of the existing equity.

After the subscribing process is finished, the unsold shares are transferred to the Development Fund, which has to offer them to the PIFs.

Supply side of the MPP

The Law on Ownership Transformation determined the supply side of the MPP. The equity of 1545 socially owned companies was available for privatization. Due to organizational and financial restructuring within the privatization process, some non-operating assets were excluded from the balance sheets and transferred to the Development Fund, reducing socially owned equity and thus creating the special form of supply for the MPP. These assets are sold to PIFs for vouchers [4].

As mentioned before, the equity of 55 public utility companies has been offered in the MPP. The infrastructure has been excluded from the company's balance sheet and transferred to the State. The State participates as a shareholder in these companies, determining their stake on a case-by-case basis.

Each of the 1,545 companies had to prepare an opening balance sheet on January 1, 1993, where the tangible assets were apprased. The provisions for ecological rehabilitation could be formed on the liability side. The value of equity from the opening balance sheet could be the basis for the share price. Additionally, a company could determine the share price on the basis of a special valuation report [5], prepared by a certified appraiser, who often chose the discounted cash flow method. This way of determining the share price was chosen in 829 cases, while 716 companies decided the value on the basis of the opening balance sheet.

The exact book value from the opening balance sheets will be available when all the companies have finished their preparation phase [6]. To date, 1,365 companies have finished the preparation phase, 30 have gone bankrupt, while others are still working on the required documentation. If we take into consideration the performance of these companies, the negative cash flow and losses are typical.

However, the estimation of book value from the balance sheets, as well as the financial statements for all companies which are subject to the MPP, have been taken into analysis. By multiplying the number of all issued shares by their initial price, which is sometimes determined on the appraisal basis and sometimes on the opening balance sheet basis, we get a new, probably the most important category, called 'actual' value of the equity.

The estimation for all 1,545 companies is shown in the Figure 3.1. The lower figure of the 'actual' value can be explained by the rational decisions of the workers' councils and management. When the apprised value was higher than the book value, they decided on the cheaper alternative.

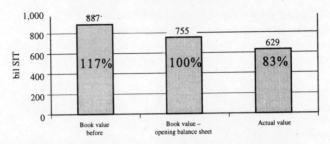

Figure 3.1   Estimated value of social capital in 1,545 companies

Figure 3.2 compares the value of offered shares method by method. It is clear that internal buyout is the prevailing method in the Slovenian privatization program.

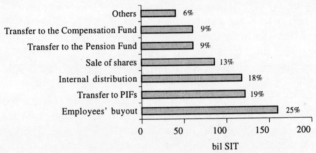

Figure 3.2   Value of social capital by privatization method

Demand side of the MPP

At the beginning of the MPP, all the Slovenian citizens who were born before the time of adopting the Law on Ownership Transformation were eligible to receive vouchers. Two million voucher accounts at the SDK (Social Accounting Service) were opened in a dematerialized form. The vouchers were distributed depending on the age of the holder and were nominated in Slovenian currency. Each citizen of Slovenia received a voucher whose nominated value varied from 150,000 SIT up to 400,000 SIT (from 2,000 DM up to 6,400 DM).

Vouchers were issued on the same day (January 1, 1993), as the shares from the MPP, to avoid problems. Problems, however, occurred in cases of cash payments, because of inflation. Revaluation[7] of share prices was done in such cases.

There was no registration fee for opening a voucher account. Voucher holders received notification from the SDK, providing them with information on their account number and amount deposited in the account.

The vouchers are not tradable. Due to a centralized and dematerialized system of vouchers, there was no possibility of transferring them from one account to another. But the prohibition of trading was avoided by using future contracts and proxies. The buyer bought, usually for a very small amount, the authorization and the right to invest a voucher in the seller's name. The seller also signed a blank contract, where an undefined number of shares of an undefined company were sold to the buyer.

Generally speaking, an individual has two ways of investing a voucher:

- To buy shares of a company undergoing privatization.
- To buy shares of a PIF.

PIFs have attracted approximately 310 billion SIT (5.1 billion DM) of vouchers, due to well-prepared advertising, promotion and aggressive marketing aiming at the voucher holders. Insiders employed in the companies undergoing privatization have mostly used vouchers in internal distribution and internal buyout, investing directly in companies. After completing the MPP, it is expected that more than 40 billion SIT (700 million DM) will be left in the accounts and thus lost (see Figures 3.3 and 3.4).

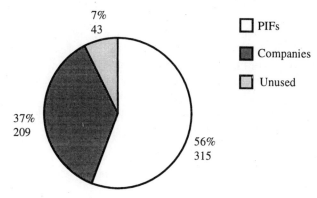

Figure 3.3   Expected investment of vouchers (in billion SIT)

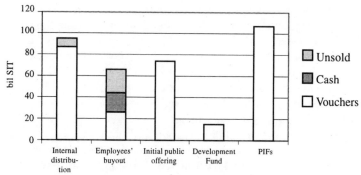

Figure 3.4   Means of payment by privatization method

The question of the total value of issued vouchers and the balance with the book value is the most important one. The Law on Ownership Transformation determined the overall nominal value of issued vouchers at 567 billion tolars (9.3 billion DM). That amount should represent at that time 40% of the opening book value of equity supplied.

As the MPP is approaching its end, it is estimated that from 160 to 175 billion SIT of vouchers will not have the coverage on the supply side, postulated in the Law on Ownership Transformation. Fewer than 10% of voucher holders believe that vouchers have no value, and therefore are not interested in investing them in the MPP at all.

Such a gap between the supply and demand is the result of many factors on both the supply and demand side. There were a lot of variables that were not known at the time of the voucher issue. On the supply side, two main features are as follows:

- Only the book value from the pre-opening balance sheets was known. It served as a basis for determining the nominal value of vouchers. The relevant value for privatization is the so-called actual value of social capital, which determines the share-selling price. The difference of 258 billion SIT can be derived from Figure 3.1.
- The exact list of companies eligible for privatization, as well as the stake of equity to be privatized, were not determined by the Law. The first estimate made by the government officials responsible was incorrect. They made a mistake by including subsidiaries of the socially-owned companies on the privatization list as well. Proof for such an assertion can be found in the notification of opening the voucher account. It says that within the ownership transformation process 'more than 2000 companies will be privatized in Slovenia'.

On the demand side, there were major changes as well. Due to political pressure from the unions, promissory notes for unpaid wages were additionally issued to the employees in socially owned companies. A promissory note has exactly the same characteristics as a voucher. The total amount of promissory notes is about 40 billion SIT and thus the total demand is increased by that amount.

The last, but not the least important problem, comes from the technique of implementation of the privatization methods, prescribed by the legislation. The price of shares in the initial public offering (IPO) method can vary depending on the demand and supply for an interval of plus/minus 30%, otherwise the share price is fixed and is determined by the opening balance sheet or valuation report.

The conclusion is obvious. At the time of the issue of vouchers, the supply side was not properly estimated. This and additional political pressures caused an inflation of vouchers. The problem is especially serious for the PIFs since they have collected over half of all issued vouchers, which do not have corresponding coverage in the privatization shares.

THE ROLE OF PRIVATIZATION INVESTMENT FUNDS IN THE PERIOD OF PRIVATIZATION AND POST-PRIVATIZATION

The Objectives of PIFs

The objectives of PIFs were introduced by the Law on Ownership Transformation and the Law on Investment Funds and Management Companies. Following these Laws, the purpose of PIFs is to collect vouchers and purchase shares issued in the MPP, thus minimizing and dispersing the investor's risk. PIFs were very successful in the process of collecting vouchers. The collected vouchers amounted to over 310 billion SIT (5.1 billion DM), which is more than half of the total voucher issue.

The share of PIFs in the companies, prescribed by the Law, implicitly reveals the second objective; an active ownership role of PIFs in the companies. Together with state-owned funds, PIFs are entitled to hold a 40% share[8] in the company's equity. Because of the similarity of interests, PIFs can play an important role in the corporate governance of privatized companies. The professional background of the management company's managers, which is requested by the Law, backs up this intention.

Legal Framework

The special provisions of the Law on Investment Funds and Management Companies define the legal and regulatory framework of the Authorized Management Companies and Authorized Investment Companies. Further in the text, the abbreviation PIF is used instead of Authorized Investment Companies and MC instead of Authorized Management Company.

Privatization Investment Fund

A PIF is a joint-stock company. This legal form is prescribed by the Law. A PIF can be transformed to some other legal form, if three quarters of the PIF shareholders make such a decision at the general shareholders' meeting. The shares of PIFs are registered shares and cannot be transferred until they are listed on the Stock Exchange. Under the Law, the PIF's nominal value of equity may range between 100 million and 10 billion SIT.

The PIF can only be established by the MC, which has also the right that in a period of 5 years, it can annually increase the equity of the PIF by 1% without the Agency's approval, and thus receive a part of the management fee.

Irrespective of the limitation imposed to the regular investment funds, PIFs may invest in real estate up to 20% of their total investments. There are additional limitations to PIFs' investments. The most important is that the PIF cannot have more than 10% of its investments in securities of the same company and a maximum of 20% shares of an individual company that owns more than 10% of the MC. Otherwise, the PIF can have a100% ownership share in the individual company.

Management Company

On the other hand, the MC may be set up as a joint-stock company or a limited liability company and the management of PIFs may be its only activity. MCs have to obtain an operating license from the Securities Market Agency, which regulates the securities market.

Shareholders and sponsors of MCs may be any individual and legal person, except the following legal entities:

- legal entities owned by the Republic of Slovenia;
- socially owned companies which are subject to MPP; and
- foreign individuals or legal persons may jointly acquire up to 10% of shares of a MC. To acquire more than 10% of shares, they need the approval of the Securities Market Agency and the responsible ministry.

Banks and insurance companies may become shareholders of an MC, irrespective of their ownership structure.

Mechanism of Collecting the Vouchers

The PIFs issued[10] shares in accordance with the provisions of the Law on Commercial Companies. The PIF's share can be paid in vouchers or cash. So far all shares have been purchased in exchange for vouchers.

All shares have a par value of 1,000 SIT, which is the minimum amount prescribed by the Law. The actual purchasing price was increased by 3% (30 SIT) to cover set-up costs. The surplus belongs to the MC in the form of shares. Consequently, on the liability side of their balance sheet PIFs had only common stocks, 1,000 SIT par value and no excess of par value as well as no retained earnings.[11]

The shares are sold in the public offering procedure, so each PIF has to prepare the prospectus, where all relevant information is disclosed. The prospectus is available at all subscription places. Usually, the subscription was performed at post office, bank and insurance counters, through their network of branches throughout the country.

A majority of MCs backed up their public offerings by large and impressive promotion actions. Well-known individuals promised safe and profitable investments on TV and other media. Since there was pressure from a lot of MCs to set up and manage as many PIFs as possible, a large part of the population was attracted. In addition, some MCs organized special teams that visited households and convinced voucher holders to give them the authorization to subscribe the PIF shares in their name and for their account.

More than one million individuals, that is over half the entire population of voucher holders have invested vouchers (approximately 315) in PIFs. The exact amount of invested vouchers in PIFs still cannot be defined, since a few PIFs have concluded their share subscription process just recently.

The rest of the vouchers have been invested either directly in companies or are still on voucher accounts and probably won't be invested at all. We expect about 43 billion SIT (7%) of vouchers will be left in the accounts and thus lost.

PIFs' Characteristics

So far, 72 PIFs have been established by the 23 MCs, mostly in 1994 and 1995. The dominant owners of management companies are the domestic legal entities. The foreigners owned minority shares in two management companies.

The state has indirect ownership share in 2 MCs through the state-owned banks, and 2 MCs are still owned by the partly socially owned sponsors (insurance companies). They control 16 PIFs which account for 28% of total PIFs' assets. Until now, the state has not taken advantage of their ownership position and if the banks (sponsors) are going to be privatized in the near future, there will be probably no interference from the state.

The banks are the major owners of MCs. They control 34 PIFs, which account for 62% of total PIFs' assets. That means that banks' MCs manage on average large PIFs. The second biggest group is the individuals, controlling 19% of PIFs and 17% of the assets. The MCs owned by the non-financial and insurance companies are a little bit smaller and amount to 33% of PIFs and 21% of PIFs' assets (see Figures 3.5 and 3.6).

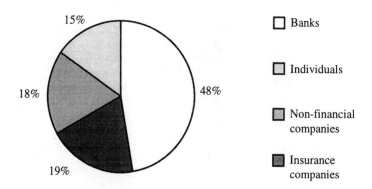

Figure 3.5   Number of PIFs owned by different groups of MC owners

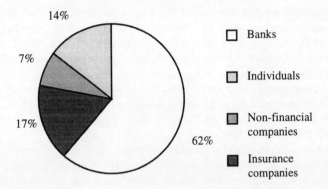

Figure 3.6   Value of assets controlled by different groups of MC owners

It is evident that banks and insurance companies control over threequarters of PIFs' total assets. On the other hand, these financial institutions also have the majority stake in banking and insurance services in the Slovenian market. So, it is often a situation that MCs manage the PIF, which have a large portion of the company's shares and at the same time, its sponsors (banks and insurance companies) have other business interests (credit and insurance contracts) with the same company. That may lead to a conflict of interest where the PIF would rather follow the interests of the MC or its sponsors than the PIF's shareholders.

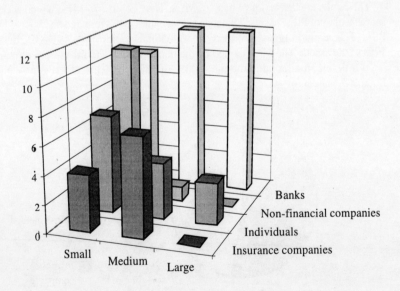

Figure 3.7   Distribution of PIFs by MC sponsors and size of PIFs

Additional information on PIFs' characteristics can be obtained if the funds are broken down by their size. The PIFs have been split up into three groups, according to the size of registered or approved equity: small (up to 4 billion SIT of equity), medium (4–8 billion SIT) and large (more than 8 billion SIT). The same division has been applied in the questionnaire, which is discussed later.

Figure 3.7 shows that the main characteristic of the large PIFs is that their MCs are mainly sponsored by the banks. The banks and insurance companies are prevailing sponsors of MCs managing medium-sized PIFs, while the small PIFs are managed primarily by the non-financial companies and individuals.

Despite the fact that an MC shall not be engaged in any activity other than the management of PIFs, a conflict of interests cannot be avoided as the financial institutions have been allowed to establish and own MCs.

Primary Allocation of Companies' Shares to PIFs

The MPP has lasted for almost five years. It is quite a lot longer than the lawmakers expected.[12] As discussed earlier, the autonomous approach has resulted in the delay, which reflects in the slow primary allocation of companies' shares to PIFs. In order to provide PIFs with the companies' shares as soon as possible, the Development Fund periodically offers packages of shares to PIFs. The Development Fund, which acquired and temporarily owns 20% of shares of each company and, additionally, unsold shares from internal distribution and employees' buyouts of some companies, has to offer these shares to PIFs.

At the beginning of the MPP, a combination of classic auction and Dutch action has been selected as a sales technique. The Development Fund has designed the packages of shares, where the shares of one company usually have composed one package, while the large blocks have been broken down in more packages. The initial prices of shares have also been determined by the Development Fund. It has calculated the price as the weighted average of prices, where the quantity of shares weights the realized price in other privatization methods.

The rationale of such a sales technique can be found in the assumption that the overall supply and demand sides are balanced. Consequently, the competition among PIFs would lead to the positive or negative price changes in accordance with companies' performance in the post opening balance sheet period. Such an approach would clear the market.

But the false assumption on balance between the supply and demand side has lead to the so-called privatization gap. According to the current data, about 27% of the social capital of approximately 685 billion SIT were bought out by PIFs. Comparing this amount with the amount of vouchers collected by the PIFs, the difference of 130 billion SIT arises. Therefore, PIFs will be left with approximately 130 billion SIT vouchers on the asset side. The PIFs were well aware of the problem in 1995 and forced the state to promise them additional state-owned assets to fill the gap.

The direct consequence of the privatization gap is the formation of the cartel agreement among PIFs. They found out that the share prices could go up as a result of excessive demand. They reached an informal price agreement on their participation in primary auctions. As a result, the shares price have been almost identical to initial prices. After the five auctions, The Development Fund and PIFs have reached an agreement on changes to the sales technique. The Development Fund began with offering a package of the shares of all companies having finished their privatization procedures by tender to the association of PIFs, which in turn proposes a price which should be at least equal to the offered price. The shares are then exchanged among the PIFs according to their internal rules. Adopting this method, PIFs have also agreed to buy all offered companies, whatever their performance is. After completing the tender procedure the real primary allocation of shares takes place. To get any relevant information of investment policy the post-tender trading among PIFs has to be taken into consideration.

However, the performance analysis for 1996 of portfolios obtained at five auctions[13] shows that the large PIFs have made the best portfolio selection (see Figure 3.8). The analyzed portfolio is positive and seems to be good. But, before making such a conclusion, we have to be aware that the best companies have been privatized first and thus have been auctioned at the beginning of the process.

The reasons for better performance of large PIFs' portfolio companies have probably the same roots as mentioned before. Since the large PIFs have been established at the beginning of the MPP, they have had access to the early auctions where shares of better companies were offered.

The request of PIFs to fill the privatization gap in order to make it possible for them to buy shares at the same price as other 'investors' in privatization can be justified and legitimized by the provisions in the Law on Ownership Transformation which fixes the share price in internal distribution and employees' buyout, being the prevailing methods of privatization in Slovenia.

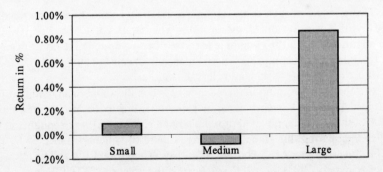

Figure 3.8   Performance of companies acquired by different sized PIFs in five auctions in 1996

To date, the Development Fund has organized five auctions and two tenders, where 100 billion SIT of shares have been sold, while about 85 billion SIT of shares from the MPP still have to be offered.

Comparing the share of unused vouchers in the total portfolio, the difference between small and larger PIFs can be found (Figure 3.9). The small ones have invested the larger portion of their portfolio, which could be accounted for by a smaller portfolio in absolute terms in this group as opposed to the other two groups of funds.

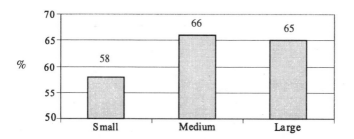

Figure 3.9   Average share of unused vouchers by size of PIF at the end of 1996

Investment Policy

In order to obtain relevant information on the investment policy and other characteristics of PIFs, a special questionnaire was prepared and sent to all MCs. The answers for 27 PIFs have been received. The sample of almost 40% [14] of PIFs is quite a representative one if we take into consideration the size and the book value of PIFs. In order to find out the significant characteristics in PIFs' investment policy, we ranked PIFs by their size and grouped them into three groups.

It is interesting that only small PIFs have on average decided to concentrate their portfolio (56%) (see Table 3.1). Large and medium size funds implement both policies they – concentrate as well as diversify.

Table 3.1   Prevailing investment policy

	Concentrating	*Diversifying*	*Both*
Small size	56	22	22
Medium size	44	44	12
Large size	33	33	33
PIFs together	45	33	22

So far, the investment decisions confirm the declared investment policy. The average size of the stake in one company measured by the percentage of the portfolio is smaller in diversifying PIFs, according to the answers from the questionnaire. It represents 0.62% of portfolio, compared to the 1.01% in PIFs applying concentrating investment policy.

A similar result is discovered by observing in how many companies PIFs have invested in controlling ownership stake.

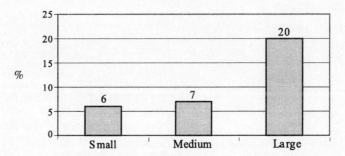

Figure 3.10   Percentage of investments in controlling ownership shares

Figure 3.10 proves that the small funds really implement the diversifying investment policy to a larger extent than medium and large funds. Or to put in another way, the funds which declared their investment policy as concentrating, have 9% of investments in controlling ownership shares.

The common characteristic of most PIFs is that they invest country-wide. Only the small ones also invest locally. Such policy decisions can best be explained by the fact that Slovenia is a small country and the managing costs are the same, regardless of the company's location.

PIFs are forced to invest to a large extent in illiquid shares and even in the shares of limited liability companies. Due to the autonomous privatization model, only 110 companies decided to go public while others find it more convenient to transform into closed joint-stock companies that are not to be traded on the organized market. The current situation on the stock exchange reveals that about a half of the listed companies' shares are illiquid. To put in another way, only 40 to 50 companies' shares will be liquid in Slovenia if the situation on the capital market remains unchanged.

Since the primary allocation of companies to PIFs is still in its first half, the relevant conclusion on investment policy cannot be made at this moment. The consolidation of the PIFs' portfolio will happen after the primary allocation by swapping or trading the portfolio.

The Role of PIFs in the Corporate Governance of Privatized Companies

As discussed in the first chapter, the PIFs are eligible to get 20% or some additional percentage of socially owned shares. However, the PIFs' share of the total equity is sometimes smaller. The explanation can be found especially in provisions of the Law on Ownership Transformation, which entitles state, local communities and agriculture cooperatives to take an equity stake in the public utility companies and in the food processing companies. The expropriated ex-owners also acquired an ownership share in almost 100 companies.

The initial ownership structure of companies that have completed the MPP is presented in the pie chart in Figure 3.11.

The state, local communities, cooperatives, owners from restitution and owners from the pre-privatization period make up the largest group of owners, called 'others'. They own almost a third of the equity in privatization. However, if the top ten companies by size of equity are excluded,[15] the picture is quite different.[16]

The PIFs exercise control over the companies to a large extent by voting at the annual shareholders meetings (ASM) and less through the representatives on supervisory boards. External control (through trading on the secondary market) can be applied in only 110 companies, which are or will be listed on the Ljubljana Stock Exchange. There is of course the possibility of selling or buying the shares of non-public joint-stock companies, but in the majority of cases it is hard to find willing buyers. An effective and fair exit strategy for PIFs in such companies has to be found.

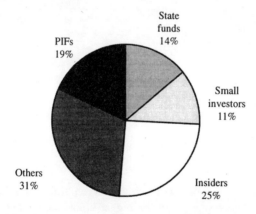

Figure 3.11   Initial ownership structure of privatized companies

The performance of privatized companies is still very bad. Analyzing the financial statements of those companies, we have found out that they have negative profitability in 1995 and 1996. In order to assess the problem carefully, we have divided the companies into three groups:

- public joint-stock companies;
- closed or non-public joint-stock companies;
- limited liability companies.

The return on equity ratio has been calculated for privatized companies and the results are shown in Figure 3.12.

The limited and closed joint-stock companies represent more than a half of the PIF portfolio. If the negative trends continue in the future, the PIFs' assets will be devalued, thereby reducing the value of PIFs' shares. Restructuring actions are necessary in these companies. Consequent to the ownership structure, where insiders have the prevailing share, the PIFs are the only likely owners who can make any changes and restructuring actions. It cannot be expected that employees will lay themselves off. On the other hand, the reasons for such a bad situation in non-public companies may be also found in the managers of these companies, who lack managerial, marketing and other knowledge.

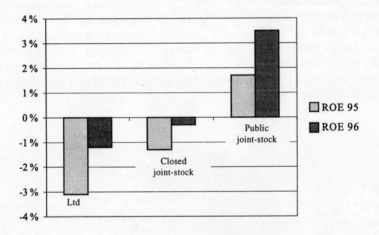

Figure 3.12   Return on equity ratio for different groups of companies for 1995 and 1996

The situation in public joint-stock companies is a little better, but still bad. The skilled managers converged in the bigger companies, where they have been stimulated by higher salaries and have more power. Due to the companies' size, they have decided in many cases publicly to offer their shares in privatization.

So far, the PIFs have not been involved in restructuring actions in the companies. Taking into consideration the companies' performance we discussed before, such actions will be necessary if PIFs want to survive in the long term.

On the other hand, the trading of the PIF portfolio has been carried out to a greater degree. The dominant buyers as well as sellers of the companies' shares that the PIFs are trading, are PIFs, followed by the Compensation and Pension

Fund, while about a quarter of transactions are carried out by the other institutions, employees and managers. In contrast to the small and medium sized PIFs, which trade mostly among themselves by swapping the shares, the large ones trade mostly with the state-owned Pension and Compensation Funds. Typically, PIFs buy shares from them and therefore concentrate. From the long term perspective, the Compensation Fund will be the biggest supplier of shares, since it has to service the liabilities to the restitution claimant and consequently liquidate their portfolio.

From the PIFs' point of view, the external control mechanism can be implemented in the public joint-stock companies through the trading of shares, while in other companies only an internal control mechanism by voting at an annual general meeting may be applied.[17]

According to the results from the questionnaire, the small and middle-sized PIFs have decided to play a passive role in corporate governance of the companies from their portfolio. They own smaller packages of shares, and often together with other PIFs. The active approach is characteristic of the large PIFs. In the companies' supervisory boards, they appointed representatives in 25% of companies from their portfolio.

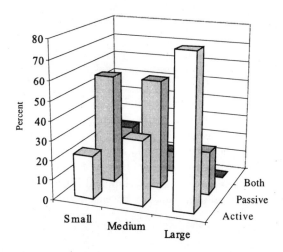

Figure 3.13   Prevailing shareholders' monitoring function implemented by PIFs in corporate governance of companies

What is the story behind Figure 3.13 above? The small PIFs can be much more selective in the portfolio selection process. Despite the fact that the capital market is not developed and only about 110 companies are going to be listed on the Ljubljana Stock Exchange, the smaller funds have the larger portion of their portfolio filled by the tradable securities, due to the relative small size of their portfolio. Therefore they can have a more passive approach toward the monitoring function than the large ones, which are doomed to play a more active role in non-public joint-stock and limited liability companies.

The specific ownership structure in privatized companies (see Figure 3.11) forces PIFs into an alliance with other groups of owners. It is indicative that all PIFs have a positive attitude to managerial ownership. Their attitude to state ownership is quite the opposite. More than 65% of them believe that the state should not hold its ownership position in privatized companies, while the rest of PIFs are indifferent.

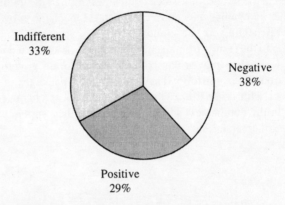

Figure 3.14   Attitude to employees' ownership

The PIFs do not agree regarding employee ownership. On average they have a slightly negative attitude. By deepening the analysis, the significant difference was found between small and large PIFs. Small funds and especially those which invest locally, have a primarily negative attitude to employees' ownership. Quite a different attitude can be found in large sized PIFs. About 60% of them support employees' ownership, and PIFs which implement the active shareholders' monitoring function have an even more positive attitude.

NOTES

1. The Compensation Fund and the Pension Fund are state-owned.
2. Only a surplus of the vouchers from internal distribution can be used in an internal buyout. Consequently, the internal buyout is a complementary method to internal distribution.
3. According to the Law, up to 100% of shares can be sold through this method. In that case, instead of shares, 40% of the proceeds (which have to be in cash) are transferred to the funds from the first point.
4. By comparing supply by the form (shares vs. assets), we decided to take into account shares only, due to the fact that the assets supply accounts for less than 1% of the total supply of the MPP.

5. Companies that sold shares by the sale of shares method had to determine the share price on the basis of the valuation report.
6. The preparation phase is completed when the Agency for Privatization issues the first approval. Before that, the opening balance sheet has to be prepared and checked by the Agency, restitution claims have to be solved, and organizational and financial restructuring has to be finished.
7. The price from January 1, 1993 was multiplied by the inflation rate from January 1, 1993 to the subscription's date.
8. 20% of each company's shares are transferred to PIFs (through the Development Fund), 10% of shares to the Compensation Fund and 10% of shares to the Pension Fund.
9. There are two state-owned banks and a few socially owned insurance companies in Slovenia.
10. Vouchers were to expire at the end of June 1997. Consequently, PIFs can expect to sell the shares until then. From a legal point of view, the shares are issued when the Clearing Depository House books the shares, due to the dematerialization of securities in Slovenia.
11. By the Law on Commercial Companies, a company must create at least 10% of reserves from retained earnings and revaluation adjustment of them.
12. The special provision of the Law determines the end of 1994 as the deadline for the companies to submit the privatization programs to the Agency for the Privatization, which supervises and monitors the privatization process.
13. At that moment, PIFs had 28% of their portfolio in shares and 72% in vouchers.
14. 68 PIFs were registered as per December 31, 1996.
15. Telecom Slovenia is the largest 'privatized' company. It represents about 9% of total capitalization of privatized companies. The 26% share has been privatized, while the rest of equity is still state owned.
16. The stake of others (state, local communities, cooperatives, ex-owners) is lower than 15% of total equity.
17. The trading among PIFs does not make any extra pressure on the management and thus does not solve the problem, since the total ownership share of PIFs remain unchanged.

II.   Transformation of Privatization Funds

Marko Simoneti

INTRODUCTION

Based on the model of certain other transition countries, privatization funds were established in Slovenia as institutions for implementing massive distributional privatization. They are expected to help achieve different objectives: (i) fast and simple privatization, (ii) fair and free-of-charge distribution of shares amongst the population at large, (iii) balance between internal and external owners, and (iv) development of new capital market institutions.

Mass privatization in Slovenia has been far from 'fast, simple and fair', but the current position of investors in privatization funds, originally intended to benefit from privatization and now the most dissatisfied group, is perhaps the most serious problem. At the moment, the main source of their dissatisfaction is the privatization gap, but soon shareholders will recognize that they are incapable of protecting themselves against non-performing fund managers. The large number of dissatisfied fund investors simply cannot be ignored if the capital market is to develop. Rather unexpectedly, privatization funds have been very successful in Slovenia. Together, they have about 1,350,000 shareholders. They gathered 56% of all certificates, while enterprises directly collected 37%, and 7% remain unused. From the citizen-shareholder perspective, privatization funds definitely have the most important role in privatization. Most Slovenian citizens will obtain their first shareholding experience in privatization funds, which operate as diversified institutional investors owned by dispersed groups of small investors. It is deemed necessary for both further capital market development and the launching of pension funds as part of pension reform, that privatization funds preserve at least minimum credibility with their shareholders.

The privatization gap may not have been identified without the successful collection of certificates by privatization funds. But whilst the gap is fund managers' major problem at the moment, it is paradoxically helping to maintain privatization momentum in the country. Privatization fund managers represent a strong interest group that supports the completion of privatization, and the over-issued certificates serve as the state's commitment to continuing privatization. Since there has never been a real commitment to privatization in Slovenia and residual state property is omnipresent and omnipotent after mainstream privatization, the unplanned role of privatization funds is in fact their major contribution to the accomplishment of economic transition.

Privatization funds are not very important for the corporate governance of privatized companies since, in the Slovenian privatization model, they could acquire 20% of companies' shares, which is equal to the shareholdings of the two para-state funds – the restitution and pension funds. The ownership structures of privatized companies reflect balances between the stakes of state-managed funds and privately managed funds on the one hand and insiders and outsiders on the other hand (see Figure 3.15). Despite the relatively small ownership stakes, privatization funds are quite active in the corporate governance of companies. They have repeatedly proven themselves, jointly with the para-state funds, to be committed agents of external shareholders, protecting their interests against internal shareholders. Initial analyses reveal that conflicts of interests between the two groups of owners are often dealt with in a way that adversely affects the development of companies. In small enterprises with dominant internal owners, the available cashflow is often used to buy shares from funds and therefore the relations between the funds and the managers of those enterprises are less conflicting. The managers of large companies which remain mostly externally owned are maintaining their negative attitudes towards the funds as the owners and potential source of financing.

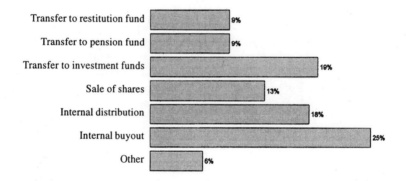

Figure 3.15   Distribution of social ownership by method

In view of their limited role in the new financing of companies, many economists in Slovenia argue that there would be no damage if privatization funds failed altogether. But as they have been entrusted with the certificates of 1,350,000 investors there is no way back. The same is also true for the privatization gap. It has emerged as the result of mistakes in designing the privatization model, but now it cannot be merely ignored by giving vague promises of its fulfillment. Adverse effects on the trust of citizens in financial institutions would be too damaging. The problem of the privatization gap has lately become quite paradoxical, since the government has begun to consider using the proceeds from sale of its property to fill the budget deficit. But the introduced path can no longer be reversed. It could be strongly argued that the least damaging solution for the state would be to fill the gap as promptly as possible with property of an appropriate quality. The gap must be filled as the precondition to start solving other institutional problems in the operations of privatization funds, which in practice have led to the poor protection of shareholders from irresponsible and ineffective fund managers.

PERFORMANCE OF PRIVATIZATION FUNDS

The institutional problems in the governance of privatization funds in Slovenia are quite obvious: (i) the fund managers are not adequately controlled by shareholders due to limited share trading and constrained consolidation of shares and votes, (ii) since establishment, fund managers have not competed to keep or acquire investors, (iii) management contracts and fee structures do not give adequate incentives to fund managers to actively search for ways of increasing the value of property for shareholders, (iv) management of privatization funds is the most lucrative business in Slovenia despite the huge accounting losses in privatization funds. The inadequate institutional framework of privatization funds can only be perpetuated because the attention of the public and shareholders is still focused on filling the privatization gap. Fund managers are very committed in representing the interests of shareholders in the unequal fight with the state and accordingly corporate governance problems appear unimportant.

But the lack of concern is inappropriate, as seen in the simple analysis of the overall performance of privatization funds based on their annual accounts given in Tables 3.2 and 3.3. At the end of 1996, the total investments of funds amounted to 157 billion SIT and the accounting loss was 40 billion SIT or 25% of the total value of assets. The main reason for this performance of privatization funds is the overvalued net asset value (NAV), which not only results in capital losses but also allows excessive management fees charged on the basis of the overvalued NAV. There could hardly be any debate that the NAV as currently used is not an appropriate basis for calculating management fees.

In 1996, management companies altogether charged 9.5 billion SIT in fees and made a combined profit of 5.1 billion SIT for their owners after covering all costs and expenditures from the fees. If one believes that NAV is a real category, then something must be very wrong if managers are rewarded with 5.1 billion SIT when they realize a loss of 40 billion SIT out of 157 billion SIT worth of property. But if one is convinced that NAV is not realistic and that losses are the result of overvalued NAV, then the same NAV simply could not be the basis for management fees.

Greater unlisted securities and fewer market transactions would provide a more realistic portfolio valuation than NAV. The calculation of management fees on the basis of such a NAV implies a basic flaw in the rewards of fund managers – the less they are active and the larger is the unlisted part of their portfolios, the bigger are their rewards in the short run. This flawed logic was even more obvious when the management companies were charging management fees for the unused certificates which then represented the best part of the funds' investments as far as the management fees were concerned. When about 80% of all investments represent unlisted securities, NAV is just an accounting category without any true economic meaning. It is not an indicator of managers' performances and hence it is not an appropriate basis for charging management fees. It cannot be estimated to what extent capital losses are the result of the poor performance of funds' managers. That the big losses of privatization funds, which accrue due to more realistic valuations of investments, are even beneficial for investors as a more realistic basis of management fees in the future is thus established. But big losses of privatization funds could also be the result of the cheap selling off of assets, as in the case of many Czech funds. There is no transparency in the performance of funds and the link between the interests of fund managers and fund investors is entirely cut. The only logical solution offering itself after the investments have been realistically valued is that the management fees should begin to be charged on the basis of the market prices of fund shares or on the basis of a fund's 'real' income.

Table 3.2   Balance sheet of privatization funds, 1996

A. ASSETS (billion SIT)		
1. Certificates	304,596	(66.5%)
2. Unlisted securities	125,863	(27.3%)
3. Listed securities	31,341	(6.2%)
Total	458,882	(100%)
B. SOURCES (billion SIT)		
1. Total capital	446,217	(97.4%)
– basic capital	284,597	
– loss from previous years	–2,998	
– current loss	–40,519	
– revaluation of capital	203,450	
2. Total liabilities	13,458	(2.6%)
– financial liabilities	1,742	
– liabilities to management co.	8,849	
– purchase of securities	2,817	
Total	458,874	(100%)

Source   ATVP data

Table 3.3   Profit and loss statement of privatization funds, 1996

A. INCOME (billion SIT)	
1. Interest	265
2. Dividends	2,904
3. Realized capital gains	1,872
4. Other income	1,055
Total	6,097
B. EXPENDITURES (billion SIT)	
5. Management fees	9,542
6. Net unrealized capital losses	24,271
7. Realized capital losses	4,203
8. Other	8,601
Total	46,617
C. Loss (A – B)	**–40.519**
D. Loss* (A – (5 + 7 + 8))	**–16.248**
E. Loss** (1 + 2 + 4 – 5)	**– 5.318**

Source   ATVP data

It is practically impossible to make an accurate market valuation of invested assets. But it is possible to give a rough estimate on the basis of data available for 1996, subject to certain assumptions. In 1996, the 'real' income of privatization funds was 4,225 billion SIT with the implicit simplified assumption that total capital losses and gains were exclusively the result of unrealistic valuations. If it is assumed that the total returns will also be equal in the future, the value of such property depends only on the expected rate of return. Assuming that the fund managers expect 3% returns in the long run and investors expect the same rates of return as bank return rates (i.e., 5%), then the estimated real value of invested assets would be 66.3% lower than the NAV at the end of 1996, which was then the basis for calculating management fees.

With the given 'real' income of funds, payment of returns to investors would only be possible if prior reductions to the values of investments are made and thereby management fees would be decreased. If investors had expected bank interest rates, the values of assets and management fees would have to be decreased by approximately 66%. These rough estimates are made on the assumption that the state will quickly fulfill its promises to fill the privatization gap with property of comparable quality. But if the state attempts to directly or indirectly avoid this, meaning that two thirds of all certificates would therefore be void, and the investors would still expect bank rates of return in the long run from total invested certificates, the required decrease in the asset values would have to be dramatic, i.e., by 85%. The fund managers would hardly survive the simultaneous huge fall in their fees and therefore they are 'fighting for their lives' for the privatization gap to be bridged or to have investors at least well informed about its size. The state is trapped and will not be able to avoid its promises of closing the gap.

The above estimates are only indicative and are intended to point out the huge risks of postponing solutions to the basic problems of the privatization gap, asset valuations and managers' rewards. Sooner or later, these problems will be properly evaluated by the market prices of funds' shares and the hypocrisy of managers, the state and supervisors will be unveiled. General dissatisfaction and public revolt with privatization funds can also be predicted with certainty to take place in Slovenia.

Lessons from other countries which do not face the privatization gap problem are highly relevant: the assets of a number of privatization funds were promptly stripped off as a result of poor or irresponsible management. Finally, the question is whether all fund managers are genuinely interested in instantaneous and full (100%) covering of the privatization gap. This would require them to shift their attention from the non-existing property to the property that needs to be managed. The responsibility for the performance of privatization funds would clearly be transferred from the state to the fund managers. By withering away the privatization gap as the common enemy, the cartel-type stance of privatization funds against the state and shareholders would also inevitably disappear. The fund managers would no longer have any good reasons allowing them to effectively hide away from control of shareholders. Therefore, the prompt bridging of the privatization gap and listing of funds should be essentially in the interests of the state so that the attention of all concerned would start focusing on the question of how well the fund managers are managing the property of fund shareholders.

TRANSFORMATION OF PRIVATIZATION FUNDS

One general question is what the fund managers should do with the privatization shares to keep the value or to add to the value of the property for the shareholders. They have at least three possibilities: (i) passive ownership and trading with listed securities, (ii) active supervision of portfolio companies, and (iii) active restructuring of the portfolio companies in which they hold larger stakes.

While it was perhaps realistic to initially expect that privatization funds would operate as diversified institutional investors, it became obvious later on that they would not be able to do so. According to data of the end of 1996 (see Tables 3.2 and 3.3), the funds gathered certificates of a total value of 446 billion SIT, which was much higher than the initial estimates. At the end of 1996, the average part of unused certificates in fund portfolios was still 66.5% or 305 billion SIT. In the invested part of portfolios (157 billion SIT), 82% is represented by unlisted securities. After the privatization gap is filled, the part of unlisted securities would likely increase.

It is objectively impossible that fund managers could effectively manage their entrusted property by actively trading with unlisted securities. There is practically no sufficient maneuvering room in Slovenia to allow the majority of funds to adjust their portfolio structures in order to operate as diversified institutional investors in listed securities in the long run. Inevitably, they would have to start behaving as active and responsible owners of portfolio companies. However, the funds' active management of companies would require: (i) a different organizational set up, (ii) different incentives for managers, and (iii) different authorities of the supervisory agency. By insisting that the privatization funds operate as diversified institutional investors under the supervision of the Agency, the false impression is given that the shareholders are well protected although the managers cannot and do not do anything useful for them except charge high fees.

The present organizational set up is inadequate even for those privatization funds which will operate in the long term as passive institutional investors. Typical closed-end funds, which invest in domestic securities, practically no longer exist in the world precisely because that form does not ensure the effective protection of small investors. Formally, small investors do have voting rights but because of widely dispersed ownership they are entirely powerless in relation to the fund managers. Possibilities to enhance the role of supervisory boards in overseeing the fund managers are very theoretical. As the exit of investors from closed-end funds is via the market, in the case of poor managers' performances the market price of fund shares would fall significantly below NAV and investors would have to absorb the resulting capital losses.

The open-end funds have an entirely different logic of control and operation. Investors can exit from one fund and enter into another at any time and there is continuous competition between the fund managers for the existing and new investors. Successful funds record net entries and thereby the basis of managers' fees is increased. Unsuccessful funds record net exits and thereby the fees are decreased as they are forced to sell off listed securities and progressively they can be eliminated altogether from competitive fights for investors. The supervisory authorities oversee the structure of investments to provide the high liquidity of open-end funds, and for the accurate calculation of NAV. The entry and exit prices for investors and managers' fees are based on the NAV. The interests of managers and shareholders are mutually consistent and there is no incentive nor the possibility of manipulation of NAV. Supervisory authorities only perform the type of supervision that they can effectively enforce. Nevertheless, the characteristics of open-end and closed-end funds tend to converge in the case of those funds which are open in intervals. Such interval funds provide better protection of investors, i.e., exit at pre-fixed intervals. At the same time, they create less liquid investments which bear higher returns.

In developed financial markets it has been widely evidenced that the only effective protection of investors in portfolio funds is the possibility of claiming redemption directly from fund managers, which threatens ineffective managers with smaller sized portfolios as a result of net exits. In that sense, if the privatization funds are transformed into investment funds they will continue facing the same type of problems that they face now. The proposals seen in other chapters of this study for improving the governance of privatization funds in Slovenia will fail to solve that inherent problem which characteristically applies to all forms of closed-end funds. The solution would have to find a way of allowing the shifting of investors from one closed-end fund to another closed-end fund. The underdeveloped capital market and the large proportion of unlisted securities in portfolios of privatization funds in Slovenia represent serious constraints for ensuring continuous competition among the fund managers for existing and potential investors. But that is not entirely impossible. The following premises would apply for both forms of closed-end funds (privatization funds and normal investment funds):

(i)   Management fees should not be calculated as a percentage of NAV but as a percentage of the market values of fund shares which are listed on the organized market. Alternatively, fees could be defined as a percentage of a fund's income. Such changes would ensure mutual coherence between the interests of fund managers and shareholders and would reduce the interest of fund managers to manipulate the NAV.

(ii)   Shareholders of privatization funds would have the possibility, in addition to selling shares on the organized market, to shift in intervals (e.g., a few times per year) to any privatization fund managed by other management companies. The shifts would take place automatically at the nominal values of shares, as the re-capitalization of the receiving funds with the shares of the exiting funds. The funds which record the new entries would become partial owners of the funds recording the respective exits and would have the opportunity to change their management.

In order that such 'acquisitions' are possible, the restriction on ownership concentration beyond 5% and on the cross-ownership of funds managed by different management companies would have to be abolished. Management fees would have to be calculated on a basis which would be proportionally decreased by those shares acquired by other funds. Ineffective fund managers would receive smaller fees because of decreased market prices of shares and net exits. They would automatically obtain active owners who would be other funds, and direct pressures for the liquidation of portfolios of less successful funds would be decreased. Similar concepts of competition within the group of specialized institutions have been applied in the case of pension funds. Participants in privately managed compulsory pension schemes have the possibility of selecting a new manager of their pension savings in intervals. Whilst exits from the compulsory pension scheme are not possible, it is possible to re-select among licensed managers in certain intervals.

It is proposed that shifts of shareholders among privatization funds should be at nominal values to simplify them, but this would also serve as an important incentive in the proposed scheme. The essence of such a proposal is that all funds are equal from an investor's viewpoint as long as they operate as privatization funds. In the present conditions, when fund portfolio investments are unrealistically valued and unused certificates prevail, such a starting premise could be justified in economic terms, too. Due to the existence of the privatization gap, the situation for investors is the same as in the period of initial investment of certificates in funds. They would shift from one fund to another at equal prices, as they cannot objectively verify the promises of fund managers. Because of the long delay in filling up fund portfolios, it would make sense if the investors, as a way of their protection, were given the opportunity to select new managers. This would encourage competitive behavior by fund managers to attract new investors and to keep the old ones. The fund managers have responded to the privatization gap with a cartel agreement for common action. As there is no realistic potential for self-organization and collective shareholder action, they can only be effectively protected by amendments to the law allowing for shifting between funds.

In the proposed mechanism, the implicit solidarity amongst investors due to shifting at nominal values is limited only until the privatization funds are transformed. If funds estimate that the advantages of growth as the result of additional entries are smaller than disadvantages due to new investments of lower quality, they will have a strong incentive to transform the fund in order to prevent new entries at nominal values. In order to allow funds to be transformed, the current conditions for transformation should, however, be simplified.

(iii)   The shareholders of funds which have already been transformed into ordinary closed-end investment funds should also be provided, when the gap between NAV and market values of fund shares is wide, with the opportunity to change managers. The solutions must be based on the principle of the equal possibility for all shareholders considering that fund investments are generally not liquid. One possibility could be to mandate the compulsory and automatic opening of all those funds with market prices of shares 40% or more below NAV. Technically, such automatic openings would have to be accomplished so that poor portfolio liquidity would be fully taken into account, i.e., with partial opening, with opening in intervals or with redemption of big shareholders directly from fund property. Another possibility where there are large discrepancies between market prices and NAV would be a mandatory tender for new fund managers.

The above premises would significantly reduce those interests in having privatization funds continue in their present form indefinitely and also that they are transformed into ordinary closed-end investment funds. On the other hand, the interest in transforming them into open-end funds and ordinary joint-stock companies (financial holdings) would be increased. Both institutions prevail in advanced market economies. This is exactly the aim of the proposed approach: closed-end funds should not be the organizational rule but rather the exception in Slovenia because of the institutional weaknesses of that form.

Recently proposed amendments to the Law on Privatization Funds in Slovenia adopt an entirely different approach to the transformation of privatization funds: transformation into financial holding companies is first prohibited and later on severely constrained with restrictive regulations and procedures. The strategy implied in the proposed amendments is to promote the transformation of privatization funds into ordinary closed-end funds which would continue to operate under the Agency's supervision. Closed-end funds with peculiar investment structures would thus exist for a long time. The protagonists of those legal amendments indirectly hold the view that the honest privatization funds are those which do not intend to transform themselves into financial holding companies. It can be strongly argued that constraining the transformation into financial holdings is a completely wrong approach to solving these problems. The institutional form of privatization funds with all the restrictions on portfolio structures, credit financing, managers' rewards, owner-ship consolidation, public reporting and agency supervision is completely inadequate for motivating the active supervision of companies and even less so the active participation of funds in company restructurings. There should be no concern that the transformed privatization funds would perform poorly since most shares sold by their shareholders would be bought by management companies and their sponsors and the decision-makers would thus risk their own property. The problem is the non-transparent way of such transformation on the gray market, which needs to be adequately and promptly regulated.

The protagonists of legal amendments implicitly support the idea that the supervision of the Agency over the operations of funds brings more benefits to the shareholders than would have accrued to them from active management of portfolio companies. Restricting such a transformation, as a matter of principle, would be absurd if it is widely supported by informed shareholders that the financial holding company would be the most appropriate institutional form for preserving their property.

It is deemed essential that decisions on transformation into a financial holding are taken in a transparent way and that the shareholders who disagree with such transformation are fully protected. The following are proposed terms for such transformation:

(i) At least three months before any transformation, the privatization funds must be listed on the organized market.

(ii) Current legal restrictions on the concentration of ownership in funds must be abolished and the regular disclosure of intended acquisitions by large shareholders (e.g., above 5%) should be mandatory.

(iii) Privatization funds must have at least 70% of their certificates invested, meaning that they cannot have more than 30% of unused certificates. The current understanding by regulators that privatization funds must have all certificates invested before transformation should be changed as it completely blocks transformation or forces management companies to treat the shareholders of different funds managed by them in a discriminatory way.

(iv) Any decision on transformation must be taken by a threequarter majority vote in the assembly; the management company must not vote with its shares obtained as partial payment of management fees and must not act as a proxy for other shareholders.

(v) Those shareholders who voted against transformation have the right to convert their shares into financial claims against the transformed company at the average share market price over the previous three months. The claims are redeemable in one year.

(vi) The transformed holding is a public joint-stock company for which all provisions of the Law on the Securities Market apply.

(vii) The management company cannot claim any indemnity upon the transformation of privatization funds.

(viii) The management company can establish a subsidiary company which takes over the management of the transformed privatization funds under a new contract.

(ix) The Agency approves the transformation and oversees that all the above conditions for transformation are fully observed.

Transformation of privatization funds into ordinary closed-end or open-end funds would be much simpler from the perspective of shareholder protection since the Agency's supervisory authorities over them would be enhanced. It would not be required to redeem the unsatisfied shareholders voting against transformation. The Agency's supervision in the approval of such transformation would focus on checking the compliance of the structure of investments with the applicable portfolio regulations.

While transformation into ordinary closed-end funds would entail an *ex ante* adjustment in the structure of investments, transformation into holding companies would require *ex ante* adjustment in the structure of ownership. No legal constraints exist to impede the adjustment of investment structures as it was already initially contemplated that privatization funds would be gradually transformed into ordinary diversified institutional investors. It should be recognized that reality has proven to be different from what was originally expected and that the transformation of privatization funds into holdings should be facilitated. The existing legislation does not allow adjustments in ownership, which would be required for taking a decision on transforming into a holding company. This would therefore have to be changed.

Large privatization funds would face major problems in transformation as objectively they would find it more difficult to adjust their structures because of the large number of shareholders on the one hand, and the large values of investments on the other. It is therefore no coincidence that the managers of large funds express discontent with the transformation of small funds as they are aware that under different institutional conditions they could themselves manage portfolios with greater success. In order to benefit from the potential of large funds, the idea for the transformation of privatization funds with the split of portfolios should be given full support. The minor listed part of their portfolios would be used to transfer into open-end funds and the larger unlisted part would be used to transfer into financial holdings. The shareholders of the former privatization funds would become investors in the same proportion in the new institutions. The institutions which emerge after transformation with the split of portfolios would no longer be able to operate as closed-end funds but would have to choose from the standard forms – open-end fund or financial holding company organized as a public joint-stock company.

CONCLUSION

It should be emphasized in conclusion that in the changed conditions, mainly due to substantial delays in the privatization process, many restrictive 'golden' rules from the past for the transformation and operation of privatization funds need to be revised. But denying the important role of the supervisory agency over privatization funds would be a big mistake. Regulations and supervision ought to receive a different focus, which does not imply that there should be less supervision. The Agency should have the key role in overseeing the transformation of privatization funds. However, the shareholders of privatization funds that take investment risks must be the key players in taking decisions on transformation. The role of the Agency should be to ensure transparency and the observance of the prescribed procedures and rules.

III.   Management Companies and Issues of Governance of Privatization Funds

Božo Jašovič

INTRODUCTION

Effective corporate governance of newly privatized enterprises is essential to their successful performance and further development. In the search for newly introduced owners to carry out mass privatization programs, institutional investors – privatization funds – were conceived in order to bring the ownership structure of companies close to those in developed economies. In addition, they were viewed as counterparts to dispersed individual shareholding, which was the corollary of the accomplished privatization programs in many companies in Slovenia. Namely, privatization funds were supposed to take on a leading role in exerting external ownership control in the context of widespread insider shareholdings.

Given the general view about privatization funds' role in the context of corporate governance, it mainly depends on the institutional structure and extent of regulatory restrictions whether their alleged role will be implemented in practice. Highly regulated privatization funds with intricate relationships between dispersed shareholders and management companies and manifold portfolio restrictions might prove inappropriate and even prohibitive for carrying out effectively corporate governance matters. Moreover, in such a regulatory environment it is unlikely that privatization funds themselves will be managed properly and diligently to fulfill the expectations of their principals – individual shareholders. That is how the governance of privatization funds comes to the fore and becomes the focal point of our concern. In this regard, the question arises of which mechanism of ownership control would best serve the purpose of governance of privatization funds – internal or external. Is there a trade-off between the two mechanisms or they should be used as complementary tools to exert ownership control over the privatization fund?

We argue in this chapter that governance of privatization funds is decisively determined by regulation in the first place and the level of capital market development in the second. The more small shareholders' rights are protected and the less room there is for abuse of shareholder passivity (e.g., proxy rules) the more potentially efficient is the internal corporate control, which could be exercised by voting at shareholders' meetings or supervisory boards. External control, on the other side, crucially depends on the possibilities of the market to impose pressure on the fund management teams and to enable small shareholders to demonstrate their dissent via their exit. It is very likely that both temporary trading restrictions on privatization fund shares and an illiquid capital market would merely impair the external control mechanism to the detriment of fund shareholders. In addition, their situation could be aggravated by the non-existence of or weak regulations dealing with conflict of interest issues and insider trading.

Inefficient corporate governance should not give rise to the broadening of supervisory competencies of supervisory institutions. This may be tempting for regulatory bodies but such an approach may cause misperception among small investors who will thus hold the supervisory institution responsible for privatization funds' performances. Therefore, the supervisory authority should be clearly assigned the role solely to check whether privatization funds abide by the regulations whereas the responsibility for the corporate governance and related risks should be borne by investors.

In the following text, some of the selected aspects of governance of privatization funds in Slovenia will be dealt with in details reflecting the current practice and deficiencies. Regulatory and other recommendations will be summarized at the end of this chapter with the aim of contributing to the enhancement of the operational capabilities and trustworthiness of these important institutional investors.

METHODOLOGY

Empirical data for this research were derived from two sources:

- the Agency for Securities Markets which on the basis of the Law on Securities Market periodically collects publicly available financial data of individual privatization funds; and
- a questionnaire which was sent to all privatization funds (management companies); responses were subsequently used to conduct a statistical analysis.

The questionnaire was sent to management companies of all privatization funds. The response rate was satisfactory given that 39.7% (27 privatization funds out of 68 registered as at December 31, 1996) of all funds returned answered questionnaires.

For the sake of the reliability of statistical results, the representation of the sample was checked on the basis of both distribution according to the size of the funds and quartile rank according to the book value. Tables 3.4 and 3.5 present the respective numbers of both distributions for the sample compared with the distributions for the basic population. Given the very negligible differences between the population and the sample, it can be concluded that the latter is sufficiently representative to provide reliable results.

Table 3.4   Population and sample of privatization investment funds broken down by fund size

Size	Population (%)	Sample (%)
Small-sized (to 4 billion SIT)	39.7	33.3
Medium-sized (over 4 billion to 8 billion SIT)	23.5	33.3
Large-sized (over 8 billion SIT)	36.8	33.3

Table 3.5   Book value of assets of privatization investment funds broken down by quartile rank

Quartile	Population (%)	Sample (%)
First quartile	4.7	5.3
Median	13.7	16.7
Third quartile	29.3	30.1
Maximum	52.3	47.9

GOVERNANCE ISSUES OF PRIVATIZATION INVESTMENT FUNDS

Governance issues of privatization investment funds are manifold and much more complicated than problems involving the corporate governance of enterprises. The root cause lies in the regulatory framework which imposes ownership restrictions on this type of investment vehicle. In particular, the principle of diversified ownership structure and restrictions on individual shareholdings in closed-end investment companies implies that the ownership role of shareholders is, at a glimpse, confined only to the market exit route. It is hardly believed that the activism of individual owners would pay off given their negligible ownership stakes and relatively high costs related to information gathering efforts. Therefore, other control mechanisms should properly be put in place in order to compensate for weakened internal corporate governance. In the following sections, some of the most important aspects of the governance of privatization funds are addressed with a strong emphasis on the current state of affairs of industry in Slovenia.

Voting Rights in Privatization Investment Funds

From the regulatory standpoint, investment funds are designed to have numerous restrictions both on investment portfolio and investment funds' shares. It is the latter which decisively entails some specific features in the governance of those investment vehicles. According to the Slovenian Law on Investment Funds and Management Companies, the dispersal of funds' shares is required by Article 58 which states that 'an individual natural person or legal entity may own, directly or indirectly, not more than 5% of all shares' of an investment fund.[1] All shares held by those persons in excess of the stipulated limitation do not entitle the holders to participate in profits and exercise their voting rights.

Although this rule is widely used in different jurisdictions and stems from the fact that shares of funds are publicly offered to the public at large, it implies some specific features as regards governance of those institutions. To be more specific, dispersal of investment fund shares causes on the other hand the dispersal of shareholders' power since there is no possibility for a single shareholder to accumulate larger blocks of shares and to actively exercise a monitoring function. Relatively small ownership holdings of individuals and entities automatically entail their passive role in corporate control matters since the costs of ownership activism would be much greater than the potential gains of such efforts.

The requirement for the dispersal of fund shares has its rationale in the fact that these institutions are designed to tap financial resources by means of public offerings. Fears that shareholders with large ownership stakes would take over the control of the fund and that minority shareholders could suffer do not make much sense. If we draw a parallel between investment funds and public joint-stock companies, we see that in the latter case there are less stringent restrictions on investors accumulating shares if they obey the rules and procedures for such acquisitions (e.g., takeover regulation, disclosure requirements). Why would privatization funds be regulated any differently to public joint-stock companies?

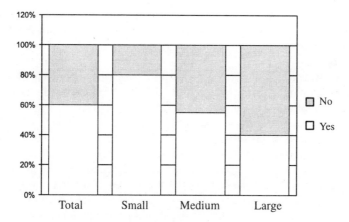

Figure 3.16   Does management company act as proxy?

Moreover, the dispersal requirement can be easily circumvented by proxy arrangements, which do not impose any limitations on the percentage of votes which can be represented by proxies. To the question of whether their management companies represent the fund shareholders as proxies, almost 60% of funds replied positively (see Figure 3.16). Among small-sized funds, the respective percentage is even higher, which means that the great majority of them are controlled by their management companies. More detailed empirical evidence of such behavior is summarized in Table 3.6 which reveals data concerning proxy representations broken down by size distribution of funds.

Table 3.6   *Average ownership shares represented by proxies and management companies acting as proxies*

Groups of funds	All proxy representation (% of votes)	Management companies as proxies (% of votes)
Small-sized funds	91	72
Medium-sized funds	52	51
Large-sized funds	84	70
Total funds	76	65

The figures in the table are self-explanatory and prove that management companies basically control the funds they manage. In other words, shareholders of funds that did not confer their voting rights to proxies are 'voiceless' given their relative position *vis-à-vis* company management. Restriction on the ownership stakes of individual shareholders designed to prevent the accumulation of shares and thus to protect small shareholders against the dominance of majority owners have turned out to be futile. If one were even more critical, such regulation could be regarded as being detrimental to shareholders. Namely, it is not difficult to understand that dispersal of ownership shares and pertinent ownership rights may translate into weakened shareholders' monitoring roles and is likely to strengthen management positions. Worse still, through the abuse of proxy arrangements management companies can firmly entrench themselves and protect their interests.

From this point of view, the question arises as to the importance of owners' monitoring roles. Are they supposed to be alert and keep an eye on the performance of the management? What about those investors who just seek a lucrative financial investment and would rather use an exit route by selling the shares than be concerned with shareholder activism? It is obvious that restrictions on the ownership holdings of the privatization fund shares preclude shareholders from using their 'voices' against management companies as potential benefits of such efforts would probably be negligible or would even not pay off. On the other hand, if such restrictions were discarded, ownership concentration would become feasible and active monitoring would gain importance, as interested investors would exercise continuous pressure to ensure satisfactory performance.

Corrective adjustments to the legislation in this regard might benefit shareholders but will certainly not further weaken their position. So there is only an upside potential. As far as fears of potential takeovers or creeping acquisitions are concerned, some comfort may be provided by the fact that obligatory disclosure of share acquisitions is required when prescribed thresholds are reached. This regulation is merely intended to inform other shareholders about ownership changes and to give them the chance and time to decide whether to react (e.g., to sell their shares) or not. In addition to that, more restrictive use of collecting proxy votes should be put in place or management companies should even be forbidden to engage in such activities.

Undoubtedly the weakened power of shareholders due to the restrictions on ownership holdings in privatization funds has an impact on the functioning of other statutory bodies. If we go by order of importance, then the supervisory board is the supreme governing body when the shareholders' meeting is not in session. In accordance with Article 65 of the Law on Investment Funds and Management Companies,[2] an investment fund's supervisory board shall consist of three members who shall be elected from among independent experts. The same Article also stipulates who shall not be members of the supervisory board of an investment fund:

- management, employees and members of supervisory boards of management company, depository institutions and banks which provide services to the privatization fund;
- members of supervisory boards of other privatization funds and management companies; and
- members of governing bodies of the stock exchange.

With many restrictions, the provision is at first glance sensible but in reality does not make much sense. It is merely a pro forma regulation aimed at introducing some safeguards in governance relations. But, on the other hand, such a provision may obscure the real picture as to whose representatives are appointed members of supervisory boards. Slovenian privatization funds were asked the very same question and in spite of the fact that 'by the law' the members shall be independent individuals (whatever this means) many of them revealed who they really represent. Table 3.7 summarizes the responses received. Surprisingly enough, although the law requires members of supervisory boards to be independent experts, many of them decided to tick the categories of management companies or companies from a portfolio. The respective percentages for these two categories are significantly higher in the groups of small-sized funds and those who invest locally. The explanation for this may lie in the fact that these two groups of funds have a greater predilection for forming alliances in a triangle between management companies, privatization funds and local companies.

Table 3.7   Whose representatives are members of the supervisory boards by size distribution of privatization funds ?

Representatives of:	Small sized (%)	Medium sized (%)	Large sized (%)	Local (%)	Total funds (%)
Management companies	26	17	13	36	19
Shareholders	16	37	26	0	28
Companies from portfolio	11	9	8	14	9
Independent individuals	47	37	53	50	44

What lessons can be learnt from Table 3.7? First, an 'independent expert' is something which always has some other content as well. Independent individuals in the last row of the table could be representatives of other institutions at the same time and vice versa, representatives of the management company could also be independent experts as required by the law.

Second, it is better not to pretend to have all necessary restrictions in place to prevent conflicts of interest, insider trading, and so on, if those restrictions are difficult to enforce or conversely could easily be circumvented. The supervisory authority would be too concerned with formal compliance with the law instead of being capable of detecting and preventing transactions and activities which could be deemed as fraudulent. Is it really important to check whether supervisory board members meet the requirement of being 'independent experts' or will the shareholders be better off if the supervisory authority develops the capabilities to prevent illicit activities?

Last but not least, the role of the supervisory boards of privatization funds should not be underestimated. They represent the funds in relations against the management companies and this is why it is surprising that the first supervisory boards were appointed by management companies.[4] With such a provision, a perfect compounding effect was achieved having in mind that management companies control the majority of shareholders' votes as well. Moreover, such mutually reinforcing provisions would be very difficult for authorities to adjust or rectify since management companies have very strong incentives to keep them non-tackled and thus ensure they stay in business for a long time to come. In contrast, shareholders should be worried as they lack an effective control mechanism to put pressure on the management company and to assure satisfactory performance.

Market Control Mechanism

As it can be concluded that it is quite difficult for privatization funds' shareholders to actively exercise any monitoring role[5] within the existing regulatory framework, one might consider external market control over a fund's performance. There are in principle two ways in which the market can react to the performance of public companies:

- through the mechanism of relative prices of publicly-traded shares; and/or
- through threats of takeover activities.

Are both mechanisms appropriate for privatization funds and applicable without any modification?

The lack of internal monitoring controls should undoubtedly result in stronger external mechanisms to exercise performance monitoring. However, this crucially depends on the level of capital market development. There should be no illusions that the shallow capital market could provide an efficient mechanism of governance. As a matter of fact, prices in such a market would be very sensitive to relatively small changes in supply and demand. Notably, it is hardly conceivable that demand and supply for a particular security would be information-driven reflecting the financial standing and performance of the issuer.

Undoubtedly, the Slovenian capital market closely resembles the above description. In such an environment, one should wonder whether the market exit mechanism might effectively supersede inefficient internal governance. Obviously the legislator used the same reasoning when he decided to ban the transfer of privatization fund shares through legal transactions until they are listed on the stock exchange (Article 135 of the Law on Investment Funds and Management Companies). Supposedly, with the phased and, in the future postponed, inclusion of privatization funds on the stock exchange, the problem of an upsurge of shares on the market should somehow be overcome.

Unfortunately, the mass privatization process is not only severely delayed but the government is running out of property which it can earmark for privatization. Privatization funds which collected more than half of issued ownership certificates from citizens are thus suffering from the privatization gap, i.e., the lack of property to be exchanged for ownership certificates at auctions. As at year-end 1996, they exchanged on average only 36% of vouchers in their portfolio for company shares while the rest (64%) is still represented by unused vouchers, which have yet to be exchanged when the government provides additional property. As a corollary to the privatization gap and delays in the ownership transformation process, the Agency for the securities market adopted a resolution to allow listing of privatization fund shares on the official open market in order to provide the transferability of shares. To demonstrate their dissent, privatization funds have shown strong reluctance to list their shares until the government provides additional property.

For the time being, shareholders of privatization funds in Slovenia are deprived of the basic right to be able to dispose of the shares which they received in exchange for ownership certificates. Since the shares are non-transferable until they are listed on the official market, those shareholders wanting to sell shares have to resort to bizarre transactions on the gray market (sale of options on currently non-transferable shares). Due to the privatization gap (on average only 36% of vouchers were exchanged for shares) and high risks involved in such transactions, shares are traded in the manner described at substantial discounts. There is no reliable data on prices and volumes, but one can second-guess that some privatization funds might be perfect takeover targets in such an opaque environment. Some investors or even management companies themselves might take over control of the funds by acquisitions through related entities and subsequently convert them into holding or closely-held companies.

It seems that shareholders of privatization funds are trapped in those institutions. They can exercise neither internal monitoring of the management company via voting, nor external control by means of an exit via the market. It appears that management companies are complete masters of the situation. Namely, they are in a position to reap generous management fees without giving an account of the fund's performance, and erosion of the assets will continue for a long time to come if there is no adjustment of the regulations. Although the government should be blamed for the privatization gap, a great deal of guilt can also be attributed to the regulators. Their efforts to list the shares of privatization funds on the official market turned out to be futile. Moreover, they are not even in a position to cope with collusion between funds that want to show their defiance of the inclusion of the funds' shares on the official market. As a result, fund shareholders have not yet received share certificates as proof of their ownership stakes in privatization funds and cannot therefore trade with non-existing shares.

Currently there is little prospect in Slovenia that the mechanism can provide an efficient way of controlling management companies. They are well organized in their struggle for additional property and they can efficiently extort the government by not issuing shares and defying the inclusion of privatization funds on the organized market. Unfortunately, all these actions, no matter how justifiable they may be, are merely to the detriment of fund shareholders. It is for this reason that we asked in the questionnaire when they expect the shares of their funds to be quoted on the stock exchange. It is not only that this question may give very straight answers about when shareholders will be given all their vested rights but also it implicitly indicates the perception of management companies as to when the state will fill the privatization gap. Namely, the first prerequisite of the privatization funds for listing on the stock exchange is that all vouchers collected are exchanged for company shares. On average, more than 41% of all funds (management companies) estimate that their shares will be quoted on the stock exchange in one year's time and the same proportion (41%) think that this will happen at the latest in two years (see Table 3.8). Results are indicative especially as regards the group of large privatization funds who are rather pessimistic about quotation on the stock exchange. Most of them think that their shares will be traded on the stock exchange only after three years (44%), whereas

22% of funds responding to the answer think that this could happen in one year's time. Such restraint of the large privatization funds could be explained by the following considerations: first, they are not confident that the government will fill the privatization gap in due time, second, even if additional property is promptly provided some additional time will be needed to restructure the portfolios according to proclaimed investment policies, and third, they are well aware of the pressure which the market imposes on participants.

Table 3.8   Estimated time shares will be quoted on the stock exchange by size distribution of privatization funds

Group of funds	In one year (%)	In two years (%)	After three years (%)
Small-sized	44	44	12
Medium-sized	56	44	–
Large-sized	22	34	44
Total funds	41	41	18

The latter could be underpinned by combining two questions which were posed to the funds. The first was related to the dividend payments and consequential influence on share prices and the second was inquiring whether there is any causation between the relative prices of fund shares and performance. Most funds answered separately to both questions positively and even when we combined the answers to both questions, most thought that both dividend payments and the success of the fund's performance have an influence on the price of shares (see Figure 3.17).

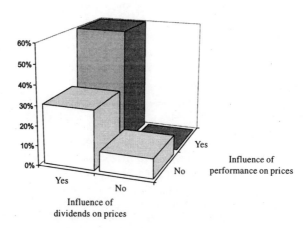

Figure 3.17   Do dividend payments and successful performance influence the market prices of fund shares?

As far as market control is concerned, too many restrictions on share acquisitions of privatization funds prohibit its flourishing. To be more specific, not only is the accumulation of shares prohibited by the dispersal rule, but privatization funds are also precluded from acquiring the shares of other funds. This rule can make sense for management companies which should not be engaged in self-dealings with funds and between the funds they manage. But there are certainly not many reasons to prevent funds from buying the shares of other funds on the market. That is the way the market for corporate control works and imposes pressure on efficient management. Let's imagine that the shares of a particular fund are traded with big discounts. If the shareholders sold their shares at such prices they would have to bear capital losses. Without an efficient market for corporate control, there is no prospect for them other than selling shares or waiting for better times to come, which are unlikely under the same management company. But on the other hand, if there were an efficient market for corporate control, some other fund would be willing to acquire the shares at given prices and introduce more efficient management. There is no need to explain what would benefit the concerned parties most. This could also be a solution for the regulators concerned with the idea of how to spur the concentration in industry, especially given the small, inactive funds which are very likely either to eat up their capital through over-generous management fees or to convert themselves into closely held companies and escape strict supervision.

To this end, some legislative corrections should be taken. One has already been mentioned in the proposal to abate the dispersal rule (the rule which precludes fund shareholders owning more than 5% of the outstanding shares). The other is related to the ban on investments of privatization funds in the shares of other investment funds, which should also be discarded in order to provide an efficient market for corporate control. If there are fears of corporate raiders, more stringent rules regarding information disclosure should be put in place in order to make shareholders aware of developments. On the whole, permitting privatization funds to invest in the shares of other privatization funds should not only be viewed as a way of introducing the market to corporate control but also of increasing market demand. The latter might translate to price increases and would thereby benefit privatization fund shareholders.[6]

Management Contracts

Management contracts represent the last set of governance issues related to privatization funds. Shareholders' voting rights can easily be diluted by entrusting great powers to the managers of the fund or to make the termination of the contract very costly or practically impossible. There is little sense for shareholders to exercise voting rights if they cannot punish sub-standard management by replacement or, in other words, if competition between management companies is dampened. Continuous threats to management companies of being pushed out of business could impose some pressure on their endeavors to enhance management.

There are two serious flaws in Slovenian regulation with regard to management contracts: first, there are no termination and obligatory renewal clauses in the law and, second, management fee structures should be substantially adjusted in order to introduce incentives for better performance and minimizing costs.

The Slovenian Law on Investment Funds and Management Companies deals extensively with management contracts and the supervisory authority is entrusted to prepare regulations prescribing the form and obligatory contents of management agreements to be concluded between the fund and management company. Although extensive care was given to this matter, the provisions on the termination of the contract are very poor and too much in favor of management companies. In addition, severance payments in the case of contract interruptions are not addressed at all. Both lessons could be learnt from U.S. regulatory practice which stipulates that a contract must be terminable at any time (without penalty) by a vote of the mutual fund's board of directors.[7] Further, annual approval of management contracts is required in order to reinforce accountability and better performance of management groups. The only exception is a starting up period (the first two years) to make room for management to cope with potential obstacles during the foundation and immediately after the start-up.

Slovenian reality on the other hand is quite different in this respect. All privatization funds which returned the questionnaire indicated that they do not have defined termination procedures in the management contract. Worse still, an average 74% of shareholders' votes are required to break a management contract. This already high threshold is further safeguarded in 40% of the funds by severance payments in the case of interruption (see Table 3.9). It is the lack of experience and consequently clearly defined provisions regarding these sensitive matters which allowed management companies to shackle the privatization funds under their management for an indefinite time. The regulatory authority will undoubtedly have a hard time introducing necessary adjustments to the law and other regulations dealing with termination of management contracts, obligatory annual renewals and bans on severance payments in cases of interruption. As long as the said regulation is effective, there will be no competition between management companies. Conceivably, they will feel safe in relation to fund shareholders no matter how efficiently privatization funds are managed.

Table 3.9   *Percentage of votes to interrupt management contract and percentage of contracts with severance payment clause*

Group of funds	% of votes to interrupt contract	% of contracts with severance payment
MC act as a 'proxy'	72	14
MC does not act as a 'proxy'	78	26
Total funds	74	40

Management fees represent another area needing scrupulous consideration and overhauling from a regulatory point of view. According to Slovenian law, management companies can be reimbursed for the foundation costs of an investment fund with up to 5% of the share capital. This reimbursement can only be realized by means of additional shares issued to the management company. In addition, a maximum 3% management fee on the net asset value can be charged on an annual basis as compensation for the services rendered according to a management contract. In the first five years, one third of the management fee is payable in the privatization funds' shares.

It is rational behavior if one can take as much as allowed. A ceiling on management fees is something which makes sense in a competitive environment where competition continuously compels participants to offer services at prices which keep them in business. The Slovenian environment is far from this and managing privatization funds is apparently the most lucrative business given the juicy management fees and inadequate regulations which make management companies too powerful in relation to shareholders. In order to reshuffle part of this power and to introduce more performance-linked compensation, the fee structure should be adjusted accordingly. To be more specific, the existing 3% flat fee should be split into two parts:

- management fee which is paid at a flat rate annually or in a proportion which varies according to performance; and
- reimbursable costs which are reimbursed upon presentation of the relevant documentation and after approval of the supervisory board.

Performance-related management fees would certainly impose some pressure on management groups to put more effort into successful management. As far as reimbursable costs are concerned, the only advantage of the proposed structure is to ensure that these costs are properly evidenced, justified and can be contested or approved by board members. This is the simplest way to introduce the culture of accountability. For the time being, this virtue is relatively weak as management companies need not give an account of costs involving the management of privatization funds.

FINAL OBSERVATIONS – LIST OF REGULATORY REMEDIAL ACTIVITIES

At the end of this chapter, we wish to list those regulatory areas of privatization funds which require immediate attention and corrective measures in Slovenia. To provide a competitive environment for efficient governance and to reshuffle the extraordinary power of management companies in favor of shareholders, all concerned areas should be addressed properly and simultaneously. A piecemeal approach will not yield the expected results, as the whole regulatory framework is as weak as the weakest link in it.

Ownership dispersal rule. The requirement that no shareholder can hold more than a 5% ownership stake in a fund is difficult to justify. It dissipates the potential shareholders' power and precludes them from accumulating shares. Such a regulation does not make much sense if it is difficult to enforce and can easily be circumvented. If shareholders were allowed to accumulate shares above the 5% ceiling, the internal control mechanism could be used more effectively in governance matters.

Stringent disclosure requirement. If the 5% ownership ceiling is abandoned, the stringent disclosure requirement will have to be put in place (e.g., obligatory disclosure for every additional acquisition of shares over a defined threshold).

Proxy rules. Rules regulating the use of proxy arrangements should be adjusted to prevent the collection of proxy votes by management companies which can result in abuse and the possibility of taking over the controlling package of votes at a shareholders' meeting.

Appointment of the first supervisory board. In accordance with our law, the first supervisory board should be appointed by a management company for a term of four years. This provision should be adjusted to nominate the first supervisory board only until the first shareholders' meeting takes place, which then must appoint a new supervisory board.

Listing of funds' shares on official securities markets. This provision, which prevents share transferability, should be immediately discarded. Shares of privatization funds should from the beginning be listed on the official market (e.g., open market C in Slovenia) in order to ensure transferability and transparency of trading. Quotation on the stock exchange is to be subject to general admission rules.

Allowing privatization funds to invest in shares of other privatization funds. The prohibition of investing in other funds (except funds managed by the same management company) is meaningless or even wrongful if the target is to promote a market for corporate control. The latter could provide both additional market strain and increased demand for shares, which in turn would benefit the original shareholders.

Term of management contracts. The law should clearly state that management contracts are terminable. Further, the term of the first management contract should be two years (with the founding management company), whereas thereafter obligatory annual renewals of the contract should be required. Severance payments in case of interruption should be forbidden. Such adjustments would introduce a more competitive environment between management companies.

Adjustment of management fee structure. The aim is to introduce more performance-linked compensation and to promote accountability of management groups. The existing fee should be split up into two parts: flat-rate or performance-linked fees and reimbursable costs.

The above list of necessary corrective measures is by no means exhaustive and only the most striking and urgent issues have been addressed. As time passes and the existing regulatory framework becomes more established, it will on the other hand be more and more complicated to introduce changes to the law. In other words, the regulator is running out of time.

NOTES

1. *Investment Funds as Intermediaries of Privatization*. Edited by Marko Simoneti and Dušan Triska. Central & Eastern European Privatization Network, C.E.E.P.N. Workshop Series, No. 5, Ljubljana 1995, page 233.
2. *Investment Funds as Intermediaries of Privatization*, 1995, page 234.
3. In this column, data are represented for the funds that declared they invest locally.
4. See Article 66 of the Law on Investment Funds and Management Companies. *Investment Funds as Intermediaries of Privatization*, 1995, page 234.
5. Even with additional regulation put in place in the U.S., fund shareholders remained passive and large mutual fund families have generally dominated the boards of their funds (Coffee, 1996).
6. Coffee, 1996.
7. Coffee, 1996.

IV. The Governance of Privatization Funds with Special Reference to the Role of Supervisory Boards

Andreja Böhm

INTRODUCTION

This chapter is based on a survey of the members of supervisory boards of privatization funds in Slovenia. A comprehensive questionnaire comprising 65 questions was mailed to 120 members. Responses were submitted by 51 members or 43% of all addressees. The sample represents 37% of the total population and is fairly representative in terms of the size of the total basic capital of funds. The collected data can therefore be compared on that basis.

The results of the survey were analyzed with twin objectives: (a) to define the effectiveness of supervisory boards in controlling management companies given the inconsistency between the company law (based on the German model) and the legal and regulatory framework of privatization funds (with Anglo-Saxon origins), and (b) to reveal the opinions and awareness of members of supervisory boards about some critical aspects of privatization funds in Slovenia.

This chapter is in four parts dealing with issues critical to the governance of privatization funds. The first part discusses the primary investment policies and portfolios of privatization funds which, it is argued, are the crucial source of their (in)effective governance. The second covers management contracts and management fees, which in principle are the most direct mechanisms of shareholder control and for motivating fund managers, but have been designed in such a way that they discourage competition between managers. The third part deals with the mutually re-enforcing internal control of fund shareholders ('the voice') and their external control ('the exit'). The last emphasizes the imperative of transforming the funds after privatization and sets out a number of possible scenarios.

INVESTMENT POLICIES AND GOVERNANCE OF PRIVATIZATION FUNDS

It was expected that privatization funds in countries in transition would, as experienced in recent years by institutional shareholders in advanced market economies, notably pension funds, provide incentives for company restructuring by ensuring them better access to financing cheaper than bank loans. However, many critics argued, on the other hand, that their role would mostly be limited to monitoring. They expressed serious doubts that the privatization funds would add value to portfolios (reducing existing values instead) and particularly that they would be capable of raising fresh money on primary markets.

Financial intermediaries can be distinguished by different investment policies and contrasting portfolio structures which represent the key for setting up effective institutional, legal and regulatory frameworks. In compliance with the prevailing investors, who are either short- or long-term, small or large, they either widely disperse their investments in mostly liquid assets and securities or, as long-term institutional investors, they concentrate investments in a small number of companies and also invest in illiquid and unquoted assets. Dispersed portfolio structures do not ensure active supervision of portfolio companies (which is even prohibited in their case) but give incentives for active portfolio trading. Concentrated and illiquid portfolio structures do not produce active portfolio trading but allow and give incentives for active supervision and management of portfolio companies.

In the survey, two-thirds of responding members of supervisory boards of privatization funds in Slovenia described the privatization funds as being minority shareholders in most portfolio companies. It is, however, impossible to draw any definite conclusion on the basis of Table 3.10 as to whether any correlation exists between investment policies and portfolio management styles of individual funds. Nevertheless, the size of funds seems to have some importance in that respect, as large funds appear to involve more than small funds in active monitoring, and support more successful management of companies whereas small funds engage themselves more in active portfolio trading.

Table 3.10   Effective ways of maximizing assets value

	All (%)	Large (%)	Small (%)
Active portfolio trading	51	47	58
Income maximization	47	47	47
Active monitoring of companies	27	34	16
Restructuring of companies	16	16	16
Supporting successful management	18	22	11
Recapitalization of companies	12	16	5
Real Estate Fund	2	3	0

In all three countries, privatization funds began with secondary portfolio trading immediately after privatization. It would be difficult, though, to give any final view on the nature of fund secondary trading, whether it is intended as income (or cashflow) maximization or as adjustment of portfolio structures for either passive or active portfolio management. Secondary portfolio trading of Polish funds is most likely intended to reduce the number of companies in portfolios by selling off minority stakes thus enhancing the capability of funds to actively restructure the remaining companies. There are many cases of cheap selling off of portfolio assets in the Czech Republic. In Slovenia, there are no legal constraints on the consolidation of fund stakes in companies for the active control of portfolio companies and, indeed, privatization funds could in fact play an important role in improving the corporate governance of companies after privatization by selling their stakes to strategic buyers or by buying stakes from other shareholders to consolidate their own stakes in companies. But, generally speaking, secondary trading of privatization shares is severely limited in the country.

One interesting question not addressed in the survey is how much privatization funds use insider information obtained from their representation on the boards of companies (which are reportedly frequent) for portfolio trading and how much their board representation and portfolio trading serve to promote the commercial interests of their sponsors.

MANAGEMENT CONTRACTS AND FEES

Long-term management contracts and legal upper limits on fixed management fees in transitional economies were intended as measures to protect small shareholders and to give incentives to fund managers in initially non-competitive markets. They are clearly the major flaws in the privatization funds' legal framework. Long-term management contracts have effectively closed the markets to new entrants and impeded competition among the existing management companies.

The main impetus for competitive markets of fund managers would be short-term management contracts which could be terminated immediately at no major cost to shareholders in proven cases of managers' frauds or non-performance. Regular annual renewals of contracts should be the norm in non-competitive markets. According to the survey, about 85% of privatization funds have either concluded indefinite or long-term management contracts, but two thirds of the responding members would support short-term contracts. About one half of respondents believe (more of them from large funds) that the management contract represents an effective mechanism for shareholder control. CEEPN's survey of the management companies of privatization funds in Slovenia pointed out that the management contracts of 40% of privatization funds included provisions for high payouts or required a large majority vote for the termination of contracts. Such statutory or contractual self-defenses of managers are prohibited elsewhere in the world.

In view of the non-competitive market in Slovenia it could be predicted that all management companies would charge the highest management fees allowed by law, i.e., 3% of NAV. More than two thirds of respondents (three quarters from large funds and less than one half from small funds) agreed that competition would reduce management fees and almost all of them argued that management fees should be approved annually by the assemblies or supervisory boards. Ninety per cent of respondents do not support the borrowing of funds to pay management fees.

There is wide evidence that fixed fees as lump sums are inappropriate incentives for active management of portfolio companies or for improving managers' performances. In Slovenia, they actually serve as a strong incentive for passivity as the fund managers maximize profits by minimizing operational and management costs. Fixed fees representing 3% of NAV are high in comparison to the fixed fees of Western closed-end investment companies, which are on average only 0.6% of NAV and range between 0.25% up to 1%. By the logic of the economy of scale, larger funds charge fewer per cent (but on the basis of larger NAV). In addition to fixed fees, about 0.5% of NAV are reimbursable costs. The supervisory agency exercises tight control over such costs and has the authority to approve increases of certain costs which may reduce market competition (e.g., in marketing). Two thirds of survey respondents agreed that a larger part of management fees should represent reimbursable costs. Since apart from brokers supervisory boards have also to approve auditors and directors of privatization funds, it would make sense that their cost be reimbursed as with the costs of brokers.

Moreover, NAV serves as an appropriate basis for calculating management fees of open-end mutual funds as it provides an incentive for improved performance by way of extending the size of the funds or increasing the efficiency (i.e., cost reduction). But NAV is a less appropriate incentive for short-term improvement of the management performance of closed-end investment companies. In their case, NAV can basically only be increased with capital gains, which means that long-term performance fees as a percentage purely of realized capital gains would motivate improved manager performances. In the short run, however, market prices of fund shares may be more appropriate and be the incentive for improved performances and also serve to protect shareholders.

Since about 80% of fund portfolio companies in Slovenia are not quoted on organized markets, NAV is largely just an accounting figure consisting of grossly overvalued company book values, and capital losses and gains accruing from 20% of quoted companies. NAV is not only the source of excessive management fees but in no way relates to managers' performances. It therefore could not serve as an incentive for improving management performance. Because privatization funds are not quoted it can only be very crudely estimated to what degree NAVs are overvalued.

Table 3.11 compares the views of the responding members of supervisory boards on what the appropriate bases should be for evaluating the performance of fund managers and calculating their fees. According to them, NAV by itself does not serve any of those purposes. Managers' performances are reflected not only in NAV but also in income, profit, market prices of shares and, to some degree, in dividends paid. In that sense, they claim that all those performance indicators should be taken into consideration in defining managers' fees, too. Although it seems that no major correlation exists between the indicators of performance and the bases for calculating fees, the respondents from large funds do give priority to NAV for both purposes and the respondents from small funds to share market prices.

Table 3.11 *Performance evaluation criteria (a) and bases for calculating management fees (b) of privatization funds*

	All (%)		*Large (%)*		*Small (%)*	
	(a)	**(b)**	**(a)**	**(b)**	**(a)**	**(b)**
NAV	17	28	25	29	14	26
Market price of shares	26	26	23	24	32	30
Profit	18	21	18	18	18	26
Income	24	18	20	18	29	17
Dividends	15	7	14	11	18	0

INTERNAL AND EXTERNAL CONTROL OF SHAREHOLDERS

The institutional framework of privatization funds in Slovenia combines the elements of two models – the company law based on the German model and the investment company law originating in the model of relevant Anglo-Saxon regulations. The question is therefore whether that framework ensures consistency between the rules and regulations concerning internal and external controls. Since external control does not exist as funds' shares are not yet registered and therefore cannot be quoted or traded on organized markets, the question is whether internal control can substitute for the lack of external control and by itself provide effective protection of fund shareholders. The question is to what extent do the assemblies and supervisory boards favor fund managers' interests rather than protect shareholders given that fund managers (or their sponsors) are naturally most interested in acquiring control over privatization funds?

Internal Control

All strategic matters such as changes and amendments to statutes and management contracts, dismissals of supervisory boards, termination of management contracts, major changes in investment policies, change of legal status etc., require approval of the shareholders and hence voting in the assemblies. Such decisions are taken by majority vote.

The shareholders of privatization funds are small investors who are typically passive and do not vote. They have neither the incentives nor means to undertake the collection of proxy votes. German banks have their own stakes in companies and serve as the custodians of small shareholders and also act as their proxies in assemblies. Elsewhere in the world, votes of small investors could easily be abused by raiders or management if they are not effectively protected in proxy contests and voting.

Most management companies in Slovenia collected proxy votes from citizens with vouchers together with general proxy statements valid for one and a half years. Since with later legal amendments, proxy votes have had to be separately collected for each voting session, management companies are now attempting to amend statutes to include various self-defensive measures. Ninety per cent of survey respondents expressed the view that the representatives of management companies should not be allowed to be proxies of shareholders. Since the law does not preclude anybody serving as proxy because of conflicts of interests, it also does not require the presence of a quorum in the assemblies for voting on strategic matters it is a very common practice that the representatives of management companies serve as proxies of fund shareholders and can take any strategic decision with a vote which represents only a small percentage of total share capital. The survey of management companies confirmed that in 60% of privatization funds representatives of management companies serve as proxies of shareholders.

The procedure for appointing members of the first supervisory boards of privatization funds in Slovenia is similar to the Anglo-Saxon practice. Given the 'bottom-up' origin of privatization funds, the candidates for board members were selected by management companies and the names were advertised in issuing prospectuses. In this way, the selected members of supervisory boards were formally approved by the shareholders. However, most citizens did not even take notice of these candidates but invested their vouchers in response to the marketing campaigns mounted by management companies. As the candidates subsequently were appointed members of the first supervisory boards, the question arises as to where their loyalty lies – to the management companies or to the shareholders? According to the survey, almost all members feel accountable to the shareholders, only a very few (5%) to the management companies and none to the government or society at large.

The independence of supervisory boards cannot be questioned in Slovenia because of the peculiar appointment procedure, but the unique start-up advantages of the 'bottom-up' origin of privatization funds and highly competitive management companies were totally wasted in that procedure. Since with the postponed quotation of shares management companies have failed to become competitive and the shareholders have no exit, the members of boards are quite unlikely to be dismissed on the initiative of new shareholders. It would therefore be interesting to know why some members of the first supervisory boards were dismissed during the mandate, as the survey revealed that a number of respondents have already replaced previous members. In the same way as management companies had selected members in the first place, undisciplined members can only be dismissed later on by management companies themselves.

As management companies selected the supervisory boards that were to monitor them, the supervisory boards in turn did not have any choice in selecting the management companies, but could only conclude management contracts with the companies that had previously selected them. A vicious circle of inter-dependence between the management companies and supervisory boards was thus established.

By law, members of supervisory boards do not represent the owners but are independent professionals. This is common legal terminology used for the members of supervisory boards of companies with widely dispersed ownership in the Anglo-Saxon world, too. In legal terms, an independent professional is a person whose protection of shareholder interests in a given company is not in conflict with his/her interests as a member of a supervisory board or management team in competitive or related business entities. Interestingly, according to the law, owners of such entities do not have such conflicts of interests. Formally, it is therefore totally correct if the owners of management companies serve as the members of supervisory boards of privatization funds. The survey revealed that this does happen in 10% of all cases.

The survey showed that more than one half of responding members (53%) also sit on one or two other boards. Most of them (85%) are members of the supervisory boards in privatized companies whose important shareholders are privatization funds. The respective management companies appointed more than one quarter of them. A few (11%) are members of the supervisory boards of the owners of management companies. Questionable members in terms of independence could include the managers (or employees) in portfolio companies of the respective fund (16%) and the owners of the respective management company (8%).

But in practice, independence is less a matter of law and regulation as laws and regulations are always incomplete in capturing conflicts of interests. In the countries with a long tradition of supervisory boards, independence is the result of a synergetic compound of personal characteristics and motivations of individuals, public images of companies, societal norms, effective courts and so on.

As experience with supervisory boards is still very limited in Slovenia, it was interesting to learn what the personal motivations of responding members were in agreeing to serve on the supervisory boards of privatization funds. Table 3.12 shows that invitations by management companies were important for most of them. Opportunities to learn and professional competence of management were important for many. But in general they do not consider that membership of boards of funds would bring any personal reputation. Similarly, a good public image of the respective funds was not important for acceptances. Rewards were almost unimportant.

Table 3.12   Important factors in agreeing to membership

	All (%)	Large (%)	Small (%)
Invitation by management company	65	59	68
Learning opportunity	47	47	47
Competence of management	43	41	42
Professional challenge	39	44	29
To contribute to transition	35	47	26
Personal prestige	22	22	21
Public image of the fund	27	31	21
Own shareholding	16	13	21
Rewards	4	3	5

In advanced market economies, supervisory board members are usually retired directors, directors of other companies or distinguished academics who know the respective industries and professions well. Judging from the survey, members of supervisory boards of privatization funds are on average highly educated (80% hold a university degree) and have management experience (half occupy top management positions). But relatively few have experience with the strategic management (22%), financial management (18%), accounting and business valuations (14%) which would be needed for informed evaluation of how well fund managers purchase companies at the voucher auctions and sell stakes or consolidate them in portfolio companies afterwards.

What characteristics, in the respondents' opinions, are required to be members of supervisory boards of privatization funds? Most consider experience with enterprise management, financial competence and contacts with enterprises to be important. But contacts with the government also appear to be important for board members.

Table 3.13   *Important characteristics of members of supervisory boards of privatization funds*

	All (%)	Large (%)	Small (%)
Experience with enterprise management	82	84	79
Financial competence	78	81	68
Contacts with enterprises	65	59	74
Public image	53	56	47
Contacts with the government	53	57	47

Tables 3.12 and 3.14 show distinctive characteristics of members of supervisory boards of large and small funds. The characteristics of respondents from large funds fairly closely resemble those of the board members of reputable large companies in advanced market economies. Professional challenges, opportunities to contribute to transition and good public image of the funds were important for more members of large funds in agreeing to serve on a board. Experience with enterprise financial and operational management, personal reputation and government contacts are considered important characteristics of board members from large funds. The distinctive characteristics of the board members of small funds are that they are themselves shareholders in respective funds and that they maintain close contacts with both portfolio companies and management companies.

The survey identified a number of areas in which professional competence of supervisory boards of privatization funds (and thereby their independence) could be strengthened. The members would require less experience with securities trading since portfolio trading is not the major value-maximization activity of managers of privatization funds, given the structure of funds' portfolios. Moreover, it is not the task of supervisory boards to control managers' frauds such as insider dealing, which is the inherent task of the Agency. Asymmetry of knowledge and understanding of relevant frameworks between management companies and supervisory boards appears to be a large problem especially with respect to the legal and regulatory loopholes of which the managers can avail themselves for their own benefits. The many rather peculiar responses in the survey were due to the lack of knowledge of the frameworks or lack of understanding of the specific problems of privatization funds. Privatization funds are a new industry in Slovenia and board members who meet in session only about twice a year according to the survey devote only a few days yearly to enhancing their understanding and knowledge.

The task of supervisory boards is to oversee management and not to manage themselves. If management performance is to be evaluated by a supervisory board, the managers would have to have day-to-day autonomy and the boards would have to refrain from interfering in their operational decisions. Supervisory boards must limit themselves to taking strategic decisions, approving plans and reports, appointments and dismissals of top management, checking the legal and moral conduct of managers actions and so on. The respondents agreed that protecting the interests of shareholders is the most important task of supervisory boards (see Table 3.14).

Table 3.14   Most important tasks of supervisory boards

	All (%)	Large (%)	Small (%)
Protection of shareholders interests	94	91	100
Performance evaluation	69	72	63
Defining strategy	69	66	74
Control of management	59	53	68
Legal conduct of management	59	63	53
Influencing dividend policy	53	56	47
Advising management	47	41	58

Table 3.15   Frequent agenda items

	All (%)	Large (%)	Small (%)
Investment policy	69	72	68
Strategic matters	65	66	63
Assembly agenda	39	41	37
Management fees	33	44	19
Restructuring of companies	31	38	21
Borrowing	24	19	32
Statutory matters	24	19	32
Share values	24	25	21
Dividend policy	24	25	21
Evaluation of management performance	18	25	12
Appointment of broker and auditor	6	6	5
Appointment of director	2	0	5

The frequency with which various items are included in board agendas is an indication of how the rather vaguely defined task has been translated into fund boardrooms. Table 3.15 points to the considerable passivity of supervisory boards in that respect. It looks as if the supervisory boards of privatization funds have not yet begun focusing on the tasks by the order of importance established in the survey by themselves. They appear to understand the task of protecting shareholders' interests in quite abstract terms and in very different ways. They consider big themes such as investment policy and strategic matters but fail to deal with some basic responsibilities such as defining the agendas of assemblies, appointments of auditors, brokers and directors. They do not seem to tackle the issues which most directly concern the interests of shareholders such as management fees, borrowings, quotations, dividend policy or evaluating the performances of fund managers.

The distinctive characteristics of the supervisory boards of small and large funds can also be observed in Tables 3.14 and 3.15. The board members from large funds understand the protection of shareholders' interests more as performance evaluation, defining strategy and checking whether managers' conduct is legally and morally correct. The supervisory boards of large funds appear to be less passive and more accountable to the shareholders by discussing more frequently various items and especially investment policies, restructuring of companies, and management fees. They also evaluate performances of management more often. For the respondents from small funds, protecting the interests of fund shareholders means quite different things: defining strategy, advising and controlling management, which could already entail interference with day-to-day management. Moreover, statutory matters and borrowing are more frequently on the agenda of small funds' boards.

The passivity of supervisory boards of privatization funds is also confirmed by responses regarding voting in sessions. Members of supervisory boards are crucially dependent on fund managers in acquiring information. They claim to be dissatisfied with the information and materials received from management companies, but they do not feel responsible for defining the reporting requirements to them. Most argue that it is the responsibility of the Agency to define and enforce such reporting and information requirements. Quite a few would leave it to the management companies themselves. On the other hand, it is very seldom that members receive materials such as the auditors' reports or management proposals before sessions which are critical for their voting. A number of them claim that they do not even receive standardized reports required by the Agency (see Table 3.16).

Table 3.16   Information received for sessions

	All (%)	Large (%)	Small (%)
Agenda	82	84	79
Minutes	82	81	79
Financial plan and report	71	72	68
Director's report	59	63	53
Standardized reports	53	59	42
Management proposals	39	38	42
Auditors' report	37	44	26

Of factors critically influencing voting, respondents emphasized the interests of shareholders and long-term performance of funds as being almost equally important. The opinions of directors seem unimportant in that respect. Table 3.17 points out the rather distinct voting practices of supervisory boards of small and large funds. Members of large funds give greater consideration to various factors in voting. More of them are concerned about long-term performance of the respective fund and its competitiveness. More of them feel accountable to the general public. Fewer from small funds take into account the interests of shareholders and more of them listen to the director's opinion.

Table 3.17   Factors influencing voting

	All (%)	*Large (%)*	*Small (%)*
Shareholders' interests	84	94	63
Long-term performance	82	88	74
Competition	66	41	32
Public accountability	61	66	53
Legal norms	57	50	68
Director's opinion	29	25	37
Own investments	6	3	16

Although most members interviewed claim that managers' opinions are not important to their voting, the survey reveals that in practice this is not exactly so. It appears that members seldom require changes to management's voting proposals and even less often do they vote against such proposals. The voting of supervisory boards of small funds appears as even more passive approval of management proposals (Table 3.18).

Table 3.18   Changes requested to management's voting proposals (a) and voting against managers' proposals (b)

	All (%)		*Large (%)*		*Small (%)*	
	(a)	**(b)**	**(a)**	**(b)**	**(a)**	**(b)**
Frequently	6	0	6	0	5	0
Seldom	63	39	72	50	47	21
Never	31	61	22	50	48	79

Consistent with many studies which examined the effectiveness of supervisory boards, the respondents evaluated the influence of supervisory boards on management companies as small or none (see Table 3.19). Similarly, most of them assess their own contributions in the board sessions as being modest.

Table 3.19   *Influence of supervisory boards on management (a) and members' individual contributions (b)*

	All (%)		Large (%)		Small (%)	
	(a)	(b)	(a)	(b)	(a)	(b)
None	18	29	13	25	26	37
Small	76	61	78	63	74	58
Large	6	10	9	13	0	5

It would be possible to enhance the active role of boards by strengthening the professional competence of members and with better information. Performance-related rewards would in principle help strengthen the personal motivation of members and their accountability to the shareholders. The survey revealed that not even one privatization fund has availed itself of the legal provision to reward members with performance fees payable in shares.

The effectiveness of supervisory boards could be enhanced with several technical and procedural improvements. Recent events in Slovenia have shown that supervisory boards play important roles in public companies with widely dispersed ownership when managers do not perform, but supervisory boards can be dismissed and non-performing management replaced only by large institutional investors. In order to allow such owners of privatization funds to be consolidated, privatization funds must be listed on organized markets.

External Control

Quotation of companies on organized markets is a *sine qua non* condition for any management competition, which is in turn the guarantee that shareholders' interests will be observed. While market values of shares accurately reflect the performances and values on developed liquid markets, on less liquid emerging markets a comparison of share prices of companies within the same industries is a reliable indication of different management performances. More than 85% of respondents from large funds and fewer than 60% from small funds agreed that market share prices will reflect different performances of management companies in the long run.

It was ensured that the Polish national investment funds were listed on the highly organized and regulated Warsaw Stock Exchange from the very beginning by way of exchanging certificates for shares on that market. The Czech investment privatization funds have also been quoted on the organized (albeit less regulated and transparent) OTC markets from the very start by extending the system of voucher auctions to post-privatization securities markets. Until recently, none of the Slovenian privatization funds was quoted on the organized market, several years after their establishment. The responding members were pessimistic that their fund's quotation would take place in two years (50%) or in several years only (50%). More than two thirds of them would, however, support immediate quotation.

The management companies vigorously resist the quotation of privatization funds on formal markets with the argument that because it is not known in public what the government will offer as additional supply to fill the privatization gap, the market shares prices would be too low. In the meantime, the shares of privatization funds are traded at very low prices on the gray markets anyway and the common buyers are reportedly the management companies themselves. The shares of funds should in principle trade at higher prices in formal markets. There is wide evidence for such an argument, based on the relevant experience from Poland where prices continuously rose as the trading of certificates and funds shares was shifted from less to more regulated markets.

In an attempt to facilitate the quotation of privatization funds, the Agency has issued an instruction that the shares of privatization funds be registered at the Central Depository. That instruction effectively supersedes the law which allows the quotation of privatization funds only after the certificates have been fully used up.

Market quotation is a necessary condition for effective external control of shareholders but it is not sufficient in itself. Several legal restrictions on fund ownership have been intended as standard measures for protecting small shareholders. Such restrictions are justifiable when companies are floated on highly liquid markets and concentration of shareholding can impede liquid exits of small shareholders. In the case of privatization funds, which have illiquid portfolios and impede liquid exits of small shareholders, such restrictions are more likely to have a counter-effect. It could be argued that consolidation of active owners would in fact be beneficial for small shareholders exiting and for those withholding shares. Namely, shareholders would be selling at higher prices as ownership consolidation would take place in a transparent way and, consequently, the internal control would also be enhanced.

The law does not allow management companies or the owners of other privatization funds to purchase shares of privatization funds. But it is exactly those who are reportedly the buyers of fund shares on the gray market and most interested in acquiring control over them. Similar legal restrictions on the ownership of privatization funds in the Czech Republic have forced management companies to redeem fund shares through legal entities that are related to their sponsors. The emerging corporate control of Czech funds is therefore not very transparent. A rather unpredicted outcome of the Polish mass program was the discovery at the time of the exchange of certificates for fund shares that one fund had already acquired 10% of another fund during secondary trading of certificates. The Polish law does not impose any restrictions on fund ownership and in fact promotes the gradual consolidation of active owners. Such owners are required, as they would be in a position to control fund managers in their intended active management of portfolio companies. The Polish law details the procedure for ownership consolidation. It requires public disclosures of each additional 10% acquisition during the first three years and a mandatory purchase offer when the 30% threshold is achieved. The ownership consolidation thus takes place in a transparent and orderly way, and the emerging corporate control of funds is also transparent.

If restrictions on the ownership of privatization funds in Slovenia were abolished, the management companies would be given a strong incentive to consider prompt quotation of funds. The secondary trading in funds shares would thereby be shifted from gray markets to organized markets and corporate control acquisitions of funds would become transparent and could be regulated.

TRANSFORMATION OF PRIVATIZATION FUNDS

Privatization funds are hybrid institutions because of their peculiar portfolios which do not allow for effective shareholder control nor do they give incentives to the managers for effective portfolio management. They cannot be sustained in the present form and prompt transformation is an imperative. It must, however, be properly regulated to ensure that shareholders are protected whilst the managers are allowed and given adequate incentives to undertake adequate adjustments of their portfolios for effective management.

Under the law in Slovenia, privatization funds have to adjust their portfolios in five years or convert themselves into ordinary joint-stock companies. In the Czech Republic, no such deadlines for the transformation of privatization funds were initially given. The common trend in both countries is that privatization funds are converted into ordinary joint-stock companies by voting in the assemblies. The emerging structures preserve all the hybrid characteristics of privatization funds since only the legal status is changed but transitional portfolio structures remain largely unadjusted. The incentive for fund managers for this kind of transformation is exactly to avoid the oversight of supervisory agencies and to enjoy large autonomy in later adjustments to their portfolios.

In view of those developments, it was rather a surprising outcome of the survey that a large number of respondents claimed that the funds will continue as closed-end investment companies in the future. The holding form is practically not considered by them as being a likely or possible transformation route (see Table 3.20).

Table 3.20   Possible forms of transformation of privatization funds

	All (%)	Large (%)	Small (%)
Investment company	67	76	53
Mutual fund	17	12	26
Venture capital fund	5	1	11
Holding company	3	4	0

Transformation of privatization funds would require that they adapt with the institutional, legal and regulatory framework of one of the standard forms of financial intermediaries: financial holding company, mutual fund, venture capital fund, etc. That would entail mutual adaptation of ownership and portfolio structures to one another. The change of legal status *per se* would be insufficient but would allow for the adjustment of portfolio structures. The sequence of both adaptations will, however, be different in the holding or mutual funds transformation routes.

Since any transformation should be subject to voting in the assemblies, specific rules for that voting ought to be defined as a special precaution for protecting shareholders' interests. It would be correct that a high numbered quorum be required and that management companies be excluded from it either as shareholders or as proxies of small shareholders. This would be a clear signal of shareholders' activism. Nevertheless, it might be more correct than forcing such shareholders into voting activism, which anyway could be manipulated to allow for the exit of unsatisfied shareholders on the organized market prior to transformation. Mandatory quotation of privatization funds as a condition of transformation would probably serve as a strong incentive for the management companies to consider it promptly.

CONCLUSION

The twin objectives of privatization funds in mass privatization programs – to reduce the risk for small investors and to improve governance of privatized companies – have been accomplished inconclusively. The managers of privatization funds are neither accountable agents to their principals (fund shareholders) nor are they responsible principals to the company managers.

The fund managers' ineffectiveness and unaccountability is less the result of managers' negligence and more due to the inherent inconsistency between the two levels of corporate governance driven by the peculiar portfolios of privatization funds. It seems that the privatization funds will have to have different portfolios to allow better control of their current shareholders or be subject to different controls and given different kinds of incentives to act as responsible owners of the portfolio companies.

The specific problem of privatization funds in Slovenia is the privatization gap, which is the reason for the long-delayed quotation on organized markets, as the main impetus of the efficiency and effectiveness of managers and the effective protection of small shareholders. Without such quotation, standard measures to protect the interests of small shareholders are applied in vain or even have adverse effects. The peculiar portfolios of privatization funds are strong incentives for corporate control acquisitions. The legal constraints on fund ownership are rather awkward forms of small shareholder protection if they are denied a (liquid) exit on transparent markets. Such legal constraints force the corporate control transactions on non-transparent markets and here shareholders do not enjoy even the most basic protection otherwise applicable.

Further, since the shares of privatization funds are not traded on organized markets, any shareholder activism (including proxy contests) cannot be promoted on the shareholders' initiatives and is likely to be captured by the fund managers.

CEEPN's survey shows that the supervisory boards respond to their awkward task of protecting the interests of shareholders by controlling the fund managers who selected (and appointed) them with passivity, and that they conveniently serve the fund mangers by approving their proposals. The evident asymmetry of information and understanding of specifics of privatization funds between the supervisory boards and managers account for the passivity of boards. This chapter strongly argues that the supervisory boards are no substitute for the lack of external control and do not compensate for the inherent inconsistencies in the institutional framework of privatization funds.

Long-term management contracts not only constrain new entries but also impede competition between existing fund managers. Those contracts also allow the continuation of fund managers' high earnings charged on the basis of overvalued portfolios regardless of both management performance and costs. The postponed quotation of privatization funds also conveniently disguises managers' high earnings and helps maintain shareholders' belief that fund shares have value.

Various procedural and technical improvements could be attempted in the current framework of privatization funds, but the achieved efficiency and control gains would compensate for only a minor part of the overall inefficiency and the control losses incurred due to the awkward portfolios of privatization funds which give incorrect incentives to fund managers. Those losses not only diminish shareholders' returns but also have significant multiplier effects across the economy at large, considering the fact that privatization funds are important shareholders in practically all privatized companies in Slovenia. It does appear, as the critics of privatization funds correctly argued, that fund managers have 'selfishly' drained existing values at the cost of fund shareholders and portfolio companies.

The need to transform privatization funds is now recognized across the region but the proposed solutions are so far incomplete. They have not yet solved the Gordian knot of how to protect the interests of shareholders whilst not forgetting the incentives given to fund managers for portfolio adjustments. While the privatization funds in Slovenia and the Czech Republic have many common initial characteristics, the Polish funds offer a model that could be followed in the holding transformation route in both countries. That route is likely to prevail over others (especially the mutual fund one) if it is taken into consideration that the initial portfolio structures of privatization funds closely comply with the overall structures of transitional economies. Most privatized companies need to be restructured and they therefore require active owners. Could the privatization funds be made to be such owners? The proposed mandatory transformation of privatization funds into open-end mutual funds would very likely lead to massive liquidations (which would perhaps be a convenient exit for earlier advocates of privatization funds). On the other hand, too many restrictions on the portfolios of transformed institutions are very likely to cause insider dealing and other manager frauds and effectively block the holding route which has the potential to make privatization funds the true and active owners of companies.

4. The Impact of Privatization Funds on Corporate Governance in Mass Privatization Schemes: the Czech Republic, Poland and Slovenia

Saul Estrin, Domenico Mario Nuti and Milica Uvalic

INTRODUCTION

In 1990–97, in the vast majority of central and eastern European countries, the 'transition' to the market economy has been accompanied by mass privatization schemes, i.e., the free or subsidized distribution of state assets to citizens, through vouchers or equivalent means (Nuti, 1995).[1] This was a major track for the privatization of large state enterprises, usually labeled large scale privatization, but in some countries vouchers could be used also for the 'small' privatization of flats, shops, restaurants, small plots of land. The few exceptions to date are Hungary; Azerbaijan, Turkmenistan and Uzbekistan in the former Soviet Union; Bosnia and Herzegovina, the FYR of Macedonia and Serbia in the former Yugoslav Federation (Estrin and Stone, 1996).

Apart from the political advantage of raising popular support for the transition, mass privatization had a number of clear advantages:

- overcoming the lack of domestic liquid assets, which had been pulverized in the stabilization that accompanied the early stage of transition;
- avoiding the difficulties of assessing the present value of enterprise assets in a period of changing relative prices and large scale restructuring of output and trade flows;
- distributional fairness: mass privatization was viewed as a kind of restitution to the entire population for their past consumption sacrifices; and
- above all speed, relative to other privatization methods.

The loss of potential revenue, with respect to asset sales at prices closer to market valuation, was not – perhaps wrongly – perceived as a significant disadvantage. It was felt that state enterprises would be stripped or run down in the delays of privatization and, in any case, speedy privatization was regarded as indispensable to put an end to state interference in the enterprise sector and to de-politicize the economy (Boycko, Shleifer and Vishny, 1996).

Mass privatization also had a major disadvantage, namely inadequate discipline of 'corporate governance', i.e., effective control by enterprise owners over managerial decision-making. Through share ownership diffusion, and in many cases also significant insiders' ownership (e.g., Russia, Slovenia), in combination with thin and still undeveloped financial markets, mass privatization has disabled traditional mechanisms of corporate governance, whether by actual or potential controlling ownership stakes as respectively in the German–Japanese or in the Anglo-Saxon model. Weak governance leaves old managers unchallenged and inhibits the willingness of financial markets to provide risk capital. Therefore governance is crucial to improving efficiency and promoting capacity restructuring of newly privatized enterprises; it ultimately determines the effectiveness of privatization itself.

In the course of mass privatization, investment funds have emerged. Such funds range from special 'national investment funds' (NIFs) with a centrally given role in the privatization process, as typically in Poland, to spontaneous and decentralized investment funds as typically in Slovenia and in the Czech Republic. All such funds are often called 'privatization investment funds' or PIFs, although – except for the Polish case – the association is purely incidental and the term is not always used in the relevant legislation (Simoneti and Triska, 1995). In ordinary market economies investment funds do not normally play a significant role in enhancing or inhibiting corporate governance (OECD, 1996). Fund managers usually diversify their portfolio without accumulating controlling stakes in any single company, and if they disapprove of managerial policies they tend to sell rather than force change through a takeover bid. In turn an investor would choose among funds according to their stated policy (e.g., investing in small companies, giving priority to income or capital, etc.) and track record, and also would tend to use an 'exit' rather than a 'voice' strategy if dissatisfied with performance. In transition economies, on the contrary, investment funds, which have become involved in mass privatization, have played important roles in corporate governance, both positive and negative.

In some cases, as in Poland, the promoters of mass privatization have relied on forms of investment funds in order to eliminate or at least alleviate both the potential loss of corporate governance and other disadvantages such as reduced access to capital and management. This has been achieved by specifically assigning to a particular 'lead' fund a large minimum stake (one third) of each enterprise subjected to mass privatization.

Reliance on investment funds for the activation of corporate governance of privatized enterprises, in turn, raises the additional question of governance within the funds: 'who monitors the monitors?' (Stiglitz, 1994). Thus the agenda is extended from first level governance – of firms – to second level governance – of funds; transforming the problem rather than solving it. This problem arises also in those investment funds, which have not been given a 'lead' and indeed have been prevented from taking a lead by the imposition of maximum ceilings to their shareholdings in any single enterprise. It turns out that Czech funds are themselves often subject to control by leading investors, in the guise of state banks which are still bearers of those interests and behaviors that the mass privatization intended to eradicate.

By and large, actual experience with investment funds to date, though short-lived, is sufficiently heterogeneous, problematic, and different from initial expectations, to justify detailed scrutiny and investigation, such as it has been attempted in the ACE project P–95–2110–R undertaken by the Ljubljana CEEPN, on 'Governance of Privatization Funds: Experiences of the Czech Republic, Poland and Slovenia'. The purpose of this chapter is that of providing a comparative overview of these countries' experience (the next section on general features of mass privatization schemes; the third section on specific features of investment funds), and drawing implications for both corporate governance and enterprise performance (the fourth and fifth sections, respectively), as well as some general conclusions.

A COMPARATIVE OVERVIEW OF MASS PRIVATIZATION

General differences between the mass privatization schemes in the Czech Republic, Poland, and Slovenia concern primarily their timing and speed; size relative to state-owned assets, GDP, or other indicators; and their mode of implementation. These general differences are reviewed in this section, whereas the following section compares more specific features of investment funds design.

Timing and Speed

Mass privatization was always presumed to be much faster than conventional methods, but in the end it was implemented with delays in all three countries (particularly in Poland), due to a series of problems – intense debates about some of the controversial issues, times of implementation longer than expected, unanticipated technical problems, complicated and long procedures of approval of privatization programs, and so forth (Nuti, 1995).

In the Czech Republic, mass privatization was part of the overall privatization strategy adopted in the early stage of transition by the former Czechoslovak government, to be implemented immediately after small-scale privatization and the restitution of property to former owners was terminated in 1991. The basic legal framework for mass privatization was provided in the February 1991 Law on large-scale privatization, which envisaged the use of various methods for privatizing medium and large-scale firms, including privatization via vouchers.[2] However, the law failed to specify a number of technical details regarding the voucher scheme, which was done only in amendments and additional laws adopted in 1991–92. As initially conceived by the Czechoslovak government, mass privatization was to be implemented in two waves, and this provision was maintained by the Czech Republic after the split (in Slovakia, on the contrary, there was only one wave, with already distributed vouchers for the second wave redeemed for government bonds). The two waves were supposed to be completed over a two-year period, but were somewhat delayed: the first was implemented in 1992, the second only in 1994. It turned out that the whole process of compiling, processing, and approving privatization projects, as well as the transfer of property to the new owners, was rather lengthy (see Kotrba *et al.* in this volume). In this way, speed in implementation, which was one of the main goals of voucher privatization, was greatly compromised.

Mass privatization (and privatization in general) has taken even longer in Slovenia. A voucher scheme was not part of the first privatization program launched by the former Yugoslav government, implemented also in Slovenia for a brief period in 1990, but was included as one of the methods only in the new privatization law adopted after the Yugoslav split (Uvalic, 1997b). The strong initial opposition to mass privatization by some major political parties had prolonged the privatization debate, and after several draft laws which were rejected in Parliament, a new privatization law was finally adopted in November 1992. The law was again amended in June 1993 and effectively started being implemented in the second half of 1993, when further delays were caused by the long and complicated procedure of preparing, submitting, and approving enterprise privatization programs, including problems linked to unsettled restitution claims and procrastination by management in the expectation of more favorable legislative changes. Out of a total of 1,543 enterprises planned for privatization, by the end of 1994 as many as 90% had submitted their privatization programs, and by February 1997, 92% (1,347) had also obtained approval, but by the end of 1996 only 58% (900) of privatizing firms had actually completed the entire privatization procedure (Jaklin and Herič, 1997: 473). Because of the slow pace of privatization, the validity of ownership certificates distributed in 1993 to Slovenian citizens has been extended several times, but they should have definitely expired in mid-1997. A major problem emerged in the meantime, in Slovenia this is known as the 'privatization gap' or a vouchers overhang (a huge discrepancy between capital disposable for privatization and ownership certificates distributed to the population). The problem arose because the authorities initially took the book value of enterprise property to be privatized as the basis for calculating the value of vouchers to be distributed to citizens; but after their distribution they revised the value of property downwards. Consequently, contrary to initial intentions of implementing mass privatization in one wave as part of the global privatization program, a 'second wave' is expected in the near future. The government has recognized its legal obligation to provide additional property in exchange for excess ownership certificates, but by mid-1997 had not yet decided which sectors or enterprises to add to the privatization list.

The longest delays in implementing mass privatization have occurred in Poland (Nuti, 1995). The debate on mass privatization started during the early phase of the transition in 1990–91, but its actual implementation incurred substantial delays due to long controversies about a number of specific issues. The first law enabling mass privatization was passed in June 1991, but only on April 30, 1993 was a law specifically dealing with the details of mass privatization adopted by Parliament ('Law on national investment funds and their privatization'). Thereafter, due to a combination of technical and political problems, it took another twenty months for the national investment funds to be created, effectively established only in December 1994, while the other provisions of the law were not implemented until 1996–97. In particular, the actual privatization of the national investment funds has been taking much longer than expected. The passage from the first phase of the program of 'single shareholder', during which the funds are owned by the State Treasury, to the second phase of conversion of certificates distributed to the population into shares of national investment funds, started only in June–July 1997. The deadline for converting certificates into shares was prolonged several times and expired at the end of 1997. It is expected that the first shareholders' meetings will be held only at the beginning of 1998. Thus contrary to the other two countries' experience, mass privatization in Poland is being implemented in a rather late phase of transition. Several rounds of mass privatization were initially planned, but the Polish government has decided that residual state assets will be devoted to funding pension system reform, rather than to further mass privatization.

Size of the Mass Privatization Program

In all three countries mass privatization was not the exclusive method of privatization, but was used along with other techniques within a multi-track privatization strategy; it had a much more important role in the Czech Republic than in both Slovenia and Poland, in terms of the most important indicators (enterprise number and value, their share in total state-owned and national assets or relative to GDP, proportion of enterprise capital privatized through vouchers).

In the Czech Republic, the large-scale privatization program involved around 70% of the then 4,800 state-owned enterprises in Czechoslovakia. The program was implemented through a combination of different methods, but voucher privatization was quantitatively the most important. During the first wave, mass privatization involved the offer of some 1,491 joint-stock companies (988 Czech and 503 Slovak), of a nominal value of CSK 299 billion; and during the second wave, of another 861 joint-stock companies (only Czech), of a nominal value of CSK 155 billion (Cermak, 1997: 100). The actual amount of property privatized through voucher privatization was somewhat lower than the amount initially offered: over the whole period 1991–96, the nominal value of shares privatized through the vouchers method amounted to CSK 342 billion, which corresponds to 55% of the value of all property privatized within the large-scale privatization program (Cermak, 1997: 99).

In addition to these global indicators, confirming the importance of mass privatization for property transformation of the Czech economy, for individual firms voucher privatization was not only one of the most frequently used methods but in many cases involved a very high percentage of total enterprise capital. Contrary to the regulations in Poland or Slovenia, where the proportion of enterprise capital to be privatized via vouchers was fixed for all firms in advance (60% in Poland and 20%–40% in Slovenia, see below), in the Czech Republic it was up to the enterprise to propose the desired combination of different methods, including the portion of equity to be privatized through vouchers.[4] Apart from 3% of equity that had to go to the restitution fund, an enterprise could in principle propose to have privatized all remaining 97% of its equity using the voucher scheme. This seems to have been indeed a frequent practice: during the first wave, 39.7% of projects used vouchers as the only privatization method (see Kotrba *et al.* in this volume). On average, during the first wave, enterprises used voucher privatization as a method to distribute 81% of their shares, representing 63.5% of the total stock value; while in the second wave, the corresponding figure was almost 70% of stock value (Coffee, 1996: 120).

The mass privatization scheme was of more limited importance in Slovenia, although it automatically involved, unlike the Czech or Polish case, all 1,543 enterprises planned for privatization. These firms in 1992 represented around 30% of total capital of the Slovenian economy, 40% of revenues, 50% of employment and 40% of GDP (the private sector already accounted for 30%, and the state sector for another 40% of GDP; see Uvalic, Rems and Jašovič in this volume). However, mass privatization as a method was quantitatively much less important in Slovenia than in the Czech Republic, due to a very different general privatization procedure. According to the 1992 privatization law, each enterprise had to transfer 20% of its shares to the Development Fund, which was to offer them at auctions to investment funds in exchange for ownership certificates they had collected from citizens. This was obligatory for all privatizing firms,[5] but an enterprise could decide to distribute, in addition, up to 20% of its shares to employees (past, present, or their relatives) in exchange for their ownership certificates.[6] Thus within a single enterprise, only 20% of the shares actually had to be allocated to mass privatization (via the Development Fund), another 20% being optional. Mass privatization therefore involved a relatively low percentage of total capital or GDP of the Slovenian economy.[7]

In Poland, mass privatization was less important than in Slovenia in terms of several global indicators, although generally involving a larger proportion of an individual enterprise's capital. Some 512 large and medium-scale enterprises were included in the mass privatization program. These firms represent around 10% of sales of the Polish industrial sector, while their book value is around 7 billion zloty (or US$ 2.8 billion; see Lewandowski and Szyszko in this volume). Enterprises which entered the mass privatization program are also reported to control 10% of the production potential of all Polish state-owned companies, to account for about 4.5% of GDP, and for 8% of total assets of the Polish economy (Lawniczak, 1996: 3). At the same time, as much as 60% of total capital of enterprises included in the mass privatization program had to be transferred to national investment funds, to be later exchanged for ownership certificates distributed to the whole population.

Mode of Mass Privatization

Mass privatization was based on the same basic principle – the transfer at a low nominal fee of state property to the population at large – but the mode of implementing this unprecedented privatization method was actually very different in the three countries under consideration, in several respects: the general approach and procedure; compulsory versus voluntary inclusion of enterprises; denomination, distribution, conversion, tradability, and other features of vouchers.

The general approach followed in the Czech large-scale privatization was centrally organized (in contrast to small privatization), as the government prepared and published a detailed list of companies to be privatized during the first and second privatization wave. At the same time, an enterprise's management (and other interested buyers) had the right to propose alternative privatization projects, based on a combination of five different methods (of which voucher privatization was one), but the project had to be evaluated and approved by specific government institutions. No fixed proportion of capital had to be set aside for vouchers, but whatever was not privatized through other methods usually was privatized through the voucher scheme.

Thus the inclusion of enterprises in mass privatization was 'semi'-voluntary: the government decided which firms were to be privatized within the large-scale privatization program, but since an enterprise could propose its own privatization methods, privatization through vouchers was not obligatory.

In Poland the mass privatization program was directly sponsored and organized by the government. By ordinance of the Council of Ministers, the enterprises selected for mass privatization were formally included in the National Investment Funds Program, and their shares were transferred to the 15 funds in the following proportions: 33% was transferred to a lead fund, another 27% in equal proportions to the other 14 funds, 15% was given to enterprise employees (and in certain cases a further 15% to entitled individuals, like farmers and fishermen, who had contractual relations with the company concerned), and 25% to the State Treasury. However, the selection of firms to be included in the program was again 'semi'-voluntary, although in a different sense from the Czech Republic. The government decided which enterprises to include in the mass privatization program, to which an open invitation was sent to enter the program, but within 45 days the enterprise director or workers council could raise objections. While the voluntary basis of enterprise inclusion was regarded a serious constraint on the supply-side of the program, it was also a condition for having parliamentary majority in favor of the program in 1993 (see Lewandowski and Szyszko in this volume) and a recognition of employee stakeholder power under the old system and in the transition.

In Slovenia the government decided which sectors were to be excluded from privatization, while all the other enterprises were automatically included in the general privatization program. All enterprises slated for privatization were obliged to privatize a fixed proportion of their capital through the voucher scheme (i.e., through the transfer of 20% of shares to the Development Fund, to be later sold to investment funds in exchange for ownership certificates). Another 20% had to be transferred to two other government funds (the Pensions fund and the Compensation fund). For the remaining 60% of capital, enterprises could propose their own privatization methods where, given the long tradition of self-management, a strong preference was given to employee buyouts: 20% could be given to employees freely in exchange of their ownership certificates, another 40% could be sold to workers at preferential terms (a 50% discount and deferred payment), or otherwise privatized using conventional methods based on sales to outside owners.

In the three countries the general procedure of mass privatization consisted of a combination, in different proportions, of a centralized approach based on government regulations and some degree of decentralization delegating some decisions to enterprises. Other characteristics of mass privatization varied, particularly regarding various features of vouchers and the design of investment funds (see the next section).

Vouchers had very different specific features, from their label – vouchers in the Czech Republic, ownership certificates in Slovenia and share certificates in Poland – to more substantial features such as their denomination, nominal fee, recipients, distribution mechanism, tradability, conversion options.[8]

In the Czech Republic a 14-page book of vouchers was offered at a nominal fee of US\$ 30 to all adult citizens, entitling them to 1,000 investment points, to be invested in a maximum of 10 enterprises or in newly-established investment funds. In Poland, share certificates were offered at a nominal fee of 20 zloty (US\$ 7–8) to all adult permanent resident citizens in the form of a single share certificate, which could be converted into shares of national investment funds. In Slovenia, all citizens (not only adults) had a special account opened with the Social Accounting Service, entitling them to a nominal value of ownership certificates between 150,000 and 400,000 tolars per person (between DM 2,000 and DM 6,400) depending on age, for which a small charge in tolars (corresponding to about DM 2) had to be paid upon registration.

Vouchers were also denominated differently: in the Czech Republic in investment points, where each of the 1,000 investment points had a predetermined value at the start of the first round of bidding, in Poland and Slovenia in national currencies, zlotys and tolars respectively. Vouchers were bearer instruments (and therefore immediately tradable) in Poland, but not in the Czech Republic and Slovenia where they normally become tradable only after having been converted into enterprise shares, or investment fund equity (though in the Czech Republic they could be transferred to heirs).

In both the Czech Republic and Slovenia, ownership certificates could be used for acquiring shares of either privatizing enterprises or PIFs, but not in Poland where their use was limited to conversion into shares of national investment funds. A specific feature of the Slovenian model was that vouchers could also be invested under special terms in the employing enterprise (and therefore similarly to the Russian model).[9] However, there are also specific restrictions in Slovenia on shares acquired by employees in exchange for ownership certificates through the internal distribution scheme, as these shares are not tradable for a period of two years (whereas all shares transferred to the Development Fund are immediately tradable). In Poland, where certificates were immediately tradable, a large percentage (around 50%) of citizens sold them at once, at a significant profit (see Lewandowski and Szyszko in this volume). Another feature of Polish certificates is that during the first phase of the mass privatization program (i.e., of state ownership of funds), all dividends are allocated to a fiscal account for the benefit of certificate holders, who are entitled to receive them at a later stage, at the latest once share certificates have been converted into national investment funds' shares.

These differences in general features of mass privatization programs in the Czech Republic, Poland and Slovenia are summarized in Table 4.1. Further details on specific features of investment funds are discussed in the following section.

Table 4.1   General features of mass privatization programs (MPP) in the Czech Republic, Poland and Slovenia

	Czech Republic	**Poland**	**Slovenia**
Period of implementation	1992 (1st wave) 1994 (2nd wave)	1991–present	1991–present
Role of MPP in privatization strategy	Part of large-scale privatization program	Implemented as a separate program	Part of the privatization program
Size			
– Number of firms	1,491 (1st wave) – 988 (Czech R.) – 503 Slovakia 861 (2nd wave)	512 medium and large-scale firms	All 1,543 firms planned for privatization
– Nominal value of firms	299 bln CSK (1st wave) 155 bln CSK (2nd wave) Value of shares privatized via vouchers,1991–96: 342 bln CSK	7 bln zloty (US$ 2.8 bln)	887 bln tolars (book value of 1,370 approved projects)
– Other indicators	55% of property privatized within the large-scale program; 25% of all state-owned assets	4.5% of GDP; 10% of sales of industrial sector	40% of GDP 30% of capital
Inclusion of firms	Semi-voluntary for a selected group	Semi-voluntary for a selected group	Obligatory for all privatizing firms
General share allocation scheme	Up to 93% could be auctioned to general public in exchange for vouchers	60% transferred to funds (33% to lead fund and 27% to other funds; 15% to employees; 25% retained by state	20% transferred to Development Fund, obliged to sell them to PIFs; another 20% to employees (optional)
Auction process	Pre-established prices (in points), complex bidding process to match supply and demand	No pre-established, PIFs to bid for vouchers	No pre-established, PIFs to bid for shares offered by Development Fund
Main features of vouchers			
– Fee	US$ 30.	US$ 8	DM 2
– Denomination	Investment points (zloty)	National currency (tolars)	National currency
– Nominal value	Not predetermined	Not predetermined	Fixed in tolars (DM 2,000–6,400)
– Tradability	Not tradable	Immediately tradable	Not tradable
– Conversion options	Shares of firms or of PIFs	Shares of PIFs only	Shares of firms or PIFs

Source   Compiled by the authors, mainly on the basis of the Project's Country Reports.

INVESTMENT FUNDS COMPARED

In all the three countries under consideration, new financial institutions, usually referred to as privatization investment funds (PIFs),[10] were intended to play a fundamental role as financial intermediaries in the post-privatization period. Since the implementation of mass privatization had usually resulted in a high dispersion of ownership in the hands of numerous small shareholders, PIFs were expected to provide an opportunity for portfolio diversification, but without excessive fragmentation of individual holdings. While the rationale for their creation was similar, the design of PIFs was rather different in many respects, including the mode of their creation, legal form, management, and portfolio restrictions. These differences in legal regulations have resulted in national differences with respect to the number of PIFs and of management companies, their dominant sponsors distribution of vouchers, concentration of ownership.

Legal Regulations of PIFs

The general approach to the creation of PIFs was basically the same in the Czech Republic and Slovenia, in both countries in net contrast with the one adopted in Poland. The first two countries have relied on the free entry of investment funds to be market driven and created spontaneously by independent legal entities,[11] which were themselves most frequently established by other legal or physical persons (whether state or private banks, private enterprises, other existing or new financial intermediaries, individuals), while the government was to provide only the basic regulatory framework (the so-called bottom-up approach). In Poland the government directly organized the whole process, from the creation of funds[12] and selection of funds' management boards, to determining the allocation of enterprise assets to different funds, stipulating minimum holdings for 'lead' funds, fixing remuneration schemes, and other details (the so-called top-down approach).

PIFs' legal form also differed. In Poland, Slovenia, and initially also in the Czech Republic, PIFs could only be established as joint stock companies, and thus as closed-end investment funds. In the Czech Republic, the April 28, 1992 Law on investment companies and investment funds allowed, in addition, the form of a closed-end and open-end mutual fund or unit trust, the main difference with respect to a joint-stock company being that individuals investing their voucher points in these funds (trusts) are not given voting rights (Mladek, 1995).[13] This change in the legislation had a major impact on the legal form of PIFs established during the second wave, when a number of open-end and closed-end mutual funds were also created.[14] Further legal changes were adopted in the Czech Republic in early 1996, as it became possible to convert PIFs into holding companies, enabling them to bypass regulations covering investment companies and investment funds altogether; the government reacted by adopting new regulations, which came into effect on July 1, 1996, requiring funds to obtain the permission of the Securities Office of the Ministry of Finance for any change in their status (Hashi, 1997: 14).

The main features of PIF certificates, and therefore also voting and other rights of individual investors, depend directly on the legal form of funds.[15] In Slovenia and Poland, where PIFs can only be established as joint stock companies, citizens who have converted their vouchers into PIF shares normally have voting rights, and PIF shares are tradable once they are registered on the stock exchange. In Slovenia, PIF shares have to be registered and they are not tradable until they are listed on the Stock Exchange, which means that at least initially, fund managers are safe from the implications of shareholders' dissatisfaction and exit (which indeed has been the case).[16] In Poland, once citizens' certificates are converted into PIF shares, they are freely tradable (as shares of any ordinary joint-stock company listed on the stock exchange). In the Czech Republic PIFs can be created either as joint-stock companies or as mutual funds. If a PIF is created as a joint-stock company its shares give shareholders voting rights and are tradable but with some delay with respect to shares of normal companies, since PIFs have to apply to the Ministry of Finance to obtain public tradability status for their shares (Triska, 1995). If a PIF is registered as a mutual fund/unit trust, a frequent practice during the second wave, individuals investing their vouchers in PIFs are unit holders but without voting rights; it is reported that there is no liquid market in these units, and thus the unit holders' ability to sell their units is quite limited (Hashi, 1997: 23).

The management of PIFs is also regulated differently. In Slovenia and initially also in the Czech Republic, a contract between the PIF and an external management company, normally its founder, was compulsory. In the Czech Republic the 1992 law abolished this obligation, and thus some funds created during the second wave are self-managed.[17] In Poland, an investment fund is not obliged to have an external manager, though self-managed funds have been strongly discouraged through both formal and informal channels.[18] Another important difference regards the actual selection of PIF managers. In the Czech Republic and Slovenia usually the company founding a PIF automatically becomes its management firm; in Poland PIFs could conclude management contracts exclusively with management companies selected through competitive tender by the Selection Commission, according to publicly announced selection criteria.[19]

Regulations on PIFs' holdings and portfolio diversification also vary widely, partly revealing different perceptions of government role. In the Czech Republic a fund cannot invest more than 10% of its assets in one enterprise and cannot hold more than 20% of shares of a single firm. Thus PIFs are loosely regulated on the standard model of institutional investors with diversified portfolio, expected to engage primarily in 'passive' portfolio management (i.e., trading of enterprise shares); however, they were also occasionally, as major shareholders or in coalition with other shareholders, active on supervisory boards of enterprises. In Slovenia, PIFs are more loosely regulated with similar standard requirements for portfolio diversification, since a fund cannot invest more than 10% of its assets in a single company; but contrary to the Czech regulations, a PIF in Slovenia can hold 100% equity in an individual enterprise (only exceptionally a limit of 20% is imposed);[20] thus the choice between a passive portfolio management or more active involvement in management of enterprises is left to the funds. In Poland portfolio diversification is subject to detailed rules: each fund as 'lead' fund would hold at least 33% of shares of about 30 firms at all times, and about 2% of shares in the remaining 450 firms (Lawniczak, 1996: 2). For each privatizing enterprise the 'lead fund' is not only encouraged but effectively induced to play a significant role in raising finance, monitoring performance, managing and promoting restructuring (while another 27% of the shares are initially held by the other 14 funds). Thus PIFs in Poland are given a special governance role, similar to that of financial institutions in the German model.

Partly due to their differences in legal design, actual experience with PIFs has also been very different in the three countries considered, with respect to their creation, functioning, and later developments during the post-privatization period.

PIFs in Practice

During the first wave of Czechoslovak mass privatization, reliance on private initiative led to the creation of some 429 PIFs (over 260 in the Czech Republic); a total of 354 funds participated in the second wave (both new funds and those established during the first wave (Mladek, 1995). As already mentioned, a major development in the second wave was the appearance of a number of open-end and closed-end mutual funds or unit trusts, while some of the formerly created PIFs also changed their status to mutual funds.[21] Thus out of the 354 funds participating in the second wave, 133 were old investment funds established during the first wave; 63 were newly established investment funds; 120 were closed-end mutual funds; and 38 were open-end mutual funds (Mladek, 1995: 84). The large majority of investment companies in both waves created only one fund, but several of the most powerful investment groups established a large number of funds. During the first wave, 336 investment companies had created a total of 428 funds; but whereas 301 investment companies created only one fund each, the remaining 35 companies created the other 127 funds.[22] Similarly, during the second wave, 238 investment companies created a total of 349 funds; again, 191 investment companies created only one PIF each, while the remaining 47 companies created the other 158 funds (calculated from Kotrba *et al.*, Table 1.15 in this volume). After the early 1996 legal changes enabling PIFs to bypass existing regulations (in particular, the 20% maximum limit of any company's shares), several PIFs transformed themselves into holdings and were exempted from the 20% limit (Hashi, 1997: 14).[23]

Multiple funds are frequent also in Slovenia. Some 23 management companies established a total of 72 PIFs, mostly during 1994 and 1995 (Rems and Jašovič, 1997). The formal reason for multiple funds in Slovenia is the legal restriction imposing a maximum limit on a fund's capital (10 billion SIT, or around DM 115 million), not present in the other two countries. The Slovenian Securities Exchange Commission, also in charge of supervising investment funds, is now considering the possibility of merging PIFs which are managed by the same management company.

In Poland management companies are also less numerous than PIFs, but for different reasons; namely, Polish PIFs are not obliged to make a contract with an external manager (though self-managed funds were strongly discouraged). Of the 15 PIFs established by the government, 14 had a contract with a management company.[24] In the meantime, however, there were disputes in three cases between management companies and the funds; two ended with the cancellation of the management contract, while in the third case the Minister of Privatization dismissed most members of the supervisory board (see Lewandowski and Szyszko in this volume).

The initial allocation of vouchers differed. Only in Poland were all ownership certificates invested directly in PIFs (as this was the only option available). In the Czech Republic and Slovenia, where citizens could choose whether to invest in PIFs or in enterprises directly, funds were very active in their promotion campaigns, which proved to be successful. In the Czech Republic, PIFs managed to attract, out of all citizens' vouchers, 72% during the first wave and 63.5% during the second. Ownership was highly concentrated, however, especially during the first wave, when the top 5 founders with their 10 funds attracted over 50% of all vouchers; during the second wave, the top 10 founders with their 48 funds attracted 50% of all vouchers (see Kotrba *et al.* in this volume). In Slovenia out of the total nominal value of issued certificates (567 billion tolars, or DM 9.3 billion), by the beginning of 1997 PIFs had collected some 310 billion tolars worth of certificates, or almost 55% (Rems and Jašovič, 1997). Employees of Slovenian firms being privatized have invested their certificates mainly directly in the employing enterprise (as part of the internal distribution scheme or an internal buyout), while around 10% of ownership certificates, which have not been utilized, have expired in June 1997.

Who Controls PIFs?

A similar pattern of control of PIFs emerged in the three countries under consideration. Although PIFs are owned by private individual shareholders – citizens who have exchanged their vouchers for PIF shares – financial institutions, mainly banks as the main and dominant owners of companies managing PIFs, *de facto* control them, thus generating potential conflicts of interest.

In the Czech Republic, of the 13 largest investment companies in each of the two waves, 11 were created by financial institutions in the first wave, and six in the second (Hashi, 1997: 11).[25] The four largest banks (Ceska Sporitelna, Investicni a postovni banka, Komercni banka and Ceskoslovenska obchodni banka), all with significant state ownership stakes (40–45%), were prominently represented in this group of 13, as they are the parent institutions of the largest investment companies setting up PIFs (Hashi, 1997: 11). Consequently a number of investment companies have large state-owned stakes, though private investment companies were also represented (three in the first wave and seven in the second wave) (Hashi, 1997: 11). Extensive cross-ownership between PIFs, their sponsoring investment companies, and banks is another major problem. In principle banks' shares could not be held by their subsidiary investment companies, by setting up PIFs which were only managed by their investment companies, but banks could bypass this regulation; thus many PIFs are under the direct control of banks and hold shares of their founding 'grandparents' (Hashi, 1997: 24).

Similarly, in Slovenia, banks have been the most important indirect actors in the setting up of PIFs. The dominant owners of the 23 management companies are domestic legal entities (foreigners own minority shares in only two management companies), mainly banks which indirectly control 48% of PIFs and 62% of PIF assets, and insurance companies which control 19% of PIFs and 17% of PIF assets (Rems and Jašovič, 1997). Thus over three quarters of total PIF assets are indirectly controlled by domestic banks and insurance companies, some of which have still not been privatized. These financial institutions also have the majority stake in banking and insurance services, with potential conflicts of interest between PIFs, their management companies, and banks, sponsors and owners of management companies (Rems and Jašovič, 1997). However, the state has indirect ownership shares in only two management companies while another two are owned by socially owned sponsors (Rems and Jašovič, 1997), which suggests that non-privatized financial institutions may not have as important a role as in the Czech Republic.

In Poland, large financial groups are also the main players controlling PIFs, but the situation differs in several respects. First, contrary to the situation in the Czech Republic or Slovenia, where managing companies setting up and running PIFs are the key actors, in Poland it seems to be the other way round, given that a PIF's supervisory board can cancel a contract with a management company if it so decides (see Lewandowski and Szyszko in this volume).[26] Second, foreign financial institutions have a much greater role in Poland than in the Czech Republic or Slovenia. In the majority of cases, PIFs are managed by a management company sponsored by a consortium of domestic and international banks and consulting companies, foreign managers and consultants (see Lewandowski and Szyszko in this volume). While in the Czech Republic in many cases PIFs are controlled by semi-privatized banks in which the state still has an important stake, in Poland in several cases the majority stake is in the hands of foreign institutions. Out of the 14 funds that had concluded a contract with an external managing company, in 9 cases the management company has a single majority shareholder (with a 50% or larger stake), of which in 7 cases the owner of the majority stake of the management company is a foreign entity (usually a bank), and in 2 cases only, a Polish entity (a commercial bank and a consulting firm; see Lewandowski and Szyszko in this volume). Finally, it seems that in Poland there are no significant opportunities for cross-ownership between management companies, their sponsors and PIFs, since banks, as the main sponsors of management companies, are either already private or are too large to be the object of significant investment by PIFs, while limits on PIFs' borrowing make such cross-ownership infeasible. Polish authorities have also tried to impose a number of regulations which are supposed to reduce (if not eliminate) the possibility of cross-ownership.[27]

The specific features of PIFs in the three countries under consideration are summarized in Table 4.2.

Table 4.2   *Features of investment funds in the Czech Republic, Poland and Slovenia*

	Czech Republic	**Poland**	**Slovenia**
Basic legislation	In 1991 no specific legislation; April 1992 Law on Investment Companies and Investment Funds. New legislation adopted in July 1996	April 1993 Law on National Investment Funds and Their Privatization	Special provisions of the December 1994 Law on Investment Funds and Management Companies
General approach	Spontaneously created market driven funds ('bottom-up')	Created and sponsored directly by the government ('top-down')	Spontaneously created market driven funds ('bottom-up')
Founder	Any legal entity ('investment company'). Minimum capital requirement: US$ 33,000	State Treasury	Any legal entity ('authorized management company'). Min. capital SIT 10 mln, max. SIT 10 bln (DM 115 mln)

Table 4.2   (continued)

	Czech Republic	**Poland**	**Slovenia**
Legal forum	Joint-stock company; and since 1992 also closed-end and open-end mutual fund	Joint-stock company	Joint-stock company
Portfolio regulations	A fund cannot invest more than 10% of its assets in one firm, and of shares of a single firm	Each fund as lead fund initially has a 33% holding in some 30 firms, which cannot be reduced	A fund cannot invest more than 10% of its assets in one firm, but can hold up to 100% (exceptionally limited to 20%)
Management	After adoption of 1992 law, contract with external management company no longer compulsory	Contract with external management company not compulsory although strongly encouraged	Contract with external management company (founder) compulsory
PIF certificates	Not always assuring voting rights; tradable with some delay	Voting shares; not tradable until listed on the stock exchange	Voting shares; not tradable until listed on the stock exchange
Number of PIFs	429 (1st wave, CSSR)[1] 354 (2nd wave)[1]	15	72
Number of management companies (MCs)	336 (1st wave, CSSR)[2] 238 (2nd wave)[2]	Initially 14, reduced to 12 by mid-1996	23
Major owners of MCs	Domestic banks (mainly semi-privatized)	Domestic and foreign banks	Domestic banks and insurance companies
Vouchers invested in PIFs	1st wave: 72% 2nd wave: 63.5%	100% (obligatory for all voucher holders)	Almost 55% of total
Concentration of ownership	1st wave; top five founders with their 20 funds attracted 50%; 2nd wave: top ten founders with their 48 funds attracted 50%	Initially equally distributed, but getting concentrated	Major banks control 34 funds and 62% of total PIF assets

Notes
(1)   Mladek (1995: 84).
(2)   Calculated from Kotrba *et al.*, Table 1.15 in this volume.

Source   Compiled by the authors, mainly on the basis of the Project's Country Reports (unless indicated differently)

IMPLICATIONS FOR CORPORATE GOVERNANCE

Corporate governance in a broad sense includes both governance in the strict sense defined in our Introduction, as effective control by enterprise owners over managerial decision-making, and in addition, equality among owners regardless of their being insiders or outsiders, or otherwise bearing an interest (stake) other than ownership (Nuti, 1998). In transition economies this broader notion can be important, in view of the unexpected dominant role of insiders in the privatization of state enterprises. In this chapter, however, we shall refer to corporate governance in the stricter sense, for two basic reasons. First, ownership by insiders (or other stakeholders), however introduced, can only be expected to adversely affect corporate governance – through inside owners appropriating indirectly more than their fare share of profits and ultimately of capital – in a special case, i.e., when a controlling interest is in the hands of insiders (or stakeholders) who individually hold a smaller share in equity than in factor supply (or other stake; see Nuti, 1997). Second, the Czech Republic does not exhibit insider ownership, while in Slovenia and Poland insider ownership, significant though not as marked as in Russia, is the result of managerial and employee buyouts in the absence of alternative takers, rather than the result of mass privatization. In any case, there is no clear evidence that in these countries insider ownership has prevented or delayed enterprise restructuring.

In a normally functioning financial market, corporate governance as shareholders' control over managerial discretion relies on two major mechanisms usually associated respectively with the German–Japanese and the Anglo-Saxon models. The first is the direct monitoring and control exercised by one or several large shareholders, also indirectly benefiting other shareholders; in 1990 in Germany 80% of companies had at least one shareholder with at least 25% of the equity; additional control is exercised – especially in Japan – by banks and cross-ownership. The second is the threat posed to managers by the potential rise of a controlling interest – through a successful takeover bid – even in a situation of highly fragmented shareholding; this requires market liquidity and developed financial institutions, as in the Anglo-Saxon model.

Within such a developed and well functioning financial market, the role for investment funds is fairly limited. It is true that some role is suggested by corporate governance and finance literature. Namely, the concentration of ownership in investment funds can be seen as a mechanism to overcome the co-ordination costs of small shareholders, enabling them to internalize the economies of scale of collective action and to overcome the agency problems in monitoring management associated with highly dispersed ownership (Blair, 1995 and Shleifer and Vishny, 1995).[28] The relevance of this advantage for mass privatization schemes is clear, since by definition these lead to highly dispersed ownership structures, thus needing new structures to monitor firms and motivate managers.

However, ownership concentration by a fund does not necessarily amount to control; and in any case monitoring managers by funds does not necessarily involve funds in forcing managers to change their ways, even when they might be able to do so if they tried. Funds are more likely – as we already indicated – to choose 'exit', i.e., the sale of shares with less than satisfactory performance, rather than 'voice', i.e., fight to change managerial policy or even managers. If this is the case, investment funds will only improve company performance if capital markets are fully developed and well functioning, so that the share price of non-satisfactory companies drops, raising the probability of a take-over. Indirect methods of governance – through funds – therefore may work well only in the context of effective financial markets.

In transition economies, however, financial markets are still not fully developed; they tend to have a low capitalization with respect to GDP, a relatively low turnover – even in those countries such as the Czech Republic where mass privatization has been used extensively and capitalization is relatively high – with respect to both capitalization and GDP (the EBRD Transition Report, 1995, 1997; in 1996, for instance, market capitalization was 43.5% of GDP in the Czech Republic, 8.8% in Slovakia, 5.9% in Hungary and 5% in Slovenia; with a turnover/capitalization ratio respectively of 0.23, 0.11, 0.13 and 0.53).

In this situation, there is something to be said both against and for investment funds. First, the classic governance problem arises from the asymmetries of information inherent in the relationship between distant owners and operational management. But this is not the key problem in transition economies, where the real issues concern how to generate rents in the first place, not the allocation of those rents. The governance problem in transition economies is therefore the provision of additional capital funds for investment, and investment funds, whose funding has come in the form of mass privatization vouchers, are not in a good position to bring real capital to bear on restructuring. Slovenian funds appear to be particularly under-capitalized, their assets apparently still consisting predominantly of vouchers, illiquid and practically worthless until the next round of mass privatization.[29]

Second, not necessarily in terms of importance, the problem arises of corporate governance once removed, i.e., governance of the funds themselves. Presumably fund managers – even in the Polish case, where they are partly rewarded according to performance – should maximize the funds' yield to investors. However in some cases, notably in the Czech Republic and in Slovenia, state-owned banks appear to have had a major role in the creation of funds and still retain substantial residual ownership. Whether this is an obstacle to restructuring, i.e., whether banks are still bearers of government interests in sustaining employment at the cost of efficiency, remains to be seen. When there is no substantial ownership, fund investors are exposed to the risk of managers 'tunneling' companies, i.e., creaming off profits to their own advantage, as it is frequently reported in the Czech Republic – though this is more a question of inadequate supervision, typical of the Czech approach to state regulation, than a problem of governance as such. More generally, we can detect conflicts of interest behind the disputes between the management and supervisory boards, which appear more frequently in Poland.

Third, well managed funds may be able to generate a good rate of return for their investors by selling stock in bad firms and concentrating on high return stock (e.g., monopolies, utilities, etc.). But this will do nothing to resolve the problem that the funds are often expected to tackle, namely to ensure that the previously poorly returning enterprises improve their performance.

Fourth, even the tangible risk of takeover will not have a significant effect on managerial behavior, if the managerial market is so thin or tight that reputation has no impact on managerial remuneration in the future. Peiperl and Estrin (1997) stress precisely such thinness of the managerial market in transition economies, which combined with current and future expected significant excess demand lowers the prospects for reputational factors being significant in the short to medium run.

On the positive side, there seem to be three main redeeming features of the experience with investment funds in mass privatization in the three countries under consideration. The first is the Polish experience which relies on a fund's large shareholding, presumably amounting to a controlling interest or more easily extended to reach a controlling interest, to establish corporate governance, inject management and capital, promote restructuring – relying on the ownership incentives of a normal market economy, though in a way 'forcing' to some extent the portfolio policy of investment funds. The Polish approach embodies some kind of industrial policy, especially seeing that three of the funds have holdings concentrated in specific branches.

Second, some of the problems indicated above should be alleviated both by supervision of funds and by appropriate remuneration schemes for fund management boards. Supervisory boards differ very considerably in the three countries: for instance, in Slovenia the supervisory board consists of only three members, appointed by the management companies themselves, thus being effectively controlled by their supervisees. In Poland, on the contrary, there appear to be five to nine members on supervisory boards, and one to seven members on the management board (appointed by the supervisory board); the very fact that conflicts with management boards are reported indicates a degree of checks and balances; amidst controversy, the management contracts of three of the funds have been terminated by the government. Fund managers' fees appear to be excessively high relative to western standards. In Slovenia management boards obtain a yearly fee corresponding to 3% of the value of the assets (1% in shares and another 2% in cash), plus a flat fee to cover fixed costs. Management fees are also very high in Poland, with an equivalent formula and a slightly higher rate. It would seem much better to reward management boards according to the increase in the value of fund assets instead of their total value, indeed according to the increase in the value of fund assets relative to the stock exchange index, in order to reward only differential performance, making up with a higher percentage for the lower basis. However, the volatile nature of stock exchanges in transition economies should be taken into account.

Third, the role of investment funds must be seen as an alternative possibly preferable to a greater role for insider ownership, for the risks specified above. Indeed Slovenian investment funds were set up precisely in order to be a countervailing power to insiders, though this does not seem to have happened: from the questionnaires in the country study it appears that investment funds actually support enterprise managers. Investment funds are emerging as the major outside institutional shareholders in all countries relying on mass privatization programs – though they are very specific institutions, a combination of holding companies and mutual funds (Ellerman, 1997), whose performance therefore requires detailed empirical study.

IMPLICATIONS FOR ECONOMIC PERFORMANCE

The material in the previous sections highlights that, in an environment of perfectly functioning capital and management markets, investment funds may not be ideal institutions for the exercise of corporate governance by outsider owners; but the question remains whether this is a relevant point of comparison. The capital and financial markets of transition economies are particularly weak and almost all private ownership which is not in the hands of investment funds is instead controlled by insiders, either workers or managers. It is not clear whether the particular governance problems raised by insider ownership are more or less serious than those discussed in this study. This section is concerned with the evidence to date about the impact of ownership by investment funds on enterprise performance.

In brief, early studies on private versus state ownership, which lump together all private firms – e.g., insider owned, investment funds owned and foreign direct investments – find little evidence of differential performance in the first years of transition. The standard interpretation is that the hardening of budget constraints motivated such an improvement in performance among state-owned firms that they could not be distinguished from their privatized counterparts. Note that these studies do typically find better performance in *de novo* firms, and sometimes in particular cases in foreign owned firms. In that sense, these studies may confirm that all forms of privatization have not been particularly successful in stimulating improved performance.

All these empirical studies are bedevilled by the problem of endogeneity of ownership form; that is to say that the choice of form of privatization was not independent of the performance of the firm in the first place. In particular, it seems likely that insiders managed to obtain ownership of the best firms for themselves, except in the case of very large firms where they were unable to raise enough capital to purchase the assets from their own resources. Thus if one observes poor performance of firms owned by investment funds, relative to the group of all privatized firms, this may be explained by the fact that only the worse firms were made available to investment funds. A similar problem may apply to studies which suggest a better performance in firms taken over by foreign multinationals. In many cases, these were already the best firms in the economy, and the foreign multinationals therefore had a sound basis upon which to build with their investments.

There have been a number of studies which compare privatized and state-owned firms, but only recently have convincing results about the positive effects of privatization begun to emerge. The first major study was by Pinto *et al.* (1993), who used a survey of 75 large state-owned firms to explore the relationship between privatization prospects and restructuring. Theory suggests that the prospect of future privatization may be sufficient to induce good managers to reveal their abilities by successfully restructuring their state-owned firms. Pinto *et al.* confirmed that existing managers expected to keep their jobs post-privatization.

Most of the early studies failed to isolate any relationship between ownership form (private versus state) and the performance of firms. This finding emerges for example in Belka *et al.* (1994), Earle and Estrin (1997). The standard approach has been to include ownership type in regressions explaining productivity, the change in productivity or enterprise growth. The dummy variables for private ownership have almost always proved to be statistically insignificant. However, a few recent studies suggest privatization may be beginning to have an effect. Earle and Estrin (1997) find that privately-owned firms have a greater increase in productivity than state-owned firms in Russia in 1994. In Frydman *et al.* (1997), there is evidence from mid-sized firms in the Czech Republic, Hungary and Poland between 1990–94 that private ownership does improve company performance in terms of increasing revenue and reducing costs.

There are several interpretations of this very mixed evidence on the impact of privatization. One is that it is simply too early to make a judgment – the full effects of privatization may take many years to become established. The point is reinforced when one realizes that other aspects of the economic environment formed by firms were also changing rapidly, most notably the hardness of budget constraints. Several studies show that the hardening of budget constraints may have been a major source of improved corporate performance and productivity increases (see in particular Estrin, 1994; Alfaranderi and Schaffer, 1996).

An alternative interpretation is that privatization did not have the desired effects because ownership went into the hands of insiders, and that group cannot be expected to deliver significantly improved economic performance, relative to the state. The comparative performance of insider and state ownership is analysed in Earle and Estrin (1997), who suggest insiders may be equivalent to the state as owner, particularly in the areas of investment, and restructuring via employment reduction. Evidence is accumulating that the form of dominant ownership matters at least as much as whether the state or a private agent owned firms. Earle and Estrin (1997) report that in Russia insider owned firms increase productivity faster than outsider owners or the state, though it is managers rather than workers as dominant owners who play the significant role. However, outsiders appear to play a more positive role in Central Europe. The study by Zemplinerova (1997) highlights superior economic performance in firms which were foreign owned, or owned by a dominant investor while Djankov and Pohl (1997) find that strategic domestic investors are effective owners in the Czech Republic, Poland and Slovakia. Frydman *et al.* (1997) also find improved performance to stem primarily from outsider owners for their sample of Central European economies.

Finally, a study by Classens *et al.* (1997) explains the impact of institutional owners, notably Investment Funds. They looked at the relationship between ownership concentration and two outcome variables – profitability and Tobin's q (the ratio between market valuation and replacement cost of capacity) – in Czech privatized firms. They found that ownership concentration was increasing strongly over time, and that the significance of the concentration was increasing over time. Bank-related funds raised Tobin's q over and above the concentration variable, though it had no significant independent effect on profitability.

In conclusion, there have been a number of studies of the relationship between ownership and corporate performance in transition, but the results have so far been weak and rather mixed. Only in very recent studies are we beginning to see some evidence that privatization improves performance, and that outsider owned firms perform better than insider owned ones. The likely reason is the subject matter of this chapter, namely the weak governance mechanisms and capital market structures associated with outsider ownership via mass privatization.

CONCLUSIONS

Large-scale ownership by investment funds, generated in the course of mass privatization, may be less than ideal. Once a large, deep, liquid and efficient financial market is instituted, investment funds' involvement in corporate governance is neither likely nor necessary. Until then, with the exception of Poland where each enterprise privatized on the mass track is specifically assigned to the responsibility of a 'lead' fund, one should not expect investment funds to play a major role in the corporate governance of companies in which they invest, thus leaving greater scope for managerial discretion than was originally intended. Moreover, the unintended, residual leading role of state banks in the creation and ownership of investment funds might well exercise an adverse impact on the governance of funds and, indirectly, on the governance of companies.

At the same time, neither ideal solutions nor instant financial markets were available at the beginning of the transition. There is a theoretical presumption – until proven otherwise – that ownership by investment funds is probably better than insider ownership, and there is some evidence for this empirically. Moreover, the very limited evidence that is now emerging suggests that investment fund ownership may be associated with some improvement in enterprise performance, at least relative to other privatized firms.

NOTES

1. These definitions of mass, large scale and small privatization appear to be both widespread and sensible and will be adopted here, though there is some confusion in the literature. Mass privatization is sometimes used as a synonym for large-scale privatization, while voucher privatization is used to indicate what we call mass privatization (see Kotrba *et al.* in this volume). With reference to the Czech case, Takla (1994) uses large scale privatization to indicate voucher privatization. The World Development Report 1996 includes under Czech mass privatization also assets sold for cash; this reflects original government policy, for in 1991 CSFR large scale privatization was supposed to coincide with voucher privatization, but then additional methods were introduced – hence the confusion.

2. According to initial proposals, large-scale privatization was supposed to coincide with voucher privatization, but then the government decided not to use voucher privatization as the exclusive method for privatizating large-scale firms. This is the main reason why, in the literature on Czech privatization, there is confusion in the terminology as large-scale, vouchers, and mass privatization are sometimes used as synonyms.

3. The problem could have been avoided had the value of vouchers not been determined in advance in national currency, and had the calculations of the supply and demand side of the program been more accurate and coordinated in time. In Czechoslovakia the denomination of vouchers was in investment points, which had the advantage of eliminating expectations of redeeming vouchers at face value.

4. The differences in these regulations have crucially determined the proportion of capital that ended up being transferred, directly or indirectly, to investment funds, and consequently also the distribution of capital among different categories of new owners after privatization. Therefore they have fundamental implications also for corporate governance of privatized firms and of investment funds (see the next two sections).

5. There was only one exception to this general rule. If a firm was privatized through cash sales, it could then transfer, instead of shares, 20% of the proceeds to the Development Fund.

6. According to the general privatization scheme, another 20% had to be transferred to two government funds (the Pensions Fund and the Compensation Fund), whereas the remaining 40% could be privatized through an internal buyout at privileged terms or using other methods based on conventional sales.

7. Considering that privatizing enterprises in Slovenia represent 40% of GDP, and that 20–40% of their shares went in exchange for vouchers, mass privatization actually involved no more than 8–6% of Slovenian GDP, and even less in terms of total capital.

8. These characteristics of voucher schemes are only discussed briefly, as they are not directly relevant for issues of corporate governance.

9. Through the so-called internal distribution scheme, 20% of shares could be given to employees in exchange for their ownership certificates; in addition, certificates in excess of internal distribution could also be used in employee-management buyouts.

10. In the literature on the Czech Republic, these funds are most frequently referred to as 'investment privatization funds' (though officially called 'investment funds'); in Slovenia, as 'privatization investment funds' (though officially called 'authorized investment companies'); while in Poland, 'national investment funds' (corresponding to their official name). For convenience, we will refer to all these funds as privatization investment funds (PIFs).

11. The terminology is complicated further by the fact that companies which create and manage PIFs are referred to as 'investment companies' in the Czech Republic, and as 'authorized management companies' in Slovenia.

12. All funds were created by the Ministry of Privatization, acting on behalf of the State Treasury as the official founder, which, following state enterprise corporatization, initially owned all the enterprises included in the mass privatization program.

13. A unit trust is a closed-end fund.

14. A unit trust is a closed-end fund, which does not give its investors' voting rights. A mutual fund is an open-end investment fund, which gives investors the right to redeem the shares, but not voting rights. These forms are therefore similar with respect of investors lack of voting rights.

15. As a joint-stock company a PIF is owned by its shareholders, i.e., individuals investing their vouchers in the fund; this implies that they have voting rights and must be consulted on all important issues (mergers, acquisitions, etc.). If a PIF is founded as a mutual fund or unit trust, individual investors are unit holders without voting rights.

16. Indeed, Slovenian companies managing PIFs have jointly been resisting quotation of funds' shares, imposing informal rules which effectively hamper any competitive action (see Böhm in this volume). The main excuse for not registering PIF shares is the existence of the 'privatization gap' (i.e., vouchers overhang). Until this problem is resolved, it is clear that registering PIF shares would imply a low market price.

17. According to the April 1992 law on investment companies and investment funds, new investment funds are no longer required to be managed externally (Hashi, 1997: 6).

18. The program was designed to discourage supervisory boards of funds from managing the funds on their own. A fund, which would not employ a management firm, was 'punished' for being unaware of a special World Bank loan available only for the 'good' funds participating in the program. In addition, according to the 1993 law on investment funds, funds managing their assets without the help of a management firm are not eligible for a performance fee, unlike the externally managed funds (Lawniczak, 1996: 5).

19. Nevertheless, it is reported that there was little competition among management companies, as the number of those companies that participated in the tender was only marginally higher than the number of funds (see Lewandowski and Szyszko in this volume).

20. The limit of 20% of a fund's shareholding in a single company applies only to companies which are at the same time at least 10% owners of the fund's management company.

21. Investment companies setting up and running PIFs had discovered that a joint-stock company was expensive to administer, exposed them to the threat of hostile takeovers, and denied them full autonomy and discretion in the decision-making process (Hashi, 1997).

22. The largest 14 investment groups created a total of 71 funds, where the extreme case was Agrobanka, setting up 17 funds (Mladek, 1995: 76).

23. Thus by the time the new July 1996 regulations came into effect requiring statutory changes to be approved by the Ministry of Finance, 121 investment funds and 9 investment companies had already changed their status; and by April 1997, a further 32 funds changed their status after obtaining permission (Hashi, 1997: 14).

24. The national investment fund number 9 (the Eugeniusz Kwiatkowski Fund) has been managed without a management firm from the very beginning.

25. Harvard Capital and Consulting Investment Company was the third largest investment company in both waves and the only large private investment company without an apparent financial institution behind it.

26. Management contracts are concluded for a period of 10 years, but can be terminated at 180 days' notice.
27. For example, a management company is not allowed to own shares of any fund to which it is providing management services, without prior approval by the Anti-Monopoly Office.
28. The literature has also explored conflicts among owners, notably concerning securities with different combinations of control and cashflow claims (see e.g., Grossman and Hart, 1988, while the private benefits of control by a dominant owner have been studied empirically by Barclay and Holderness, 1989, with reference to the premium paid for a large block of shares).
29. Slovenian funds, incidentally, decide when they will be quoted on the stock exchange.

5. The Governance of Privatization Funds: Open Issues and Policy Recommendations

Marko Simoneti and Andreja Böhm

INTRODUCTION

Effective corporate governance is the key to the efficiency and restructuring of newly privatized enterprises in transitional economies in Central and Eastern Europe. Privatization funds are intended to provide a corporate governance solution to the problem of widely dispersed ownership in enterprises after mass privatization. They have emerged as the major external institutional shareholders – 'true' owners of the enterprises. They are expected to monitor management, undertake restructuring and eventually raise capital. But the privatization funds themselves exemplify the typical problems of corporate governance of public companies with diversified ownership structures. The fundamental question of their own governance therefore has to be addressed: 'Who will guard the guardians?'

Privatization funds are established to intermediate between voucher holders and companies in mass privatization programs. They are intended to mitigate between the two conflicting objectives of those programs: to reduce the risk for small investors by dispersing investments among several companies and to improve, by ownership consolidation, corporate governance of privatized companies. Effective governance of financial intermediaries requires that the fund managers are given the freedom and the right incentives to manage portfolios so as to maximize their values and so fund shareholders have adequate mechanisms to control the fund managers.

This chapter consists of four parts, which deal with the most critical issues of governance of privatization funds. The first discusses the structure of portfolios of privatization funds which is the critical source of their (in)effective governance and emphasizes the importance of the funds transformations. The second covers management contracts and management fees, which in principle represent the most direct mechanisms of shareholders' control and fund

managers' incentives. The third and fourth parts deal with the internal control
of fund shareholders ('the voice') and their external control ('the exit'). The
chapter draws extensively on relevant literature on institutional shareholders
in advanced market economies and makes comparisons of the privatization
funds in the Czech Republic, Slovenia and Poland.

PORTFOLIO STRUCTURE AND GOVERNANCE OF PRIVATIZATION FUNDS

Institutional shareholders can be distinguished by different investment policies
and contrasting portfolios structures which represent the key for setting up
their effective legal and regulatory frameworks. In compliance with the prevailing
investors, who are either short- or long-term, small or large, they either widely
disperse their investments in mostly liquid assets, or as long-term institutional
investors they concentrate investments in a small number of companies and
also invest in illiquid financial assets. Dispersed portfolio structures do not
ensure the active supervision of portfolio companies (which is often prohibited
in their case) but give incentives for active portfolio trading. Concentrated and
illiquid portfolio structures do not provide active portfolio trading but allow
and give incentives for active supervision and management of portfolio
companies (Kidwell *et al.,* 1993; Thygerson, 1993).

As to how investors control the fund managers, it is important, apart from
portfolio characteristics, whether the funds are established as open-end or
closed-end entities and if they are organized as joint-stock companies or not.
Open-end mutual funds typically do not have a legal personality and are
therefore subject to tighter regulatory supervision. They are obliged to redeem
property units directly to investors at any time. They trade simultaneously with
investment coupons and portfolio securities and their size depends on the exits
and entries of investors. Hence, the market price of coupons is in parity with
the portfolio values. Such funds have to comply with strict rules, which identify
what does and does not qualify as a proper investment for redemption. The
threat of diminishing size (and henceforth diminishing management fees) and
eventually the liquidation of the fund as a result of massive exit of unsatisfied
investors effectively forces the fund managers *ex ante* to perform. As the
investors of mutual funds who maximize benefits in the short run are largely
small, mutual funds themselves could not be large and long-term investors in
companies.

The rules for investments of closed-end investment funds, which are typically
organized as joint-stock companies, venture funds or financial holdings, are
less strict but at least the conditions for effective shareholder control must be
ensured. The number of shares of closed-end investment companies is fixed
and the shares are traded on the open markets at discounted prices in relation

to the portfolio values. This is less appropriate for the control of small investors as it does not provide for a liquid exit. The measure which disciplines the managers of institutional shareholders organized as a joint-stock company to perform is the threat of consolidation of large shareholders who have capacities and incentives to monitor more closely the managers and would terminate the management contract with the non-performing managers. Large shareholders typically maximize dividends and capital gains in the long run and, therefore, institutions owned by them can be themselves relatively large and long-term investors in the companies.

A large variety of approaches to designing and regulating privatization funds exists in the transitional economies. The 'top-down' Polish national investment funds have been designed as essentially restructuring holding companies with an elaborated system of rules for portfolio diversification and ownership concentration in individual enterprises. Experienced international investment managers selected on competitive bases are given strong incentives for restructuring while they are supervised by independent boards acting as fiduciaries of fund shareholders. A contrasting example is the 'bottom-up' Czech privatization investment funds. Allowed 'free entry' and being loosely regulated on the standard model of institutional investors with diversified portfolios, they primarily engage in passive portfolio management (i.e., trading of enterprise shares) but occasionally, as major shareholders or in coalition with other shareholders, are active on supervisory boards of enterprises. The entry of the Slovenian 'bottom-up' privatization funds has been more closely regulated, but with no restriction on ownership in individual enterprises while addressing typical situations of conflicts of interests. The choice of either a passive portfolio management or a more active involvement in the management of enterprises is left to the funds in Slovenia.

The advantage of the Polish 'top-down' approach to the creation of privatization funds is that the structuring of the portfolios and the selection of fund managers was done in a way to promote the fund role in active restructuring of the portfolio companies. On the other side, Polish national investment funds are initially 100% owned by the state and supervised by independent experts nominated by the state. In the Polish mass privatization program, restructuring of companies comes first and privatization of funds via distribution of shares to citizens comes second. This is a government-led restructuring program, where the positive effects of restructuring are privatized and distributed to the citizens at large in the second phase of the program. Due to the strong involvement of the government, the implementation of the program has been very slow and expensive in comparison to other mass privatization schemes in the region. The program was limited to a relatively small number of carefully selected middle-sized companies and the government appointees in the supervisory boards have been reportedly very reluctant to support painful restructuring measures in portfolio companies. In short, a well designed program provided capable private management groups with appropriate instruments and incentives for restructuring, but this potential was not fully utilized as the government kept an active role in the program for a long time.

The advantage of the 'bottom-up' approach to the creation of privatization funds in the Czech Republic and Slovenia is that the role of the government is limited to defining the institutional framework for funds operation and the licensing of fund managers. The program starts with privatization, whereby fund managers collect privatization vouchers to be later exchanged for privatization shares. Concentration of shares in companies and their restructuring takes place only in the second phase if the fund managers and fund shareholders are provided with the rules of the game and incentives, which support such activities. With the limited role of the government in the 'bottom-up' approach, the institutional framework for fund activities is even more important than in the 'top-down' approach. In addition, a great majority of all companies in the country were included in mass privatization in Slovenia and the Czech Republic, which made it practically impossible for the funds to later adjust their portfolios to the institutional framework provided by the law. It was, therefore, a serious mistake in these two countries that, contrary to the Polish case, so little attention was paid to the quality of privatized companies when defining the rules of the game for the operations of privatization funds.

Privatization models of various countries in transition led to a negative selection of enterprises that were offered to privatization funds. Most companies offered are underperforming and require substantial restructuring. In Slovenia, for example, better performing enterprises opted for internal buyouts and initial public offerings for certificates rather than for the transfer to privatization funds. In the Czech Republic, such enterprises reserved larger stakes for cash privatization. Moreover, the logistics of primary allocation of shares (i.e., the pricing policies) and several legal restrictions on primary investments included in funds laws or general privatization laws did not allow the funds to concentrate their stakes in portfolio companies already on voucher auctions. Only a few Czech privately sponsored funds pursued concentrated investment policies in auctions and continued such policy in secondary portfolio trading (Coffee, 1996). Nevertheless, Czech funds managed by the same managers cannot by law together hold stakes in companies larger than 20% (see Kotrba *et al.* in this volume).

Only in Poland have privatization funds become sufficiently large shareholders in companies to have incentives for their active management and restructuring. In all other countries, they have become large enough for shareholders to individually or in alliances make appointments to supervisory boards with other shareholders, but they do not have incentives to actively manage those companies. Even Polish 'lead' funds that hold 33% stakes in companies must negotiate with other shareholders on strategic decisions that require majority voting (see Lewandowski and Szyszko in this volume). All

Polish funds together have 60% stakes in individual companies. In the Czech Republic, a number of funds managed by different companies could in principle own total companies according to the 'large privatization law'. But the maximum acquired joint shareholding is about 80%, whereas on average the funds hold together 40% shares in companies. In Slovenia, the legal privatization scheme allowed one or all funds together to acquire 20% stakes of companies or 40% if the shares acquired by two state funds are also included (see Rems in this volume). Namely, state funds have concluded an agreement on cooperation with privatization funds on secondary trading of shares within the 40% limits and on common standards for corporate governance activities in companies.

In all three countries, privatization funds began with portfolio trading immediately after privatization. It would be difficult, though, to give any definite view on their secondary trading, whether it is intended as income (or cashflow) maximization or as adjustment of portfolio structures for either passive or active portfolio management. Secondary portfolio trading of Polish funds is obviously intended to reduce the number of companies in portfolios by selling off minority stakes thus enhancing the capability of funds to actively restructure the remaining companies. There are numerous cases of selling off fund portfolio assets cheaply in the Czech Republic (see Kotrba *et al.* in this volume). In Slovenia, there are no direct legal constraints (as in the Czech Republic) preventing funds from consolidating stakes in companies for their active control, but secondary trading of privatization shares has generally been severely limited. Indeed, privatization funds could in principle play an important role in improving the corporate governance of companies after privatization by selling their stakes to strategic buyers or by buying stakes from other shareholders to consolidate their own stakes in companies. Such corporate control transactions need to be promoted rather than constrained after mass privatization (Simoneti, 1998).

A general question is what can and should the fund managers do with the privatization shares to keep or add to the value of the property for the shareholders? They have at least three possibilities: (i) passive ownership and trading with listed securities, (ii) active supervision of portfolio companies, and (iii) active restructuring of portfolio companies in which they hold larger stakes. While it was perhaps realistic to initially expect that privatization funds would operate as diversified institutional investors in Slovenia and the Czech Republic, it later became obvious that they would not be able to do so. It is objectively not possible for fund managers effectively to manage the entrusted property by active trading with unlisted securities. Given the size of the mass privatization programs in Slovenia and the Czech Republic, there is practically insufficient maneuvering room to allow the majority of funds to adjust their portfolio structures in order to operate as diversified institutional investors in listed securities in the long run. Inevitably, they would have to transform and start behaving as active owners of portfolio companies. However, the funds' active management of companies would require: (i) a different organizational set up, (ii) different incentives for managers, and (iii) different authorities of the supervisory agency. By insisting that the privatization funds operate as diversified institutional investors under the supervision of the agency, a false impression is maintained that the shareholders are well protected, although the managers cannot and do not do anything useful for them except charge high fees.

The present organizational set-up is inadequate even for those privatization funds which will operate in the long run as passive institutional investors. Typical closed-end funds, which invest in domestic securities, practically no longer exist in developed market economies, precisely because that form does not provide effective protection of small investors (Herzfeld, 1993). Formally, small investors have voting rights but because of widely dispersed ownership they are entirely powerless in relation to the fund managers. Possibilities of enhancing the role of supervisory boards in overseeing the fund managers are only theoretical due to dispersed ownership. As the exit of investors from the closed-end funds is via the market, in the case of poor managers' performance, the market price of fund shares would fall significantly below NAV and investors would have to absorb large capital losses.

The open-end funds have an entirely different logic of control and operation. Investors can exit from one fund and enter into another one at any time and there is continuous competition among the fund managers for existing and new investors. Successful funds record net entries and thereby the basis of managers' fees is increased. Unsuccessful funds record net exits and thereby the fees are decreased as they are forced to sell off listed securities and progressively they can be eliminated altogether from the competition for investors. The supervisory authorities oversee the structure of investments to ensure the high liquidity of open-end funds, and for the accurate calculation of NAV. The entry and exit prices for investors and the managers' fees are based on the NAV. The interests of managers and shareholders are mutually consistent and there is neither incentive nor the possibility of manipulating the NAV (Simoneti, 1998). Supervisory authorities only perform the type of supervision which they can effectively enforce. Recently, the characteristics of open-end and closed-end funds have tended to converge in the case of the funds which are open in intervals. Such interval funds provide for a better protection of investors, i.e., exit at pre-fixed intervals. At the same time, they allow for less liquid investments which bear higher returns.

In developed financial markets, there is widespread evidence that the only effective protection of investors in portfolio funds is the possibility of claiming redemption directly from the fund managers, which threatens ineffective managers with smaller sized portfolios as the result of net exits. In that sense, if the privatization funds are transformed into closed-end investment funds, they will continue facing the same type of problems they face now. Governance of privatization funds will solve that inherent problem which characteristically applies to all forms of closed-end funds. The solution would have to find a way to provide for the effective exit of shareholders. The underdeveloped capital market and large proportion of unlisted securities in portfolios of privatization funds represent serious constraints for ensuring continuous competition among the fund managers for the existing and potential investors. But this is not entirely impossible. The following premises would apply for various forms of closed-end funds (privatization funds and normal investment funds):

(i)   Management fees should not be calculated as a percentage of NAV but as a percentage of market values of funds' shares, which are listed on the organized market. Alternatively, the fees could be defined as a percentage of a fund's income. Such changes would ensure mutual coherence between the interests of fund managers and shareholders and would reduce the interest of fund managers to manipulate the NAV.

(ii) Shareholders of privatization funds would have the possibility, in addition to selling shares on the organized market, to shift in intervals (e.g., a few times per year) to any privatization fund managed by other management companies. Those shifts would take place automatically at the nominal values of shares, as the re-capitalization of the entering funds with the shares of the exiting funds. The funds which record new entries would become partial owners of the funds recording the respective exits, and would have the opportunity to change their management. This possibility of shifting investors would be available only as long as privatization funds are not transformed.

(iii) The shareholders of the funds that have already been transformed into ordinary closed-end investment funds, should also have the opportunity to change managers when the gap between NAV and market values of fund shares is wide. The solutions must be based on the principle of the equal possibility for all shareholders considering that the funds' investments are generally not liquid. One possibility could be to mandate compulsory and automatic opening of all those funds with market prices of shares falling significantly below NAV. Technically, such automatic openings would have to be accomplished in a way that poor liquidity of a portfolio would be fully taken into account, i.e., with partial opening, with opening in intervals or with redemption of big shareholders directly from the property of the fund. A less risky possibility where there are large discrepancies between market prices and NAV would be a mandatory and automatic tender for new fund managers.

The above premises would significantly increase competition for investors amongst the funds, diminish the interests that privatization funds continue in their present form indefinitely and also that they are transformed into ordinary closed-end investment funds. On the other hand, the interest in transforming them into open-end funds and ordinary joint-stock companies (financial holdings) would be increased. Both institutions prevail in advanced market economies. This is exactly the aim of the proposed approach: closed-end funds should not be the organizational rule but rather an exception in countries in transition in the long run because of the institutional weaknesses of that form.

Recent proposed amendments to the law on privatization funds in Slovenia adopt an entirely different approach to the transformation of privatization funds: transformation into financial holding is first prohibited and later severely constrained with restrictive regulations and procedures. The strategy implied in the proposed amendments is to promote transformation of privatization funds into ordinary closed-end funds, which would continue to operate under the agency's supervision. Closed-end funds with peculiar investment structures would thus exist for a long time. The protagonists of this approach implicitly support the opinion that the supervision of the Agency over fund operations brings more benefits to the shareholders than would have accrued to them from active management of portfolio companies. The institutional form of privatization funds with all the restrictions on portfolio structures, credit financing, managers' rewards, ownership consolidation, public reporting and agency supervision is completely inadequate to motivate active supervision of companies and even less to motivate the active participation of funds in companies' restructuring. Restricting such transformation, as a matter of principle, would be absurd when it is widely supported by informed shareholders that the financial holding would be the most appropriate institutional form for preserving their property.

While transformation into ordinary closed-end funds would entail an *ex ante* adjustment in the structure of investments, the transformation into a holding company would require *ex ante* adjustment in the structure of ownership. No legal constraints exist which would impede the adjustment of investment structures, as it was already initially contemplated that privatization funds would be gradually transformed into ordinary diversified institutional investors (Simoneti, 1998). It should be recognized that real life has proven to be different from what was originally expected and that the transformation of privatization funds into holdings should be facilitated. The valid legislation does not allow the *ex ante* concentration in ownership required for taking the decision on transforming into holding. It would, therefore, have to be changed. There should be no concern that the transformed privatization funds would perform poorly since most shares would be bought by management companies and their sponsors and the decision-makers would thus risk their own property. The problem is the non-transparent way of such transformation on the gray market, which therefore needs to be adequately and promptly regulated.

Large privatization funds would face major problems in transformation, as objectively they would find it more difficult to adjust their structures because of the large number of shareholders on the one hand, and the large values of investments on the other. In order to benefit from the restructuring potentials of large funds, the idea of transforming privatization funds by splitting portfolios should be given full support. The minor listed part of their portfolios would be used to transform into open-end funds and the larger unlisted part would be transferred into financial holdings. The shareholders of the former privatization funds would become investors in the same proportion in the new institutions. The institutions that would emerge after the transformation, with the split of portfolios, would be in standard forms – open-end fund or financial holding organized as public joint-stock company.

Privatization funds are hybrid and transitional institutions because of their peculiar structure of portfolios. They therefore cannot stay in the present form for long and their transformation is an imperative. They must, however, be properly regulated to ensure that the interests of the shareholders are not abused while the managers should be given adequate incentives for effective management of the portfolio.

The Polish program of mass privatization has a limited duration of ten years which is also the life span of the respective privatization funds. The management consortia are given clear incentives for restructuring and selling off total portfolios within that time (see Lewandowski and Szyszko in this volume). In Slovenia, the law states that the privatization funds have to adjust their portfolios in five years or convert themselves into ordinary joint-stock companies. In the Czech Republic no deadlines for the transformation of privatization funds were initially given (see Kotrba *et al.* in this volume). The common practice in both countries is transformation of privatization funds into ordinary joint-stock companies by nontransparent voting in the assemblies. Specific rules for that voting ought be defined as a special precaution for protecting shareholder interests. It would be correct that a high quorum be required and that management companies would be prohibited to act as the proxies of small shareholders. Nevertheless, it may be more important to provide for the exit of unsatisfied shareholders on the organized market prior to transformation and for the transparent *ex ante* concentration of shares by those who are interested to risk their money investing in funds and will, therefore, be highly motivated to monitor their managers.

In all these countries, ownership consolidation of privatization funds is already underway but unlike in Poland it occurs in a nontransparent and non-regulated way in the Czech Republic and Slovenia. In Poland, fund managers have no real interest to purchase additional shares of funds as the initial structure of incentives has been set up in a way to promote restructuring of companies. In the other two countries, shares of privatization funds are reportedly, directly or indirectly, acquired by the companies managing them. The investors and regulators are not fully aware of the motives of management companies and their sponsors to take control over privatization funds, particularly if the sponsors are commercial banks. Should the development of an Anglo-Saxon type of corporate governance and finance system based on liquid securities markets and institutional investors or a German type of such system relying on strong universal banks capable of direct control over management be encouraged? Mass privatization programs and privatization funds have set a basis for market-based systems. Since many privatization funds are, by direct ownership or indirectly by ownership of management companies, controlled by banks, the bank-based system is likely to prevail in the end despite the fact that initially a strong economic rationale exists for a market-based system (Simoneti, 1997).

The regulation of ownership consolidation of privatization funds ought to take into account the inherent conflict of interests between the lending and investment businesses of commercial banks as sponsors of privatization funds. The problem is not new for the universal banking system and strict banking supervision is the appropriate solution for that type of conflict of interests that is inherent for such systems that appear to be emerging in transitional economies. The concentration of ownership of privatization funds by management companies and their sponsors should be encouraged as a way of improving the structure of incentives for active management of portfolio companies, but at the same time the banking supervision ought to be strengthened in order to minimize potential conflicts of interests and to avoid a surge of systemic risks that are inherent in cross-ownership structures.

MANAGEMENT CONTRACTS AND FEES

Management contracts and management fees represent mechanisms for the most direct control of fund managers and to tailor the incentives to the managers to motivate specific portfolio management.

In transitional economies, long-term management contracts and upper limits on fixed management fees have been intended as measures for protecting small shareholders and giving incentives to the fund managers in the initial non-competitive markets (Coffee, 1996). They are, however, most evidently the major flaws in the legal framework of privatization funds. Long-term contracts have effectively closed the markets to new entrants and impeded competition amongst the existing management companies.

The main impetus for competitive markets of fund managers are short-term management contracts which can be terminated immediately at no major cost to the shareholders in case of proven manager frauds or non-performance. Regular annual renewal of contracts is a norm in such markets. The survey in Slovenia revealed that about 85% of all management contracts of privatization funds are either indefinite or long-term ones (see Jašovič in this volume), although two thirds of the responding members of supervisory boards strongly support short-term contracts. About one half of all interviewed board members believe that the management contract serves as an effective mechanism for shareholder control (see Böhm in this volume). The survey with the management companies of privatization funds pointed out that management contracts of about 40% of Slovenian privatization funds include high indemnities or require large majority voting for their termination (see Jašovič in this volume). Such statutory or contractual self-defenses of fund managers are strictly prohibited elsewhere in the world.

Management contracts of Polish national investment funds were concluded for the total ten-year period of the mass privatization program. The supervisory boards have the legal authority to terminate them at any time with two months' notice. They have to justify the reasons for termination and the management companies have in principle time to adjust. All the attempts of supervisory boards to terminate management contracts have so far been futile, resulting instead in the dismissal of the board president. Interestingly, the only fund that did not sign a management contract became the target of a takeover by another. The view is held in Poland that it may be easier for the management consortia to terminate contracts than for the supervisory boards (see Lewandowski and Szyszko in this volume).

Given the non-competitive market in Slovenia, it could be predicted that all management companies would charge the highest permissible management fees, i.e., 3% of NAV. More than two thirds of interviewed members of supervisory boards agreed that competition would reduce management fees and almost all of them argued that the management fees need to be annually approved by the assemblies or supervisory boards.

In the Czech Republic, the maximum allowed management fee is 2% of NAV, but the actually charged fees range between 1.5% and 1.75% (see Kotrba *et al.* in this volume) which is proof that there is some competition among management companies, i.e., despite long-term management contracts. In Poland, fixed fees range between 1.5% and 4% of NAV and are charged in addition to reimbursable costs and generous performance fees. Polish management fees are the highest in the region. Relatively high fixed fees provide evidence that there was not much competition in the international tender for the management of Polish privatization funds. Performance fees and reimbursable costs have been carefully structured to give strong incentives to fund managers for the successful restructuring and sale (i.e., privatization) of portfolio companies. Performance fees represent a percentage of realized capital gains, meaning that the company shares must be sold for their payment (see Lewandowski and Szyszko in this volume). But, on the other hand, as management fees are the key ingredient of long-term management contracts it would be impossible to modify them in any way later on.

Fixed fees as lump sums have been widely proven as inappropriate incentives for the active management of portfolio companies or improving managers' performance. In Slovenia, they serve in fact as a strong incentive for passivity of the fund managers, since the managers' profits are maximized by minimizing operational and management costs. But 3% of NAV is a high percentage in itself in comparison to the fixed fees of Western closed-end investment companies, which are on average 0.6% of NAV and range from 0.25% up to 1% (Kidwell *et al.*, 1993). Given that economies of scale exist, larger funds charge smaller percentage amounts (i.e., on the basis of larger NAV). In addition, about 0.5% of NAV represents reimbursable cost (Kidwell *et al.*, 1993). The supervisory agency exercises control over them and approves increases in certain costs which may entail reduced market competition (Pessin, 1990). Two thirds of respondents in Slovenia agreed that a larger part of management fees should consist of reimbursable costs to be approved by supervisory boards.

Moreover, NAV represents the appropriate basis for calculating the fees of managers of open-end mutual funds as it provides an incentive for improved performance of funds by way of extending the size of the funds and increasing their efficiency (i.e., cost reduction). But NAV is less appropriate as an incentive for short-term improved performance of managers of closed-end investment companies in a short run. Since NAV can be increased basically with capital gains, long-term performance fees as a percentage of capital gains would motivate improved performance of managers of closed-end investment companies. In the short run, market prices of fund shares may be more appropriate than NAV for calculating the management fees as the fund managers would be in the same position as the existing shareholders.

As, in Slovenia, on average about 80% of fund portfolio companies are not quoted on organized markets, NAV is largely an accounting figure consisting of grossly overvalued book values of companies. NAV is not only the source of excessive management fees but it is in no way related to the fund managers' performance and therefore could not serve as an incentive for improving the performance of fund managers.

In Poland, about one quarter of 500 portfolio companies of privatization funds are already quoted and the market prices of funds shares are in close parity with NAVs (see Lewandowski and Szyszko in this volume). But different reasons could account for these prices. Since the quoted companies are obviously the better performing ones, NAVs are still likely to be overvalued. Therefore, a more likely reason is the high demand for funds shares which indeed are one of the most liquid securities traded on the highly regulated Warsaw Stock Exchange (see Lewandowski and Szyszko in this volume). The most likely reason for such strong demand is the expected high capital gain due to stronger incentives given to fund managers, and the greater restructuring potential of Polish funds due to their specific portfolio characteristics. In the Czech Republic, both funds shares and portfolio shares are quoted on organized markets, albeit less regulated than the Polish ones. The fund shares are traded with 20%–80% price discounts to NAVs (see Kotrba *et al.* in this volume) which can be definitively ascribed to different performances of fund managers.

If management fees are fixed then the management contracts can be fairly standardized and their supervision is just a matter of routine. Management contracts of active institutional shareholders are on the other hand highly contingent. Performance fees and reimbursable costs are the key ingredient of such contracts. For conclusion and monitoring of contingent contracts strong owners or strong supervisory boards are required since the asymmetry of information in active management of portfolio companies is wide and the management companies can agree on unrealistic targets to maximize performance fees. Moreover, such contracts offer wide possibilities for insider trading and other frauds by fund managers, which investors would hardly be able to control.

The management contracts of Polish privatization funds were designed as contingent contracts. The Polish government appointed the first supervisory boards exactly to negotiate and conclude those management contracts. Members of supervisory boards had to prove professional competence for the task by passing an exam and also had at their disposal detailed information on the companies. Nevertheless, overseeing the implementation of the contracts would require active shareholders of privatization funds that have already begun emerging in the secondary markets of fund shares.

INTERNAL CONTROL OF SHAREHOLDERS BY VOICE

Two basic corporate governance models are commonly quoted in the literature – German and Anglo-Saxon. They developed as the result of different constraints on financing and ownership of companies in two environments. In large American and British public corporations, institutional investors are in the minority and their stakes are typically smaller than those of institutional shareholders in those German corporations which have also offered shares to small shareholders. In both models, internal and external controls have a different importance and function in entirely different ways. There are practically no takeovers in the German model but internal control (proxy voting and supervisory boards) is firm due to strong owners. In the Anglo-Saxon world, boards of directors can only be replaced through the market.

In public joint-stock companies, internal and external control must co-exist. In order that the 'raiders' who have been acquiring shares from unsatisfied small shareholders on the market would take over control (i.e., terminate the management contract or dismiss top management) they have to have a sufficient 'voice' in the assemblies. Relative importance of external and internal controls depends on specific ownership structures. It varies depending on whether the owners are dispersed small shareholders or also include large institutional shareholders. The identity of owners is also important. Are they short-term or long-term shareholders and especially who are the large shareholders and what are their capacities and incentives to control the managers?

All strategic matters such as changes and amendments to statutes and management contracts, dismissal of supervisory boards, termination of management contracts, major changes in investment policies, change of legal status etc., require the approval of shareholders and hence voting in the assemblies. Such decisions are taken by majority vote.

The shareholders of privatization funds are small investors who are typically passive and do not vote. They have neither the incentives nor means to undertake the collection of proxy votes. German banks which have their own stakes in the companies and serve as the custodians of small shareholders act as their proxies in assemblies. Elsewhere in the world, small investors do not have such effective aligned shareholders and therefore their votes could easily be abused by raiders or management if their interests are not effectively protected by enforcing the rules for proxy contests and voting.

Most management companies of privatization funds in Slovenia collected both vouchers and general proxy statements from citizens that were valid for one and a half years. The survey of management companies confirms that in 60% of privatization funds they serve as proxies of shareholders (see Jašovič in this volume). Since the law does not define the conflicts of interests for persons serving as proxies of small shareholders and it also does not require the presence of any quorum for voting on strategic matters, representatives of management companies reportedly serve as proxies of fund shareholders and take such strategic decisions with votes representing a small percentage of the total share capital.

German two-tier boards are effective because of strong owners or banks which appoint members of supervisory boards, and which in turn appoint managers. Nobody can serve at the same time in external supervisory boards and in internal management teams, as a way of ensuring their mutual independence. The independence of one-tiered Anglo-Saxon boards of directors is less clear-cut. External directors are selected by internal directors and there is mutual loyalty and financial dependence among them. Nevertheless, both external and internal directors are appointed and dismissed by assemblies. In order to enhance boards' independence, the number of external directors is constantly increased in relation to the number of internal directors and various board committees (e.g., appointment, auditing) being set up. Moreover, precise duties of internal and external directors are provided in laws and contracts, meaning that the shareholders have at least formal possibilities of suing them in relatively effective courts.

The procedure for appointing members of the first supervisory boards of privatization funds in Slovenia was similar to the Anglo-Saxon practice. Given the 'bottom-up' origin of privatization funds, candidates for board members were selected by management companies and the names were advertised in prospectuses. In this way, the selection of supervisory board members was formally approved by the shareholders. But most citizens took no notice of those candidates and invested their vouchers in response to the marketing campaigns mounted by management companies. Since the candidates were later appointed members of the first supervisory boards the question of who the members feel accountable to – to the management companies or to the shareholders – is relevant. According to the survey, almost all members feel accountable to the shareholders, only very few (5%) to the management companies and none to the government or society at large.

A comparison with the procedure for appointment of the first supervisory boards of privatization funds in Poland is interesting despite the different 'top-down' origin of Polish funds. The first supervisory boards were appointed by the government. The members were later re-appointed in the first assemblies of shareholders. But through secondary trading of fund shares, new shareholders have already begun replacing members of the first boards with their own representatives (see Lewandowski and Szyszko in this volume).

The independence of supervisory boards from the government could not be questioned in Slovenia and the Czech Republic and this is the advantage of the 'bottom-up' origin of privatization funds. Due to the postponement of funds' quotation in Slovenia, shareholders have no exit and the board members cannot be dismissed on the initiative of new shareholders. Management companies had selected supervisory boards that were to monitor them and supervisory boards in turn concluded management contracts with the same management companies that had selected them. A vicious circle of interdependence between management companies and supervisory boards has thus been established in Slovenia. In that sense, the supervisory boards can be dismissed only by the management companies.

The professional competence of members is an important requirement for independence, but it is no guarantee of it. For example, the members of Polish boards were highly qualified and professionally competent, but their appointments were made more on political grounds. They are frequently referring to ministers. Since the change of government, the boards have lost political support and become quite controversial. They are beginning to gain credibility in controlling management consortia when the members appointed by the government are replaced by representatives of fund shareholders (see Lewandowski and Szyszko in this volume).

The effectiveness of supervisory boards could be enhanced by technical and procedural improvements. Recent experience has shown that supervisory boards also play a role in public companies with diverse ownership in Slovenia when managers do not perform. But it has also been widely evidenced that supervisory boards can be dismissed and new ones appointed to replace the non-performing management only by large inside investors. In order to allow active owners of privatization funds to be consolidated, privatization funds ought to be listed on organized markets.

EXTERNAL CONTROL OF SHAREHOLDERS BY EXIT

The most effective control small shareholders have in companies with diverse ownership is by selling shares, threatening the managers with takeover (or consolidation of active owners). Therefore, the interests of small shareholders are best protected if companies are listed on organized markets. In such markets, companies are required regularly to disclose information on the performances and share prices, and takeovers or consolidation of ownership takes place in a transparent way with full protection of the small shareholders.

Only a few German corporations that offered shares to small shareholders, are listed on stock exchanges, as small shareholders are already adequately protected by custodian banks, which control voting in assemblies and supervisory boards. On the other hand, hostile takeovers are relatively rare in Anglo-Saxon countries too, in comparison with the large number of companies listed. Moreover, takeovers are much easier and cheaper in small companies as taking over large stakes in large companies requires considerable falls in prices so that large shareholders are willing to take larger risks. Quotation of companies on organized markets is a *sine qua non* condition for managers' competition, which in turn is the guarantee that they will observe shareholders' interests. While market values of shares accurately reflect the performances and values on developed liquid markets, on the less liquid emerging markets the comparison of share prices of companies within the same industry is already an indication of their different performances.

The Polish national investment funds have been listed on the highly organized and regulated Warsaw Stock Exchange since the very beginning by way of exchanging certificates for shares on that market. The Czech investment privatization funds have been quoted on the organized (albeit less transparent) OTC markets from the very start also by extending the system of voucher auctions to post-privatization securities markets. Until recently, none of the Slovenian privatization funds has yet been quoted on the organized market, several years after their establishment.

The management companies in Slovenia vigorously resist the quotation of privatization funds on formal markets using the argument that, because the fact that the government is offering to bolster supply to fill the privatization gap is not publicly known, market share prices would be too low. The shares of privatization funds are being traded at very low prices on the gray markets anyway and the most common buyers are reportedly management companies. The shares of funds would in principle trade at higher prices in formal markets. There is widespread evidence of such assignments across the world, including in Poland where prices have continuously increased as the trading of certificates and funds' shares is shifting to more regulated markets (see Lewandowski and Szyszko in this volume).

Market quotation is a necessary condition for effective external control of shareholders but it is not sufficient in itself. Several legal restrictions on fund ownership have been intended as standard measures for protecting small shareholders. Such restrictions are justifiable when companies are floated on highly liquid markets and a concentration of shareholding can impede the liquid exits of small shareholders. In the case of privatization funds, such restrictions may even have a counter effect. It could be argued that consolidation of active owners would be beneficial for the liquid exits of small shareholders. Namely, shareholders would sell at higher prices, ownership consolidation would take place in a transparent way and, consequently, internal control would be enhanced.

By law, shareholders of privatization funds in Slovenia cannot be management companies, their sponsors (banks and insurance companies) and other privatization funds, in order to prevent cross-ownership and conflicts of interest. Reportedly, they are the main buyers of fund shares on the gray market and are most interested in acquiring control over them. Similar legal restrictions on the ownership of privatization funds in the Czech Republic have forced management companies to redeem the shares through legal entities related to their sponsors and the emerging corporate control of Czech funds is therefore not very transparent.

A rather unpredicted outcome of the Polish mass program is the discovery at the exchange of certificates for fund shares that one fund has already acquired 10% of another fund during the secondary trading of certificates. The Polish law does not impose any restrictions on fund ownership and in fact promotes the gradual consolidation of active owners who would be in a better position to control fund managers in their intended active management of portfolio companies. But the law details the procedure for ownership consolidation by requiring public disclosures for each 10% acquisition during the first three years and a mandatory tender offer when the 30% threshold is reached. Thus, ownership consolidation takes place in a transparent and orderly way, and the emerging shareholders' control of funds is also transparent.

By abolishing restrictions on the ownership of privatization funds in Slovenia, strong incentives would be given to management companies for the quotation of funds. The secondary trading with funds' shares would then shift from the gray markets to organized markets and control acquisitions of funds would become transparent and could be regulated.

CONCLUSION

The main reason for the lack of effective governance of privatization funds is their institutional structure, which is in many respects not appropriate for the various tasks of portfolio companies. In the Czech Republic and Slovenia, the funds are to be active in the supervising and restructuring of many non-listed companies. The adopted institutional framework for the closed-end diversified institutional investors in listed securities is not appropriate for the required shareholders' activism by the funds. This framework restricts and gives limited incentives to fund managers for the active restructuring of portfolio companies that would accrue benefits to fund shareholders. First, the effective exercise of ownership rights of funds in the portfolio companies with the possibilities of active trading of listed shares or with the possibilities for block voting with non-listed shares would have to be assured (as in Poland). In other words, stronger accountability of company managers to the funds is the precondition for the enhanced accountability of fund managers to their shareholders.

The second reason for the current lack of internal and external controls by fund shareholders can to a great extent be accounted for by the poor conditions of corporate governance in general in transitional economies: (i) shareholders who emerged in mass privatization programs are not yet accustomed to exercising their ownership rights either by exit or by voice, (ii) developed securities markets as a precondition for effective control of shareholders by exit do not yet exist, and (iii) concentration of ownership after free distribution of shares to citizens as a precondition for effective internal control of shareholders by voice has not yet been completed. The importance of those limitations will be gradually diminished as economic transition progresses. But currently there are still many regulations which restrict both trading and the concentration of privatization funds' shares and impede the development of effective mechanisms for their governance.

References and Bibliography

Aghion, P., O. Blanchard and R. Burgess (1994), 'The Behaviour of State Firms in Eastern Europe, Pre-privatisation', *European Economic Review,* **38**, 1327–49.

Aghion, P., O. Blanchard and W. Carlin (1994), 'The Economics of Enterprise Restructuring in Central and Eastern Europe', *CEPR Discussion Paper,* No. 1058.

Alfaranderi, G. and M. Schaffer (1996), 'Arrears in the Russian Enterprise Sector', in S. Commander, Q. Fan and M. E. Schaffer (eds), *Enterprise Restructuring and Economic Policy in Russia,* EDI Development Study 16137, Washington DC: The World Bank.

Aoki, M. and H.-J. Kim (eds) (1995), *Corporate Governance in Transitional Economies: Insider Control and the Role of Banks.* Washington DC: The World Bank.

Barclay, M. J. and C. G. Holderness (1989), 'Private Benefits from the Control of Public Corporations', *Journal of Financial Economics,* **25**, 371–97.

Baums, T., R. M. Buxbaum and K. J. Hopt (eds) (1994), *Institutional Investors and Corporate Governance,* Berlin and New York: Walter de Gruyter.

Begg, D. (1991), 'Economic Reform in Czechoslovakia: Should We Believe in Santa Klaus?', *Economic Policy,* **13**, October.

Belka, M., M. Schaffer, S. Estrin and I. Singh (1994), 'Evidence from a Survey of State-Owned, Privatized, and Emerging Private Firms', paper presented at Workshop on Enterprise Adjustment in Eastern Europe, 22–23 September, Washington DC: The World Bank.

Blair, M. M. (1995), *Ownership and Control: Rethinking Corporate Governance for the 21st Century,* Washington DC: Brookings Institution.

Blanchard, O., R Dornbusch, P. Krugman, R. Layard and L. Summers (1991), *Reform in Eastern Europe,* Cambridge, MA: MIT Press.

Böhm, A. (ed.) (1997), *Economic Transition Report 1996,* Ljubljana: C.E.E.P.N.

Boycko, M., A. Shleifer and R. Vishny (1996), 'A Theory of Privatization', *Economic Journal,* **106**, 309–19.

Brancato, C. K. (1997), *Institutional Investors and Corporate Governance: Best Practices for Increasing Corporate Value,* Chicago and London: R. D. Irwin Inc.

Carlin, W. and M. Landesmann (1997), 'From Theory into Practice? Corporate Restructuring and Economic Dynamism in Transition Economies', March, mimeographed.

CERGE-EI (1993), Annual Report, 1992–1993, Prague: Fund of National Property of the Czech Republic.

Cermak, P. (1997), 'Economic Transition in the Czech Republic – 1996', in A. Böhm (ed.), *Economic Transition Report 1996,* Ljubljana: C.E.E.P.N.

Classens, S. and S. Djankov (1997), 'Politicians and Firms: Evidence from Seven Central and Eastern European Countries', Washington DC: The World Bank, mimeographed.

Classens, S., S. Djankov and G. Pohl (1997), 'Ownership and Corporate Governance: Evidence from the Czech Republic', Washington DC: The World Bank, mimeographed.

Coffee, J. C. (1996), 'Institutional Investors in Transitional Economies – Lessons from the Czech Experience', in R. Frydman, C.W. Gray and A. Rapaczynski (eds), *Corporate Governance in Central Europe and Russia*, Budapest: Central European University Press.

Czech Statistical Office (1993), 'Statistical Yearbook of the Czech Republic 1993', Prague.

Czech Statistical Office (1995), 'Statistical Yearbook of the Czech Republic 1995', Prague.

Demb, A. and F. F. Neubauer (1992), *The Corporate Board: Confronting the Paradoxes,* Oxford: Oxford University Press.

Dimovski, V. (1995), 'Upravljanje investicijskih skladov: ekonomski vidiki upravljanja', in *Zbornik tretjega letnega sreèanja Zveze ekonomistov,* Ljubljana: pp. 105–15.

Djankov, S. and G. Pohl (1997), 'Restructuring of Large Firms in Slovakia', March, mimeographed.

Earle, J. and S. Estrin (1996), 'Employee Ownership in Transition', in R. Frydman *et al.* (eds), *Corporate Governance in Central Europe and Russia,* London and New York: Central European University Press.

Earle, J. S. and S. Estrin (1997), 'After Voucher Privatization: The Structure of Corporate Ownership in Russian Manufacturing Industry', June, mimeographed.

EBRD – European Bank for Reconstruction and Development (1997), 'Transition Report (1995, 1997)', London.

Ellerman, D. (1997), 'Voucher Privatization with Investment Funds: A Reappraisal', mimeographed.

Estrin, S. (ed.) (1994), *Privatization in Central and Eastern Europe,* London and New York: Longman.

Estrin, S. and J. Earle (1996), 'Employee Self-management in Transitional Economies', mimeographed, forthcoming in *Advances in the Economic Analysis of Participatory and Labor-Managed Firms* (1998), Greenwich and London: JAI Press.

Estrin, S., A. Gelb, and I. J. Singh (1993), 'Restructuring Viability and Privatization: A Comparative Study on Enterprise Adjustment in Transition', Washington DC: The World Bank, mimeographed.

Estrin, S., D. M. Nuti and M. Uvalic (1997), 'The Impact of Investment Funds on Corporate Governance in Mass Privatization Schemes: Czech Republic, Poland and Slovenia', Ljubljana: C.E.E.P.N: ACE Research Project, mimeographed.

Estrin, S. and R. Stone (1996), 'A Taxonomy of Mass Privatization', *Transition*, Vol. 7, Nos. 11–12, December, pp. 8–9, Washington DC: The World Bank

Fabozzi J. F., F. Modigliani and M. Ferri (1994), *Foundations of Financial Markets and Institutions*, Englewood Cliffs: Prentice-Hall International.

Fabozzi, J. F. and F. Modigliani (1994), *Financial Markets and Institutions*, Englewood Cliffs, New Jersey: Prentice-Hall Inc.

Foley, B. J. (1991), *Capital Markets*, Hampshire: Bernard J. Foley.

Fredman, J. A. and R. Wiles (1993), *How Mutual Funds Work*, New York: Institute of Finance.

Frydman, R. and A. Rapaczynski (1991), 'Markets and Institutions in Large Scale Privatizations: An Approach to Economic and Social Transformations in Eastern Europe', in V. Corbo, F. Coricelli, and J. Bossak (eds), *Reforming Central and Eastern European Economies: Initial Results and Challenges*, Washington DC: The World Bank, pp. 53–274.

Frydman, R., A. Rapaczynski and J. S. Earle (1993), *The Privatization Process in Central Europe*, Budapest, London, New York: Central European University Press.

Frydman, R., C. W. Gray and A. Rapaczynski, (eds) (1996), *Corporate Governance in Central Europe and Russia*, Budapest, London and New York: Central European University Press.

Frydman, R., C. W. Gray, M. Hessel and A. Rapaczynski (1997), 'Private Ownership and Corporate Performance: Some Lessons from Transition Economies', *Economic Research Report*, 97–28, C.V. Starr Center for Applied Economics.

Goldberg, I., G. Jedrzejczak. and M. Fuchs (1997), 'A New Tool for Privatization – The "IPO Plus"', Washington DC: The World Bank, mimeographed.

Grossman G. and O. Hart (1988), 'One Share One Vote and the Market for Corporate Control', *Journal of Financial Economics*, **20**, 2203–35.

Hanousek, J. and E. Koèenda (1996), 'Effects of the Czech Voucher Scheme on the Corporate Governance', *Economics Institute Discussion Paper, 05/ 97*, Bulgarian Academy of Sciences.

Hanousek, J. and E. Kroch (1995), 'The Two Waves of Voucher Privatization in the Czech Republic: A Model of Learning in Sequential Bidding', forthcoming in: *Applied Economics*.

Hanousek, J. and R. Lastovicka (1993), 'The First Fully Recorded Realization of a Closed Economy: A Methodology and Estimation Using Czech Privatization Data', Prague: CERGE–EI Working Paper.

Hashi, I. (1997), 'Mass Privatisation and Corporate Governance in the Czech Republic', Staffordshire University, July, mimeographed.

Herzfeld, T. J. (1993), *Herzfeld's Guide to Closed-end Funds,* New York: McGraw-Hill, Inc.

Jaklin, J. and B. Heriè (1997), 'Economic Transition in Slovenia – 1996', in A. Böhm (ed.), *Economic Transition Report 1996,* Ljubljana: C.E.E.P.N.

Kenway, P. and J. Chlumsky (1997), 'The Influence of Owners on Voucher Privatized Firms in the Czech Republic', *Economics of Transition,* **5** (1), 185–93.

Kidwell, D. S., R. L. Peterson and D. W. Blackwell (1993), *Financial Institutions, Markets and Money,* Fort Worth: The Dryden Press.

Kollo, J. (1996), 'Employment and Wage Setting in Three Stages of Hungary's Labor Market Transition', in S. Commander (ed.), *'Enterprise Restructuring and Unemployment in Models of Transition'*, Washington DC: EDI-World Bank.

Kotrba, J. (1995), 'Privatization Process in the Czech Republic: Players and Winners', in J. Svejnar (ed.), *The Czech Republic and Economic Transition in Eastern Europe,* San Diego: Academic Press.

Kotrba, J. and J. Svejnar (1994), 'Rapid and Multifaceted Privatization: Experience of the Czech and Slovak Republics', *Nomisma – MOCT 4,* pp. 147–85.

Lawniczak, R. (1996), 'A Polish Experiment in Corporate Governance of the National Investment Funds (NIFs)', Poznan University of Economics Working Paper and Reprint Series.

Lipton, D. and J. Sachs (1990), 'Privatization in Eastern Europe: The Case of Poland', Brookings Papers on Economic Activity No. 2.

Lorsch, J. W. (1989), *Pawns or Potentates: The Reality of America's Corporate Boards,* Boston: Harvard Business School Press.

Luftmann, R. (1992), 'Changes of Corporate Control and Mandatory Bids', *International Review of Law and Economics,* **12**, p. 497.

Lukovac, J. (1997), 'Provizije za upravljanje pooblašèenih investicijskih dru•b', *Agens,* **44**, Ljubljana.

Lzedzal, L., M. Singer, and J. Svejnar. (1995), 'Manager Interests, Breakups and Performance of State Enterprises in Transition', in J. Svejnar (ed.), *The Czech Republic and Economic Transition in Eastern Europe,* San Diego: Academic Press.

McCahery, J., S. Picciotto and C. Scott (1993), *Corporate Control and Accountability: Changing Structures and Dynamics of Regulation*, Oxford: Oxford University Press.

Mejstrik, M. (1997), 'The Emergence of Institutional Owners: The Role of Banks and Nonbanking Financial Institutions in the Privatization of the Economy and the Banks', in M. Mejstrik (ed.), *The Privatization Process in East-Central Europe – Evolutionary Process of Czech Privatization,* Dordrecht, Boston and London: Kluwer.

Ministry for the Administration of the National Property and Its Privatization of the Czech Republic (1993), 'Report on the Privatization Process for the Years 1989 to 1992 (1993)', Prague.

Mladek, J. (1995), 'Voucher Privatisation in the Czech Republic and Slovakia, OECD: pp. 61–86.

Monks, R. A. G. and N. Minow (1995), *Corporate Governance*, Cambridge and London: Blackwell Publishers.

Mramor, D. (1991), 'Finanèna politika podjetja: teoretièni prikaz', *Gospodarski vestnik,* Ljubljana.

Nuti, D. M. (1995), 'Mass Privatisation: Costs and Benefits of Instant Capitalism', in R. Daviddi (ed.), *Property Rights and Privatization in the Transition to a Market Economy, A Comparative Review*, Maastricht: EIPA, pp. 103–32.

Nuti, D. M. (1997), 'Employeeism: Corporate Governance and Employee Share Ownership in Transition Economies', in M. I. Blejer and M. Skreb (eds), *Macroeconomic Stabilisation in Transition Economies*, Cambridge: Cambridge University Press, pp. 126–54.

Nuti, D. M. (1998), 'Stocks and Stakes: The Case for Protecting Stakeholders' Interests', *Economic Analysis,* **1**: 7–16.

OECD (1995), 'Mass Privatization – an Initial Assessment', Paris.

OECD (1996), 'Corporate Governance in Transition Economies: Lessons from Recent Development in OECD Member Countries', Paris.

Oxelheim, L. (1996), *Financial Markets in Transition: Globalization, Investment and Economic Growth,* London: International Thomson Business Press.

Peasnell, K. V. and C. W. R. Ward (1985), 'British Financial Markets and Institutions, Englewood Cliffs: Prentice-Hall International.

Peiperl, M. and S. Estrin (1997), 'Managerial Markets in Transition in Central and Eastern Europe', March, mimeographed.

Perotti, E. (1994), 'Corporate Governance in Mass Privatization Programs', in S. Estrin (ed.), *Privatization in Central and Eastern Europe,* London and New York: Longman.

Pessin, A. H. (1990), *Securities Law Compliance,* Homewood: Dow Jones-Irwin.

Pinto, B., M. Belka and S. Krajewski (1993), 'Transforming State Enterprises in Poland: Evidence on Adjustment by Manufacturing Firms', *Brooking Papers on Economic Activity,* **1**, 213–70. Washington DC: Brookings Institution.

Pistor, K., R. Frydman and A. Rapaczynski (1994), 'Investing in Insider-Dominated Firms. A Study of Russian Voucher Privatization Funds', A Joint Conference of The World Bank and the Central European University Privatization Project, Washington DC.

Pistor, K. and A. Spicer (1996), 'Investment Funds in Mass Privatisation and Beyond', OECD Advisory Group on Privatisation, Tenth Plenary Session, in cooperation with the Private Sector Development of The World Bank, Paris: OECD.

Pohl, G., R. E. Anderson, S. Claessens and S. Djankov (1997), 'Privatization and Restructuring in Central and Eastern Europe – Evidence and Policy Options', World Bank Technical Paper No. 368, Finance, Private Sector, and Infrastructure Network, Washington DC: The World Bank

Pohl, G., S. Djankov and R. E. Anderson (1996), 'Restructuring Large Industrial Firms in Central and Eastern Europe: An Empirical Evidence', Washington DC: The World Bank and Ljubljana: C.E.E.P.N.

Portes, R. (ed.) (1993), *Economic Transformation in Central Europe. A Progress Report,* London: CEPR.

Pye, R. B. K. (1996), 'Foreign Direct Investment in Central Europe (the Czech Republic, Hungary, Poland, Romania, and Slovakia) – Results from a Survey of Major Western Investors', Chapter of Ph.D. Dissertation, The City University Business School.

Rems, M. and B. Jašovič (1997), 'The Role of Privatisation Funds in Privatisation and Post-privatisation', Part I of Draft Country Report: 'Corporate Governance of Privatisation Investment Funds in Slovenia', Ljubljana: June.

Ribnikar, I. (1990), 'Investicijska podjetja in investicijski skladi', *Bančni vestnik,* **40** (4), 137–8, Ljubljana.

Rotschild, M. and J. Stiglitz (1976), 'Equilibrium in Competitive Insurance Markets: An Essay on the Economics of Imperfect Information', *Quarterly Journal of Economics,* **90**, 629–49.

Sharpe, W. F. and G. J. Alexander (1990), *Investments,* Englewood Cliffs: Prentice- Hall International.

Shleifer, A. and R. W. Vishny (1995), 'A Survey of Corporate Governance', Harvard Institute of Economic Research, Discussion Paper 1741, October.

Siebert, H. (1991), 'German Unification: the Economics of Transition', *Economic Policy,* **3**, October.

Simoneti, M. (1997), 'Issues in Regulating Post-Privatization Securities Markets in Transitional Economies', *EDI Working Papers*, Washington DC: Economic Development Institute of the World Bank.

Simoneti, M. (1998), 'Transformation of Privatization Funds', C.E.E.P.N, Ljubljana, ACE Research Project, mimeographed.

Simoneti, M. and B. Jašovič (1997), 'Dual Approach to Regulation of Post-Privatisation Capital Markets in Slovenia', *Working Papers,* **46**, Faculty of Economics, University of Ljubljana.

Simoneti, M. and D. Triska (eds) (1995), *Investment Funds as Intermediaries of Privatization,* C.E.E.P.N. Workshop Series, Ljubljana.

Singer, M. and J. Svejnar (1994), 'Using Vouchers to Privatize an Economy: The Czech and Slovak Case', *Economics of Transition*, Vol. **2**, No. 1.

Stapledon, G. P. (1996), *Institutional Shareholders and Corporate Governance,* Oxford: Clarendon Press.

Steil, B. *et al.* (1996), *The European Equity Markets. The State of the Union and an Agenda for the Millennium,* Washington DC: The Royal Institute of International Affairs.

Stiglitz, J. (1994), *Whither Socialism?,* Cambridge MA: MIT Press.

Svejnar, J. (1989), 'A Framework for the Economic Transformation of Czechoslovakia', *PlanEcon Report,* Vol. V, No. 52.

Svejnar J. (ed.) (1995), *The Czech Republic and Economic Transition in Eastern Europe,* San Diego, etc.: Academic Press.Svejnar J., (ed.) (1995), *The Czech Republic and Economic Transition in Eastern Europe,* San Diego: Academic Press.

Takla, L. (1994), 'The Relationship between Privatization and the Reform of the Banking Sector: The Case of the Czech Republic and Slovakia', in S. Estrin (ed.), *Privatization in Central and Eastern Europe,* London and New York: Longman.

Thygerson, K. J. (1993), *Financial Markets and Institutions,* Harper Collins College Publishers.

Triska, D. (1995), 'Post-privatisation Securities Markets in the Czech Republic', in OECD, pp. 87–106.

Useem, M and C. Gager (1996), 'Employee Shareholders or Institutional Investors? When Corporate Managers Replace Their Shareholders', *Journal of Management Studies,* 33 (5), Oxford.

Uvalic, M. (1997a), 'Corporate Governance in Transition Economies', *Conference Paper,* Split, Forthcoming in Conference Proceedings.

Uvalic, M. (1997b), 'Privatization in Successor States of Former Yugoslavia', in M. Uvalic and D. Vaughan-Whitehead (eds), *Privatization Surprises in Transition Economies,* Cheltenham: Edward Elgar.

Vujovich, D. (1992), *Straight Talk about Mutual Funds,* New York: McGraw-Hill, Inc.

Zemplinerova, A. (1997), 'The Role of Foreign Enterprises in the Privatization and Restructuring of the Czech Economy', Vienna Institute for Comparative Economics Study, WIIW 238, June.

Index